OFFICIAL 1998

NFL POCKET ALMANAC

INCLUDES

SCHEDULES, STATISTICS, SCOUTING REPORTS, RECORDS, AND MORE

Andrews McMeel Publishing

Kansas City

©1998 National Football League Properties, Inc. All rights reserved. No part of this book may be reproduced or transmitted in any form or by any means, electronic or mechanical, including photocopying, recording, or by any information storage and retrieval system, without permission in writing from the National Football League.

Written and edited by Brian Peterson
Design and production by Brad Jansen, Bill Madrid, and Sandy Gordon

Printed in the United States of America.

ISBN 0-8362-6569-6

Library of Congress
cataloging-in-publication
data on file.

Andrews McMeel Publishing
an Andrews McMeel Universal company
4520 Main Street
Kansas City, Missouri 64111

www.andrewsmcmeel.com

1998 NFL PREVIEW

After four unsuccessful Super Bowl appearances, the Denver Broncos triumphed in Super Bowl XXXII, and quarterback John Elway finally got an NFL championship ring. Detroit running back Barry Sanders rushed for 2,053 yards, second most in a single season in league history. These were just two of the many memorable moments in the NFL last year. What's in store for 1998? Can the Broncos repeat, or will the Vince Lombardi Trophy return to Green Bay? Is this the year Dan Marino leads the Dolphins to victory in Super Bowl XXXIII, which will be played in Miami? *The Official 1998 NFL Pocket Almanac* will help you answer these questions. Everything you will need to prepare for the upcoming NFL season is included in the following pages.

All information in this book is correct as of 5/1/98.

CONTENTS

Arizona Cardinals	4
Atlanta Falcons	8
Baltimore Ravens	12
Buffalo Bills	16
Carolina Panthers	20
Chicago Bears	24
Cincinnati Bengals	28
Dallas Cowboys	32
Denver Broncos	36
Detroit Lions	40
Green Bay Packers	44
Indianapolis Colts	48
Jacksonville Jaguars	52
Kansas City Chiefs	56
Miami Dolphins	60
Minnesota Vikings	64
New England Patriots	68
New Orleans Saints	72
New York Giants	76
New York Jets	80
Oakland Raiders	84
Philadelphia Eagles	88
Pittsburgh Steelers	92
St. Louis Rams	96
San Diego Chargers	100
San Francisco 49ers	104
Seattle Seahawks	108
Tampa Bay Buccaneers	112
Tennessee Oilers	116
Washington Redskins	120
1998 NFL Schedule	124

ARIZONA CARDINALS

P.O. Box 888
Phoenix, Arizona 85001-0888
Telephone: (602) 379-0101
Website: nfl.com

Team Colors: Cardinal Red, Black, and White

1997 Regular-Season Attendance:
Home: 379,547 Away: 484,689
Playing Surface: Grass
Training Camp: Northern Arizona University Flagstaff, Arizona 86011

NFC East
1997 Record 4-12
Home: 3-5
Away: 1-7
Stadium: Sun Devil Stadium
Capacity: 73,273

1997 RESULTS

DATE	RESULT	OPPONENT	ATT.
8/31	L 21-24	at Cincinnati	53,644
9/7	W 25-22*	DALLAS	71,578
9/14	L 13-19*	at Wash.	78,270
9/28	L 18-19	at Tampa Bay	53,804
10/5	L 19-20	MINNESOTA	45,550
10/12	L 13-27	N.Y. GIANTS	38,959
10/19	L 10-13*	at Phil.	66,860
10/26	L 14-41	TENNESSEE	44,030
11/2	W 31-21	PHILADELPHIA	39,549
11/9	L 6-24	at Dallas	64,302
11/16	L 10-19	at N.Y. Giants	68,316
11/23	W 16-13	at Baltimore	53,976
11/30	L 20-26*	PITTSBURGH	66,341
12/7	L 28-38	WASHINGTON	41,537
12/14	L 10-27	at N.O.	45,517
12/21	W 29-26	ATLANTA	32,003

*Overtime

1998 SCHEDULE

REGULAR SEASON

Sept. 6	at Dallas	3:05
Sept. 13	at Seattle	1:15
Sept. 20	**PHILADELPHIA**	**5:20**
Sept. 27	at St. Louis	12:01
Oct. 4	OAKLAND	1:05
Oct. 11	CHICAGO	1:05
Oct. 18	at New York Giants	1:01
Oct. 25	OPEN DATE	
Nov. 1	at Detroit	1:01
Nov. 8	WASHINGTON	2:05
Nov. 15	DALLAS	2:15
Nov. 22	at Washington	1:01
Nov. 29	at Kansas City	12:01
Dec. 6	NEW YORK GIANTS	2:05
Dec. 13	at Philadelphia	1:01
Dec. 20	NEW ORLEANS	2:15
Dec. 27	SAN DIEGO	2:15

Nationally Televised Games in **Bold**/All times local

COACHING STAFF

Head Coach—Vince Tobin; Assistant Coaches—George (Geep) Chryst, Alan Everest, Joe Greene, Larry Marmie, Dave McGinnis, Glenn Pires, Vic Rapp, Bob Rogucki, Johnny Roland, Marc Trestman, George Warhop.

1998 SCOUTING REPORT

Arizona may have finished 4-12 in 1997, but there are many reasons for optimism in 1998.

The Cardinals narrowly missed winning 10 games instead of 4 last year. Three of their losses came in overtime and three others were by a total of five points.

Combine Arizona's close calls with some impressive offseason moves, and the Cardinals should contend for the NFC East title. Former 49ers offensive coordinator Marc Trestman was hired for the same role in Arizona and should enhance the development of starting quarterback Jake Plummer, who showed flashes of brilliance as a rookie.

Adrian Murrell, who surpassed 1,000 rushing yards the past two seasons with the Jets, will add life to the Cardinals' running game, the league's poorest in 1997.

1998 DRAFT CHOICES

RD. NAME	POS.	COLLEGE	RD. NAME	POS.	COLLEGE
1. Andre Wadsworth	DE	Florida St.	6. Zack Walz	LB	Dartmouth
2a. Corey Chavous	S	Vanderbilt	7a. Phil Savoy	WR	Colorado
2b. Anthony Clement	T	S.W. Louisiana	7b. Jomo Cousins	DE	Florida A&M
4. Michael Pittman	RB	Fresno St.	7c. Pat Tillman	S	Arizona St.
5. Terry Hardy	TE	So. Mississippi	7d. Ron Janes	RB	Missouri

Wadsworth arguably was best player in draft. He'll team with veterans Eric Swann and Simeon Rice to make up one of most formidable defensive lines in NFL...Chavous likely will start...Clement is huge player (6-7, 355) who is difficult to get around.

KEY ACQUISITIONS

NAME	POS.	PREVIOUS NFL TEAM	NAME	POS.	PREVIOUS NFL TEAM
Mario Bates (FA)	RB	Saints	Eric Metcalf (Trade)	WR-KR	Chargers
Lester Holmes (FA)	G	Raiders	Adrian Murrell (Trade)	RB	Jets
Van Malone (FA)	S	Lions	Patrick Sapp (Trade)	LB	Chargers

KEY LOSSES

NAME	POS.	NEW NFL TEAM	NAME	POS.	NEW NFL TEAM
Brent Alexander (FA)	S	Panthers	Eric Hill (FA)	LB	Rams
Michael Bankston (FA)	DT	Bengals	LeShon Johnson (FA)	RB	Giants
Kent Graham (FA)	QB	Giants	Kevin Williams (FA)	WR	Bills

(FA) = Free Agent

1997 STATISTICAL LEADERS

SCORING

PLAYER	TD	PAT	FG	PTS.
Nedney	0	19/19	11/17	52
Rob Moore	8	0/0	0/0	50
Butler	0	9/10	8/12	33
Sanders	4	0/0	0/0	26
Gedney	4	0/0	0/0	24
Plummer	2	0/0	0/0	14
Centers	2	0/0	0/0	12
K. Graham	2	0/0	0/0	12
McElroy	2	0/0	0/0	12
A. Williams	2	0/0	0/0	12
Cardinals	32	28/29	19/29	283
Opponents	42	35/37	30/35	379

2-Point conversions: Cardinals 3-3, Opponents 1-3

RUSHING

PLAYER	ATT.	YDS.	AVG.	TD
McElroy	135	424	3.1	2
Ron Moore	57	175	3.1	0
Centers	101	276	2.7	1
Plummer	39	216	5.5	2
Johnson	23	81	3.5	0
Bouie	11	26	2.4	0
K. Graham	13	23	1.8	2
Cardinals	395	1,255	3.2	9
Opponents	524	2,180	4.2	13

INTERCEPTIONS

PLAYER	NO.	YDS.	AVG.	TD
A. Williams	6	95	15.8	2
McKinnon	3	40	13.3	0
Wilson	1	66	66.0	1
McCleskey	1	15	15.0	0
Lassiter	1	10	10.0	0
Caldwell	1	5	5.0	0
Bennett	1	0	0.0	0
Cardinals	15	231	15.4	3
Opponents	22	289	13.1	0

RECEIVING

PLAYER	ATT.	YDS.	AVG.	TD
Rob Moore	97	*1,584	16.3	8
Sanders	75	1,017	13.6	4
Centers	54	409	7.6	1
Gedney	23	261	11.3	4
K. Williams	20	273	13.7	1
Edwards	20	203	10.2	1
McWilliams	7	75	10.7	0
Carter	7	44	6.3	1
McElroy	7	32	4.6	0
Johnson	3	4	1.3	0
C. Smith	2	20	10.0	0
Brock	1	29	29.0	0
Plummer	1	2	2.0	0
Wilson	0	0	—	0
Cardinals	317	3,953	12.5	19
Opponents	279	3,461	12.4	23

KICKOFF RETURNS

PLAYER	NO.	YDS.	AVG.	TD
K. Williams	59	1,458	24.7	0
Bouie	6	136	22.7	0
C. Smith	3	50	16.7	0
Gedney	2	26	13.0	0
Cardinals	70	1,696	24.2	0
Opponents	42	945	22.5	1

PUNT RETURNS

PLAYER	NO.	YDS.	AVG.	TD
K. Williams	40	462	11.6	0
Edwards	1	-1	-1.0	0
Cardinals	41	461	11.2	0
Opponents	40	441	11.0	1

PUNTING

PLAYER	NO.	YDS.	AVG.
Feagles	91	4,028	44.3
Cardinals	92	4,028	43.8
Opponents	94	4,130	43.9

PASSING

PLAYER	ATT.	COMP.	YDS.	PCT.	TD	INT.	RAT.
Plummer	296	157	2,203	53.0	15	15	73.1
K. Graham	250	130	1,408	52.0	4	5	65.9
Case	55	29	316	52.7	0	2	54.8
Sanders	1	1	26	100.0	1	0	118.8
Cardinals	602	317	3,953	52.7	19	22	68.6
Opponents	491	279	3,461	56.8	23	15	81.7

SACKS: Swann 7.5, M. Smith 6.0, Miller 5.5, Cardinals 34.0, Opponents 78.0

*League Leader   (All individuals may not be represented.)

RECORD HOLDERS

INDIVIDUAL RECORDS—CAREER

CATEGORY	NAME	PERFORMANCE
Rushing (Yds.)	Ottis Anderson, 1979-1986	7,999
Passing (Yds.)	Jim Hart, 1966-1983	34,639
Passing (TDs)	Jim Hart, 1966-1983	209
Receiving (No.)	Roy Green, 1979-1990	522
Receiving (Yds.)	Roy Green, 1979-1990	8,497
Interceptions	Larry Wilson, 1960-1972	52
Punting (Avg.)	Jerry Norton, 1959-1961	44.9
Punt Return (Avg.)	Charley Trippi, 1947-1955	13.7
Kickoff Return (Avg.)	Ollie Matson, 1952, 1954-58	28.5
Field Goals	Jim Bakken, 1962-1978	282
Touchdowns (Tot.)	Roy Green, 1979-1990	70
Points	Jim Bakken, 1962-1978	1,380

INDIVIDUAL RECORDS—SINGLE SEASON

CATEGORY	NAME	PERFORMANCE
Rushing (Yds.)	Ottis Anderson, 1979	1,605
Passing (Yds.)	Neil Lomax, 1984	4,614
Passing (TDs)	Charley Johnson, 1963	28
	Neil Lomax, 1984	28
Receiving (No.)	Larry Centers, 1995	101
Receiving (Yds.)	Rob Moore, 1997	1,584
Interceptions	Bob Nussbaumer, 1949	12
Punting (Avg.)	Jerry Norton, 1960	45.6
Punt Return (Avg.)	John (Red) Cochran, 1949	20.9
Kickoff Return (Avg.)	Ollie Matson, 1958	35.5
Field Goals	Greg Davis, 1995	30
Touchdowns (Tot.)	John David Crow, 1962	17
Points	Jim Bakken, 1967; Neil O'Donoghue, 1984	117

INDIVIDUAL RECORDS—SINGLE GAME

CATEGORY	NAME	PERFORMANCE
Rushing (Yds.)	LeShon Johnson, 9-22-96	214
Passing (Yds.)	Boomer Esiason, 11-10-96 (OT)	522
Passing (TDs)	Jim Hardy, 10-2-50	6
	Charley Johnson, 9-26-65, 11-2-69	6
Receiving (No.)	Sonny Randle, 11-4-62	16
Receiving (Yds.)	Sonny Randle, 11-4-62	256
Interceptions	Bob Nussbaumer, 11-13-49	*4
	Jerry Norton, 11-20-60	*4
Field Goals	Jim Bakken, 9-24-67	*7
Touchdowns (Tot.)	Ernie Nevers, 11-28-29	*6
Points	Ernie Nevers, 11-28-29	*40

*NFL Record

ATLANTA FALCONS

One Falcon Place
Suwanee, Georgia 30174
Telephone: (770) 945-1111
Websites: nfl.com and
atlantafalcons.com

Team Colors: Black, Red, Silver, and White
NFC West
1997 Record 7-9
Home: 3-5
Away: 4-4
Stadium: Georgia Dome
Capacity: 71,228

1997 Regular-Season Attendance:
Home: 375,427 Away: 437,145
Playing Surface: Artificial Turf
Training Camp:
One Falcon Place
Suwanee, Georgia 30174

1997 RESULTS

DATE	RESULT	OPPONENT	ATT.
8/31	L 17-28	at Detroit	61,244
9/7	L 6-9	CAROLINA	51,829
9/14	L 31-36	OAKLAND	47,922
9/21	L 7-34	at S.F.	60,404
9/28	L 21-29	DENVER	48,211
10/12	W 23-17	at N.O.	65,619
10/19	L 28-35	SAN FRANCISCO	53,378
10/26	L 12-21	at Carolina	54,675
11/2	W 34-31	ST. LOUIS	36,583
11/9	L 10-31	TAMPA BAY	46,018
11/16	W 27-21	at St. Louis	64,299
11/23	W 20-3	NEW ORLEANS	48,620
11/30	W 24-17	at Seattle	52,584
12/7	W 14-3	at San Diego	46,317
12/14	W 20-17	PHILADELPHIA	42,866
12/21	L 26-29	at Arizona	32,003

1998 SCHEDULE

REGULAR SEASON

Sept. 6	at Carolina	1:01
Sept. 13	PHILADELPHIA	1:01
Sept. 20	OPEN DATE	
Sept. 27	at San Francisco	1:15
Oct. 4	CAROLINA	1:01
Oct. 11	**at New York Giants**	**8:20**
Oct. 18	NEW ORLEANS	1:01
Oct. 25	at New York Jets	1:01
Nov. 1	ST. LOUIS	1:01
Nov. 8	at New England	1:01
Nov. 15	SAN FRANCISCO	1:01
Nov. 22	CHICAGO	1:01
Nov. 29	at St. Louis	12:01
Dec. 6	INDIANAPOLIS	1:01
Dec. 13	at New Orleans	12:01
Dec. 20	at Detroit	1:01
Dec. 27	MIAMI	1:01

*Nationally Televised Games in **Bold**/All times local*

COACHING STAFF

Head Coach—Dan Reeves; Assistant Coaches—Marvin Bass, Don Blackmon, Rich Brooks, Jack Burns, James Daniel, Joe DeCamillis, Tim Jorgensen, Bill Kollar, Ron Meeks, Al Miller, Art Shell, Warren Simmons, Ed West, Brian Xanders.

1998 SCOUTING REPORT

In 1997—Dan Reeves's first year as Atlanta's head coach—the Falcons began the season 1-7. But they rebounded to contend for a playoff spot by winning six of their final eight games.

Reeves hopes his team carries the momentum into 1998 it generated at the end of last season. For that to happen, Pro Bowl quarterback Chris Chandler, who finished second in the NFL with a 95.1 passer rating and threw a career-high 20 touchdown passes in 1997, needs to stay healthy. He missed two games and parts of four others with various injuries.

The Falcons are one of only three NFL teams to score at least 300 points in every season during the 1990s. Jamal Anderson rushed for more than 1,000 yards for the second successive season last year, becoming the first Atlanta player to do so since 1986.

1998 DRAFT CHOICES

RD.	NAME	POS.	COLLEGE	RD.	NAME	POS.	COLLEGE
1.	Keith Brooking	LB	Georgia Tech	6.	Elijah Williams	CB	Florida
2.	Bob Hallen	C	Kent St.	7a.	Ephraim Salaam	T	San Diego St.
3.	Jammi German	WR	Miami	7b.	Ken Oxendine	RB	Virginia Tech
4a.	Omar Brown	S	North Carolina	7c.	Henry Slay	DT	West Virginia
4b.	Tim Dwight	WR	Iowa				

It's uncertain whether Brookings will play outside or inside linebacker, but he should have an immediate impact...Hallen is versatile enough to play both center and tackle...German has not played in two years, but he runs good routes and can make tough catches.

KEY ACQUISITIONS

NAME	POS.	PREVIOUS NFL TEAM	NAME	POS.	PREVIOUS NFL TEAM
Keith Crawford (FA)	WR	Rams	Corey Louchiey (FA)	T	Bills
Matt Elliott (FA)	G-T	Panthers	Eugene Robinson (FA)	S	Packers
Brian Kozlowski (FA)	TE	Giants	Mark Rypien (FA)	QB	Rams

KEY LOSSES

NAME	POS.	NEW NFL TEAM	NAME	POS.	NEW NFL TEAM
Bert Emanuel (FA)	WR	Buccaneers	Dan Owens (FA)	DT	Lions
Roman Fortin (FA)	C	Chargers	Anthony Pleasant (FA)	DE	Jets

(FA) = Free Agent

1997 STATISTICAL LEADERS

SCORING

PLAYER	TD	PAT	FG	PTS.
Andersen	0	35/35	23/27	104
Anderson	10	0/0	0/0	60
Emanuel	9	0/0	0/0	54
Mathis	6	0/0	0/0	36
Hanspard	3	0/0	0/0	18
Santiago	2	0/0	0/0	12
Christian	1	0/0	0/0	6
Green	1	0/0	0/0	6
Haynes	1	0/0	0/0	6
Kinchen	1	0/0	0/0	6
Falcons	36	35/35	23/27	320
Opponents	45	39/39	14/20	361

2-Point conversions: Falcons 0-1, Opponents 4-6

RUSHING

PLAYER	ATT.	YDS.	AVG.	TD
Anderson	290	1,002	3.5	7
Hanspard	53	335	6.3	0
Chandler	43	158	3.7	0
Green	36	78	2.2	1
Mathis	3	35	11.7	0
Graziani	3	19	6.3	0
Christian	7	8	1.1	0
Tolliver	7	8	1.1	0
Falcons	442	1,643	3.7	8
Opponents	409	1,666	4.1	18

INTERCEPTIONS

PLAYER	NO.	YDS.	AVG.	TD
Buchanan	5	49	9.8	0
Bradford	4	9	2.3	0
Booker	3	16	5.3	0
Owens	1	14	14.0	0
White	1	11	11.0	0
McGill	1	7	7.0	0
Bush	1	4	4.0	0
Falcons	18	114	6.3	0
Opponents	11	124	11.3	1

RECEIVING

PLAYER	ATT.	YDS.	AVG.	TD
Emanuel	65	991	15.2	9
Mathis	62	802	12.9	6
Green	29	360	12.4	0
Anderson	29	284	9.8	3
Christian	22	154	7.0	1
Santiago	17	217	12.8	2
Kinchen	16	266	16.6	1
Haynes	12	154	12.8	1
Kozlowski	7	99	14.1	1
West	7	63	9.0	1
Hanspard	6	53	8.8	1
E. Smith	1	2	2.0	0
Falcons	273	3,445	12.6	26
Opponents	275	3,794	13.8	24

KICKOFF RETURNS

PLAYER	NO.	YDS.	AVG.	TD
Hanspard	40	987	24.7	2
Bolden	5	106	21.2	0
Kozlowski	2	49	24.5	0
Burrough	1	6	6.0	0
Green	1	23	23.0	0
Kinchen	1	18	18.0	0
Owens	1	9	9.0	0
Falcons	51	1,198	23.5	2
Opponents	52	1,167	22.4	0

PUNT RETURNS

PLAYER	NO.	YDS.	AVG.	TD
Kinchen	52	446	8.6	0
Buchanan	0	37	—	0
Falcons	52	483	9.3	0
Opponents	21	55	2.6	0

PUNTING

PLAYER	NO.	YDS.	AVG.
Stryzinski	89	3,498	39.3
Falcons	89	3,498	39.3
Opponents	90	3,835	42.6

PASSING

PLAYER	ATT.	COMP.	YDS.	PCT.	TD	INT.	RAT.
Chandler	342	202	2,692	59.1	20	7	95.1
Tolliver	115	63	685	54.8	5	1	83.4
Graziani	23	7	41	30.4	0	2	3.7
Anderson	4	1	27	25.0	1	1	55.2
Falcons	484	273	3,445	56.4	26	11	87.2
Opponents	496	275	3,794	55.4	24	18	81.2

SACKS: C. Smith 12.0, Hall 10.5, Archambeau 8.5, Falcons 55.0, Opponents 54.0

(All individuals may not be represented.)

RECORD HOLDERS

INDIVIDUAL RECORDS—CAREER

CATEGORY	NAME	PERFORMANCE
Rushing (Yds.)	Gerald Riggs, 1982-88	6,631
Passing (Yds.)	Steve Bartkowski, 1975-1985	23,468
Passing (TDs)	Steve Bartkowski, 1975-1985	154
Receiving (No.)	Andre Rison, 1990-94	423
Receiving (Yds.)	Alfred Jenkins, 1975-1983	6,257
Interceptions	Rolland Lawrence, 1973-1980	39
Punting (Avg.)	Rick Donnelly, 1985-89	42.6
Punt Return (Avg.)	Al Dodd, 1973-74	11.8
Kickoff Return (Avg.)	Tony Smith, 1992-94	24.9
Field Goals	Mick Luckhurst, 1981-87	115
Touchdowns (Tot.)	Andre Rison, 1990-94	56
Points	Mick Luckhurst, 1981-87	558

INDIVIDUAL RECORDS—SINGLE SEASON

CATEGORY	NAME	PERFORMANCE
Rushing (Yds.)	Gerald Riggs, 1985	1,719
Passing (Yds.)	Jeff George, 1995	4,143
Passing (TDs)	Steve Bartkowski, 1980	31
Receiving (No.)	Terance Mathis, 1994	111
Receiving (Yds.)	Alfred Jenkins, 1981	1,358
Interceptions	Scott Case, 1988	10
Punting (Avg.)	Billy Lothridge, 1968	44.3
Punt Return (Avg.)	Al Dodd, 1974	12.74
Kickoff Return (Avg.)	Sylvester Stamps, 1987	27.5
Field Goals	Morten Andersen, 1995	31
Touchdowns (Tot.)	Andre Rison, 1993	15
Points	Morten Andersen, 1995	122

INDIVIDUAL RECORDS—SINGLE GAME

CATEGORY	NAME	PERFORMANCE
Rushing (Yds.)	Gerald Riggs, 9-2-84	202
Passing (Yds.)	Steve Bartkowski, 11-15-81	416
Passing (TDs)	Wade Wilson, 12-13-92	5
Receiving (No.)	William Andrews, 11-15-81	15
Receiving (Yds.)	Alfred Jackson, 12-2-84	193
	Andre Rison, 9-4-94	193
Interceptions	Many times	2
	Last time by Ray Buchanan, 12-7-97	
Field Goals	Norm Johnson, 11-13-94	6
Touchdowns (Tot.)	Many times	3
	Last time by Terance Mathis, 11-19-95	
Points	Norm Johnson, 11-13-94	20

BALTIMORE RAVENS

11001 Owings Mills Boulevard
Owings Mills, Maryland 21117
Telephone: (410) 654-6200
Website: nfl.com

Team Colors: Black, Purple, and Metallic Gold

1997 Regular-Season Attendance:
Home: 475,236 Away: 447,488
Playing Surface: SportGrass
Training Camp: Western Maryland College Westminster, Maryland 21157

AFC Central
1997 Record 6-9-1
Home: 3-4-1, **Away:** 3-5
Stadium: Baltimore Ravens Stadium at Camden Yards
Capacity: 68,400

1997 RESULTS

DATE	RESULT	OPPONENT	ATT.
8/31	L 27-28	JACKSONVILLE	61,018
9/7	W 23-10	CINCINNATI	52,968
9/14	W 24-23	at N.Y. Giants	69,768
9/21	W 36-10	at Tennessee	17,737
9/28	L 17-21	at San Diego	54,094
10/5	L 34-42	PITTSBURGH	64,421
10/19	L 13-24	MIAMI	64,354
10/26	W 20-17	at Washington	75,067
11/2	L 16-19*	at N.Y. Jets	59,524
11/9	L 0-37	at Pittsburgh	56,669
11/16	T 10-10*	PHILADELPHIA	63,546
11/23	L 13-16	ARIZONA	53,976
11/30	L 27-29	at Jacksonville	63,712
12/7	W 31-24	SEATTLE	54,395
12/14	W 21-19	TENNESSEE	60,558
12/21	L 14-16	at Cincinnati	50,917

*Overtime

1998 SCHEDULE

REGULAR SEASON

Sept. 6	PITTSBURGH	1:01
Sept. 13	at New York Jets	1:01
Sept. 20	at Jacksonville	4:15
Sept. 27	**CINCINNATI**	**8:20**
Oct. 4	OPEN DATE	
Oct. 11	TENNESSEE	1:01
Oct. 18	at Pittsburgh	1:01
Oct. 25	at Green Bay	12:01
Nov. 1	JACKSONVILLE	1:01
Nov. 8	OAKLAND	1:01
Nov. 15	at San Diego	1:05
Nov. 22	at Cincinnati	4:15
Nov. 29	INDIANAPOLIS	1:01
Dec. 6	at Tennessee	3:15
Dec. 13	MINNESOTA	4:15
Dec. 20	at Chicago	12:01
Dec. 27	DETROIT	1:01

Nationally Televised Games in **Bold**/All times local

COACHING STAFF

Head Coach—Ted Marchibroda; Assistant Coaches—Maxie Baughan, Jacob Burney, Kirk Ferentz, Al Lavan, Marvin Lewis, Richard Mann, Scott O'Brien, Alvin Reynolds, Jerry Simmons, Don Strock, Ken Whisenhunt.

1998 SCOUTING REPORT

Ravens head coach Ted Marchibroda hopes that gritty quarterback Jim Harbaugh can do for him in Baltimore what he did for him in Indianapolis. Marchibroda was the Colts' head coach in 1995 when Harbaugh came within inches of completing a Hail Mary pass that would have given Indianapolis a last-second victory over Pittsburgh in the AFC title game.

Harbaugh and running back Errict Rhett, who eclipsed 1,000 rushing yards for Tampa Bay in 1994-95, will give the offense more consistency and toughness. Wide receiver Michael Jackson has recorded a touchdown for every 6.85 receptions during his career.

The young linebacking corps of Ray Lewis (the team's leading tackler), Peter Boulware (who led NFL rookies with 11½ sacks in 1997), and Jamie Sharper (another outstanding rookie last year) is the strength of the defense.

1998 DRAFT CHOICES

RD.	NAME	POS.	COLLEGE
1.	Duane Starks	CB	Miami
2.	Pat Johnson	WR	Oregon
5a.	Martin Chase	DT	Oklahoma
5b.	Ryan Sutter	S	Colorado
6a.	Ron Rogers	LB	Georgia Tech
6b.	Sammy Williams	T	Oklahoma
7.	Cam Quayle	TE	Weber St.

Starks excels in man-for-man coverage and should start opposite veteran Rod Woodson. Despite standing only 5 feet 10 inches tall and weighing 170 pounds, Starks plays big and can be tough against run...Johnson, former track standout, has solid receiving skills to go with blinding speed...Chase has size to be effective run stopper in middle of defensive line.

KEY ACQUISITIONS

NAME	POS.	PREVIOUS NFL TEAM
Jim Harbaugh (Trade)	QB	Colts
Roosevelt Potts (FA)	RB	Dolphins
Errict Rhett (Trade)	RB	Buccaneers
Rod Woodson (FA)	CB	49ers

KEY LOSSES

NAME	POS.	NEW NFL TEAM
Derrick Alexander (FA)	WR	Chiefs
Antonio Langham (FA)	CB	49ers
Bam Morris (FA)	RB	Unsigned
Quentin Neujahr (FA)	C	Jaguars

(FA) = Free Agent

1997 STATISTICAL LEADERS

SCORING

PLAYER	TD	PAT	FG	PTS.
Stover	0	32/32	26/34	110
Alexander	9	0/0	0/0	54
J. Lewis	8	0/0	0/0	48
Green	5	0/0	0/0	30
Jackson	4	0/0	0/0	26
Morris	4	0/0	0/0	24
Graham	2	0/0	0/0	12
Cotton	1	0/0	0/0	6
Kinchen	1	0/0	0/0	6
Langham	1	0/0	0/0	6
Byner	0	0/0	0/0	2
Ravens	35	32/32	26/34	326
Opponents	39	33/35	24/34	345

2-Point conversions: Ravens 2-3, Opponents 2-4

RUSHING

PLAYER	ATT.	YDS.	AVG.	TD
Morris	204	774	3.8	4
Byner	84	313	3.7	0
Graham	81	299	3.7	2
Testaverde	34	138	4.1	0
J. Lewis	3	35	11.7	0
Zeier	10	17	1.7	0
Montgomery	1	11	11.0	0
Cotton	2	2	1.0	1
Alexander	1	0	0.0	0
Ravens	420	1,589	3.8	7
Opponents	470	1,690	3.6	17

INTERCEPTIONS

PLAYER	NO.	YDS.	AVG.	TD
Moore	4	56	14.0	0
Daniel	3	60	20.0	0
Langham	3	40	13.3	1
Staten	2	12	6.0	0
C. Brown	1	21	21.0	0
R. Lewis	1	18	18.0	0
Jenkins	1	15	15.0	0
Ravens	17	241	14.2	1
Opponents	16	118	7.4	0

RECEIVING

PLAYER	ATT.	YDS.	AVG.	TD
Jackson	69	918	13.3	4
Alexander	65	1,009	15.5	9
Green	65	601	9.2	5
J. Lewis	42	648	15.4	6
Morris	29	176	6.1	0
Byner	28	171	6.1	0
Yarborough	16	183	11.4	0
Graham	12	51	4.3	0
Kinchen	11	95	8.6	1
Roe	7	124	17.7	0
Testaverde	1	-4	-4.0	0
Ravens	338	3,929	11.6	25
Opponents	332	3,966	11.9	20

KICKOFF RETURNS

PLAYER	NO.	YDS.	AVG.	TD
J. Lewis	41	905	22.1	0
Roe	9	189	21.0	0
Graham	6	115	19.2	0
Brew	5	88	17.6	0
Singleton	4	64	16.0	0
Ethridge	2	37	18.5	0
Byner	1	0	0.0	0
Holmes	1	14	14.0	0
McCloud	1	0	0.0	0
Ravens	71	1,435	20.2	0
Opponents	58	1,323	22.8	1

PUNT RETURNS

PLAYER	NO.	YDS.	AVG.	TD
J. Lewis	28	437	*15.6	2
Roe	8	72	9.0	0
Ethridge	5	21	4.2	0
Alexander	1	34	34.0	0
Ravens	42	564	13.4	2
Opponents	53	460	8.7	0

PUNTING

PLAYER	NO.	YDS.	AVG.
Montgomery	83	3,540	42.7
Ravens	83	3,540	42.7
Opponents	82	3,611	44.0

PASSING

PLAYER	ATT.	COMP.	YDS.	PCT.	TD	INT.	RAT.
Testaverde	470	271	2,971	57.7	18	15	75.9
Zeier	116	67	958	57.8	7	1	101.1
Ravens	586	338	3,929	57.7	25	16	80.9
Opponents	556	332	3,966	59.7	20	17	80.8

SACKS: Boulware 11.5, McCrary 9.0, J. Jones 6.0, Ravens 42.0, Opponents 37.0

*League Leader   (All individuals may not be represented.)

RECORD HOLDERS

INDIVIDUAL RECORDS—CAREER

CATEGORY	NAME	PERFORMANCE
Rushing (Yds.)	Byron (Bam) Morris, 1996-97	1,511
Passing (Yds.)	Vinny Testaverde, 1996-97	7,148
Passing (TDs)	Vinny Testaverde, 1996-97	51
Receiving (No.)	Michael Jackson, 1996-97	145
Receiving (Yds.)	Michael Jackson, 1996-97	2,119
Interceptions	Antonio Langham, 1996-97; Eric Turner, 1996	5
Punting (Avg.)	Greg Montgomery, 1996-97	43.2
Punt Return (Avg.)	Jermaine Lewis, 1996-97	12.1
Kickoff Return (Avg.)	Jermaine Lewis, 1996-97	21.8
Field Goals	Matt Stover, 1996-97	45
Touchdowns (Tot.)	Michael Jackson, 1996-97	18
Points	Matt Stover, 1996-97	201

INDIVIDUAL RECORDS—SINGLE SEASON

CATEGORY	NAME	PERFORMANCE
Rushing (Yds.)	Byron (Bam) Morris, 1997	774
Passing (Yds.)	Vinny Testaverde, 1996	4,177
Passing (TDs)	Vinny Testaverde, 1996	33
Receiving (No.)	Michael Jackson, 1996	76
Receiving (Yds.)	Michael Jackson, 1996	1,201
Interceptions	Antonio Langham, 1996; Eric Turner, 1996	5
Punting (Avg.)	Greg Montgomery, 1996	43.8
Punt Return (Avg.)	Jermaine Lewis, 1996	15.6
Kickoff Return (Avg.)	Jermaine Lewis, 1997	22.1
Field Goals	Matt Stover, 1997	26
Touchdowns (Tot.)	Michael Jackson, 1996	14
Points	Matt Stover, 1997	110

INDIVIDUAL RECORDS—SINGLE GAME

CATEGORY	NAME	PERFORMANCE
Rushing (Yds.)	Byron (Bam) Morris, 10-26-97	176
Passing (Yds.)	Vinny Testaverde, 10-27-96	429
Passing (TDs)	Vinny Testaverde, 10-20-96	4
Receiving (No.)	Many times	9
	Last time by Eric Green, 11-2-97	
Receiving (Yds.)	Derrick Alexander, 12-1-96	198
Interceptions	Many times	2
	Last time by Ralph Staten, 12-7-97	
Field Goals	Matt Stover, 11-24-96	4
Touchdowns (Tot.)	Michael Jackson, 12-22-96; Jermaine Lewis, 12-7-97	3
Points	Michael Jackson, 12-22-96	18
	Jermaine Lewis, 12-7-97	

BUFFALO BILLS

**One Bills Drive
Orchard Park, NY 14127
Telephone: (716) 648-1800
Websites: nfl.com and
www.buffalobills.com**

Team Colors: Royal Blue, Scarlet Red, and White
AFC East
1997 Record 6-10
Home: 4-4
Away: 2-6
Stadium: Rich Stadium
Capacity: 80,024

1997 Regular-Season Attendance:
Home: 523,763 Away: 469,716
Playing Surface: AstroTurf
Training Camp: Fredonia State University
Fredonia, New York 14063

1997 RESULTS

DATE	RESULT	OPPONENT	ATT.
8/31	L 13-34	MINNESOTA	79,139
9/7	W 28-22	at N.Y. Jets	72,988
9/14	L 16-22	at Kansas City	78,169
9/21	W 37-35	INDIANAPOLIS	55,340
10/5	W 22-13	DETROIT	78,025
10/12	L 6-33	at N.E.	59,802
10/20	W 9-6	at Ind.	61,139
10/26	L 20-23*	DENVER	78,458
11/2	W 9-6	MIAMI	78,011
11/9	L 10-31	NEW ENGLAND	65,783
11/17	L 13-30	at Miami	74,155
11/23	L 14-31	at Tennessee	23,571
11/30	W 20-10	N.Y. JETS	47,776
12/7	L 3-20	at Chicago	39,784
12/14	L 14-20	JACKSONVILLE	41,231
12/20	L 21-31	at Green Bay	60,108

*Overtime

1998 SCHEDULE

REGULAR SEASON

Sept. 6	at San Diego	1:15
Sept. 13	at Miami	1:01
Sept. 20	ST. LOUIS	1:01
Sept. 27	OPEN DATE	
Oct. 4	SAN FRANCISCO	1:01
Oct. 11	at Indianapolis	12:01
Oct. 18	JACKSONVILLE	1:01
Oct. 25	**at Carolina**	**8:20**
Nov. 1	MIAMI	1:01
Nov. 8	at New York Jets	4:15
Nov. 15	NEW ENGLAND	1:01
Nov. 22	INDIANAPOLIS	1:01
Nov. 29	at New England	4:05
Dec. 6	at Cincinnati	1:01
Dec. 13	OAKLAND	1:01
Dec. 19	**NEW YORK JETS (Sat.)**	**12:35**
Dec. 27	at New Orleans	12:01

Nationally Televised Games in **Bold**/All times local

COACHING STAFF
Head Coach—Wade Phillips; Assistant Coaches—Max Bowman, Bill Bradley, Ted Cottrell, Bruce DeHaven, Chris Dickson, Bishop Harris, Charlie Joiner, Rusty Jones, Chuck Lester, John Levra, Carl Mauck, Joe Pendry, Elijah Pitts, Turk Schonert.

1998 SCOUTING REPORT

A lot of change has taken place in Buffalo. Quarterback Jim Kelly retired before the 1997 NFL season, head coach Marv Levy retired after it, and for only the second time in the 1990s, the Bills, who played in four Super Bowls from 1990-93, didn't make the AFC playoffs.

Wade Phillips, Buffalo's defensive coordinator the past three years, takes over for Levy. Todd Collins tried to fill Kelly's shoes in 1997, but couldn't. The Bills finished last in the AFC in scoring and averaged only 4.86 yards per pass play, lowest in the league.

Rob Johnson, who was Mark Brunell's backup in Jacksonville last year, has promise and will be Buffalo's starter in 1998. Antowain Smith, the Bills' first-round draft choice in 1997, showed he was ready to take over for aging Thurman Thomas by leading the team in rushing yards and touchdowns.

1998 DRAFT CHOICES

RD. NAME	POS.	COLLEGE	RD. NAME	POS.	COLLEGE
2. Sam Cowart	LB	Florida St.	6. Fred Coleman	WR	Washington
3. Robert Hicks	T	Mississippi St.	7a. Victor Allotey	G	Indiana
5. Jonathan Linton	RB	North Carolina	7b. Kamil Loud	WR	Cal Poly-SLO

In Cowart, Bills got first-round caliber player in second round. He has excellent range, flies to ball, and will be outstanding middle linebacker...Despite size (6-7, 350), Hicks is better suited to play right tackle...Linton is tough runner who rarely goes down after first hit...Coleman has good speed and will sacrifice body to make tough catches.

KEY ACQUISITIONS

NAME	POS.	PREVIOUS NFL TEAM	NAME	POS.	PREVIOUS NFL TEAM
Sam Gash (FA)	RB	Patriots	Joe Panos (FA)	G	Eagles
Rob Johnson (Trade)	QB	Jaguars	Kevin Williams (FA)	WR	Cardinals

KEY LOSSES

NAME	POS.	NEW NFL TEAM	NAME	POS.	NEW NFL TEAM
Jeff Burris (FA)	CB	Colts	Corey Louchiey (FA)	T	Falcons
Jim Jeffcoat (Retired)	DE	None	Bryce Paup (FA)	LB	Jaguars
Corbin Lacina (FA)	G	Panthers	Steve Tasker (Retired)	WR	None

(FA) = Free Agent

1997 STATISTICAL LEADERS

SCORING
PLAYER	TD	PAT	FG	PTS.
Christie	0	21/21	24/30	93
A. Smith	8	0/0	0/0	48
Early	5	0/0	0/0	30
Reed	5	0/0	0/0	30
Riemersma	2	0/0	0/0	14
Holmes	2	0/0	0/0	12
Johnson	2	0/0	0/0	12
Thomas	1	0/0	0/0	6
Van Pelt	1	0/0	0/0	6
Hansen	0	0/0	0/0	2
Moulds	0	0/0	0/0	2
Bills	26	21/21	24/30	255
Opponents	37	34/35	37/46	367

2-Point conversions: Bills 2-5, Opponents: 0-2

RUSHING
PLAYER	ATT.	YDS.	AVG.	TD
A. Smith	194	840	4.3	8
Thomas	154	643	4.2	1
Holmes	22	106	4.8	2
Collins	30	77	2.6	0
Moulds	4	59	14.8	0
Van Pelt	11	33	3.0	1
Reed	3	11	3.7	0
Hobert	2	7	3.5	0
Johnson	1	6	6.0	0
Mohr	1	0	0.0	0
Bills	422	1,782	4.2	12
Opponents	493	1,792	3.6	11

INTERCEPTIONS
PLAYER	NO.	YDS.	AVG.	TD
Irvin	2	28	14.0	0
Schulz	2	23	11.5	0
Kerner	2	20	10.0	0
Burris	2	19	9.5	0
Bills	15	157	10.5	0
Opponents	25	359	14.4	3

RECEIVING
PLAYER	ATT.	YDS.	AVG.	TD
Reed	60	880	14.7	5
Early	60	853	14.2	5
Johnson	41	340	8.3	2
Thomas	30	208	6.9	0
Moulds	29	294	10.1	0
A. Smith	28	177	6.3	0
Riemersma	26	208	8.0	2
Holmes	13	106	8.2	0
Tindale	4	105	26.3	0
Cline	1	29	29.0	0
Reese	1	13	13.0	0
Bills	293	3,213	11.0	14
Opponents	287	3,405	11.9	17

KICKOFF RETURNS
PLAYER	NO.	YDS.	AVG.	TD
Moulds	43	921	21.4	0
Holmes	23	430	18.7	0
Galloway	6	130	21.7	0
Burris	1	10	10.0	0
Cline	1	0	0.0	0
Coons	1	12	12.0	0
Pike	1	11	11.0	0
Tasker	1	12	12.0	0
Bills	78	1,538	19.7	0
Opponents	55	1,385	25.2	3

PUNT RETURNS
PLAYER	NO.	YDS.	AVG.	TD
Burris	21	198	9.4	0
Tasker	12	113	9.4	0
Galloway	2	15	7.5	0
Bills	39	346	8.9	0
Opponents	44	366	8.3	0

PUNTING
PLAYER	NO.	YDS.	AVG.
Mohr	90	3,764	41.8
Bills	91	3,764	41.4
Opponents	86	3,608	42.0

PASSING
PLAYER	ATT.	COMP.	YDS.	PCT.	TD	INT.	RAT.
Collins	391	215	2,367	55.0	12	13	69.5
Van Pelt	124	60	684	48.4	2	10	37.2
Hobert	30	17	133	56.7	0	2	40.0
Mohr	1	1	29	100.0	0	0	118.8
Bills	546	293	3,213	53.7	14	25	60.8
Opponents	502	287	3,405	57.2	17	15	76.8

SACKS: B. Smith 14.0, Paup 9.5, Hansen 6.0, Bills 46.0, Opponents 46.0

(All individuals may not be represented.)

RECORD HOLDERS

INDIVIDUAL RECORDS—CAREER

CATEGORY	NAME	PERFORMANCE
Rushing (Yds.)	Thurman Thomas, 1988-1997	11,404
Passing (Yds.)	Jim Kelly, 1986-1996	35,467
Passing (TDs)	Jim Kelly, 1986-1996	237
Receiving (No.)	Andre Reed, 1985-1997	826
Receiving (Yds.)	Andre Reed, 1985-1997	11,764
Interceptions	George (Butch) Byrd, 1964-1970	40
Punting (Avg.)	Paul Maguire, 1964-1970	42.1
Punt Return (Avg.)	Clifford Hicks, 1990-92	12.2
Kickoff Return (Avg.)	O.J. Simpson, 1969-1977	30.0
Field Goals	Scott Norwood, 1985-1991	133
Touchdowns (Tot.)	Thurman Thomas, 1988-1997	83
Points	Scott Norwood, 1985-1991	670

INDIVIDUAL RECORDS—SINGLE SEASON

CATEGORY	NAME	PERFORMANCE
Rushing (Yds.)	O.J. Simpson, 1973	2,003
Passing (Yds.)	Jim Kelly, 1991	3,844
Passing (TDs)	Jim Kelly, 1991	33
Receiving (No.)	Andre Reed, 1994	90
Receiving (Yds.)	Andre Reed, 1989	1,312
Interceptions	Billy Atkins, 1961	10
	Tom Janik, 1967	10
Punting (Avg.)	Billy Atkins, 1961	44.5
Punt Return (Avg.)	Keith Moody, 1977	13.1
Kickoff Return (Avg.)	Ed Rutkowski, 1963	30.2
Field Goals	Scott Norwood, 1988	32
Touchdowns (Tot.)	O.J. Simpson, 1975	23
Points	O.J. Simpson, 1975	138

INDIVIDUAL RECORDS—SINGLE GAME

CATEGORY	NAME	PERFORMANCE
Rushing (Yds.)	O.J. Simpson, 11-25-76	273
Passing (Yds.)	Joe Ferguson, 10-9-83	419
Passing (TDs)	Jim Kelly, 9-8-91	6
Receiving (No.)	Andre Reed, 11-20-94	15
Receiving (Yds.)	Jerry Butler, 9-23-79	255
Interceptions	Many Times	3
	Last time by Jeff Nixon, 9-7-80	
Field Goals	Steve Christie, 10-20-96	6
Touchdowns (Tot.)	Cookie Gilchrist, 12-8-63	5
Points	Cookie Gilchrist, 12-8-63	30

CAROLINA PANTHERS

800 South Mint Street
Charlotte, NC 28202
Telephone: (704) 358-7000
Website: nfl.com

Team Colors: Black,
Panther Blue, and Silver

1997 Regular-Season Attendance:
Home: 523,691 Away: 489,334
Playing Surface: Grass
Training Camp:
Wofford College
Spartanburg, SC 29303

NFC West
1997 Record 7-9
Home: 3-5
Away: 4-4
Stadium: Ericsson Stadium
Capacity: 73,250

1997 RESULTS

DATE	RESULT	OPPONENT	ATT.
8/31	L 10-24	Washington	72,633
9/7	W 9-6	at Atlanta	51,829
9/14	W 26-7	at San Diego	63,149
9/21	L 14-35	Kansas City	67,402
9/29	L 21-34	San Francisco	70,972
10/12	L 14-21	at Minnesota	62,625
10/19	W 13-0	at N.O.	50,963
10/26	W 21-12	Atlanta	54,675
11/2	W 38-14	Oakland	71,064
11/9	L 0-34	at Denver	71,408
11/16	L 19-27	at S.F.	61,500
11/23	W 16-10	at St. Louis	64,609
11/30	L 13-16	New Orleans	57,957
12/8	W 23-13	at Dallas	63,251
12/14	L 10-31	Green Bay	70,887
12/20	L 18-30	St. Louis	58,101

1998 SCHEDULE

REGULAR SEASON

Sept. 6	ATLANTA	1:01
Sept. 13	at New Orleans	12:01
Sept. 20	OPEN DATE	
Sept. 27	GREEN BAY	1:01
Oct. 4	at Atlanta	1:01
Oct. 11	at Dallas	12:01
Oct. 18	at Tampa Bay	1:01
Oct. 25	**BUFFALO**	**8:20**
Nov. 1	NEW ORLEANS	1:01
Nov. 8	at San Francisco	1:01
Nov. 15	MIAMI	1:01
Nov. 22	at St. Louis	3:05
Nov. 29	at New York Jets	1:01
Dec. 6	SAN FRANCISCO	1:01
Dec. 13	WASHINGTON	1:01
Dec. 20	ST. LOUIS	1:01
Dec. 27	at Indianapolis	1:01

*Nationally Televised Games in **Bold**/All times local*

COACHING STAFF
Head Coach—Dom Capers; Assistant Coaches—Don Breaux, Billy Davis, Vic Fangio, Ted Gill, Gil Haskell, Chick Harris, Brett Maxie, Jim McNally, Chip Morton, Brad Seely, Steve Shafer, John Shoop, Kevin Steele, Richard Williamson.

1998 SCOUTING REPORT

A familiar face returns to Carolina in 1998 to try to help the Panthers regain their 1996 form when they finished 12-4, won the NFC West, and advanced to the NFC Championship Game.

In 1997, Carolina stumbled to a 7-9 record, partly because of the loss of fiery outside linebacker Kevin Greene, who signed as a free agent with the 49ers. Greene is back, and he should help put more bite in the Panthers' defense, which allowed nearly 100 more points (314) in 1997 than it did in 1996, when it surrendered only 218, second best in the league.

Quarterback Kerry Collins, who was rattled after suffering a broken jaw in preseason last year, also needs to return to his Pro Bowl form of 1996.

1998 DRAFT CHOICES

RD. NAME	POS.	COLLEGE	RD. NAME	POS.	COLLEGE
1. Jason Peter	DT	Nebraska	5. Jerry Jensen	LB	Washington
3a. Chuck Wiley	DE	Louisiana St.	6. Damien Richardson	CB	Arizona St.
3b. Mitch Marrow	DE	Pennsylvania	7a. Viliami Maumau	DT	Colorado
4. Donald Hayes	WR	Wisconsin	7b. Jim Turner	WR	Syracuse

Panthers wanted players with toughness and hard-working attitude and got three of them in Peter, Wiley, and Marrow...Hayes and Turner are big targets (6-4, 212 and 6-3, 208, respectively) who should make quarterback Kerry Collins happy...Jensen is excellent blitzer...Richardson rarely is caught out of position and can play run.

KEY ACQUISITIONS

NAME	POS.	PREVIOUS NFL TEAM	NAME	POS.	PREVIOUS NFL TEAM
Brent Alexander (FA)	S	Cardinals	Sean Gilbert (FA)	DT	Redskins
Ernest Dixon (FA)	LB	Saints	Kevin Greene (FA)	LB	49ers
Doug Evans (FA)	CB	Packers	Corbin Lacina (FA)	G	Bills
William Floyd (FA)	RB	49ers	Leonard Wheeler (FA)	CB	Vikings

KEY LOSSES

NAME	POS.	NEW NFL TEAM	NAME	POS.	NEW NFL TEAM
Chad Cota (FA)	S	Saints	Sam Mills (Retired)	LB	None
Matt Elliott (FA)	G	Falcons	Andre Royal (FA)	LB	Saints
Greg Kragen (Retired)	DT	None	Ray Seals (FA)	DT	Bengals
Ernie Mills (FA)	WR	Cowboys			

(FA) = Free Agent

1997 STATISTICAL LEADERS

SCORING

PLAYER	TD	PAT	FG	PTS.
Kasay	0	25/25	22/26	91
Lane	7	0/0	0/0	42
Walls	6	0/0	0/0	36
Carruth	4	0/0	0/0	24
Biakabutuka	2	0/0	0/0	12
Carrier	2	0/0	0/0	12
S. Greene	2	0/0	0/0	12
Ismail	2	0/0	0/0	12
Johnson	1	0/0	0/0	8
Collins	1	0/0	0/0	6
E. Mills	1	0/0	0/0	6
Muhammad	0	0/0	0/0	2
Stone	0	0/0	0/0	2
Panthers	28	25/25	22/26	265
Opponents	36	35/35	21/25	314

2-Point conversions: Panthers 2-3, Opponents 0-1

RUSHING

PLAYER	ATT.	YDS.	AVG.	TD
Lane	182	809	4.4	7
Johnson	97	358	3.7	1
Biakabutuka	75	299	4.0	2
S. Greene	45	157	3.5	1
Collins	26	65	2.5	1
Beuerlein	4	32	8.0	0
Ismail	4	32	8.0	0
Carruth	6	23	3.8	0
Oliver	1	0	0.0	0
Walter	1	-5	-5.0	0
Panthers	441	1,770	4.0	11
Opponents	497	1,973	4.0	12

INTERCEPTIONS

PLAYER	NO.	YDS.	AVG.	TD
Davis	5	25	5.0	0
Cota	2	28	14.0	0
Poole	2	0	0.0	0
S. Mills	1	18	18.0	0
Panthers	11	72	6.5	0
Opponents	24	265	11.0	2

RECEIVING

PLAYER	ATT.	YDS.	AVG.	TD
Walls	58	746	12.9	6
Carruth	44	545	12.4	4
S. Greene	40	277	6.9	1
Ismail	36	419	11.6	2
Carrier	33	436	13.2	2
Muhammad	27	317	11.7	0
Johnson	21	158	7.5	1
E. Mills	11	127	11.5	1
Lane	8	27	3.4	0
Oliver	6	47	7.8	0
Mangum	4	56	14.0	0
Rasby	1	1	1.0	0
Panthers	289	3,156	10.9	17
Opponents	260	3,253	12.5	17

KICKOFF RETURNS

PLAYER	NO.	YDS.	AVG.	TD
Bates	47	1,281	*27.3	0
E. Mills	4	65	16.3	0
S. Greene	3	18	6.0	0
Rasby	3	32	10.7	0
Stone	3	76	25.3	0
S. Mills	2	12	6.0	0
Garcia	1	11	11.0	0
Poole	1	5	5.0	0
Panthers	64	1,500	23.4	0
Opponents	55	1,276	23.2	1

PUNT RETURNS

PLAYER	NO.	YDS.	AVG.	TD
Poole	26	191	7.3	0
Oliver	14	111	7.9	0
Bates	1	8	8.0	0
Panthers	41	310	7.6	0
Opponents	38	428	11.3	2

PUNTING

PLAYER	NO.	YDS.	AVG.
Walter	85	3,604	42.4
Panthers	85	3,604	42.4
Opponents	88	3,756	42.7

PASSING

PLAYER	ATT.	COMP.	YDS.	PCT.	TD	INT.	RAT.
Collins	381	200	2,124	52.5	11	21	55.7
Beuerlein	153	89	1,032	58.2	6	3	83.6
Panthers	534	289	3,156	54.1	17	24	63.7
Opponents	490	260	3,253	53.1	17	11	76.2

SACKS: Barrow 8.5, Miller 5.5, Royal 5.0, Panthers 36.0, Opponents 44.0

*League Leader   (All individuals may not be represented.)

RECORD HOLDERS

INDIVIDUAL RECORDS—CAREER

CATEGORY	NAME	PERFORMANCE
Rushing (Yds.)	Anthony Johnson, 1995-97	1,588
Passing (Yds.)	Kerry Collins, 1995-97	7,295
Passing (TDs)	Kerry Collins, 1995-97	39
Receiving (No.)	Mark Carrier, 1995-97	157
Receiving (Yds.)	Mark Carrier, 1995-97	2,246
Interceptions	Eric Davis, 1996-97	10
Punting (Avg.)	Ken Walter, 1997	42.4
Punt Return (Avg.)	Winslow Oliver, 1996-97	11.5
Kickoff Return (Avg.)	Michael Bates, 1996-97	28.5
Field Goals	John Kasay, 1995-97	85
Touchdowns (Tot.)	Wesley Walls, 1996-97	16
Points	John Kasay, 1995-97	341

INDIVIDUAL RECORDS—SINGLE SEASON

CATEGORY	NAME	PERFORMANCE
Rushing (Yds.)	Anthony Johnson, 1996	1,120
Passing (Yds.)	Kerry Collins, 1995	2,717
Passing (TDs)	Kerry Collins 1995, 1996	14
Receiving (No.)	Mark Carrier, 1995	66
Receiving (Yds.)	Mark Carrier, 1995	1,002
Interceptions	Brett Maxie, 1995	6
Punting (Avg.)	Ken Walter, 1997	42.4
Punt Return (Avg.)	Winslow Oliver, 1996	11.5
Kickoff Return (Avg.)	Michael Bates, 1996	30.2
Field Goals	John Kasay, 1996	37
Touchdowns (Tot.)	Wesley Walls, 1996	10
Points	John Kasay, 1996	145

INDIVIDUAL RECORDS—SINGLE GAME

CATEGORY	NAME	PERFORMANCE
Rushing (Yds.)	Fred Lane, 11-2-97	147
Passing (Yds.)	Kerry Collins, 11-26-95	335
Passing (TDs)	Kerry Collins, 11-26-95, 10-13-96, 12-8-96	3
	Steve Beverlein, 11-24-96	3
Receiving (No.)	Willie Green, 11-3-96	9
Receiving (Yds.)	Willie Green, 11-12-95, 12-8-96	157
Interceptions	Eric Davis, 10-19-97; Brett Maxie, 10-22-95	2
	Pat Terrell, 11-10-96	
Field Goals	John Kasay, 9-1-96, 9-8-96	5
Touchdowns (Tot.)	Fred Lane, 11-2-97	3
Points	Fred Lane, 11-2-97	18

CHICAGO BEARS

Halas Hall at Conway Park
1000 Football Drive
Lake Forest, Illinois 60045
Telephone: (847) 295-6600
Website: nfl.com

Team Colors: Navy Blue, Orange, and White

1997 Regular-Season Attendance:
Home: 421,900 Away: 536,184
Playing Surface: Grass
Training Camp: University of Wisconsin-Platteville, Platteville, Wisconsin 53818

NFC Central
1997 Record 4-12
Home: 2-6
Away: 2-6
Stadium: Soldier Field
Capacity: 66,944

1997 RESULTS

DATE	RESULT	OPPONENT	ATT.
9/1	L 24-38	at Green Bay	60,766
9/7	L 24-27	MINNESOTA	59,263
9/14	L 7-32	DETROIT	59,147
9/21	L 3-31	at N.E.	59,873
9/28	L 3-27	at Dallas	64,082
10/5	L 17-20	NEW ORLEANS	58,865
10/12	L 23-24	GREEN BAY	62,212
10/27	W 36-33*	at Miami	73,156
11/2	L 8-31	WASHINGTON	53,032
11/9	L 22-29	at Minnesota	63,443
11/16	L 15-23	NEW YORK JETS	45,642
11/23	W 13-7	TAMPA BAY	43,955
11/27	L 20-55	at Detroit	77,904
12/7	W 20-3	BUFFALO	39,784
12/14	W 13-10	at St. Louis	66,030
12/21	L 15-31	at Tampa Bay	70,930

*Overtime

1998 SCHEDULE

REGULAR SEASON

Sept. 6	JACKSONVILLE 12:01
Sept. 13	at Pittsburgh 1:01
Sept. 20	at Tampa Bay 4:05
Sept. 27	**MINNESOTA 3:15**
Oct. 4	DETROIT 12:01
Oct. 11	at Arizona 1:05
Oct. 18	**DALLAS 3:15**
Oct. 25	at Tennessee 3:05
Nov. 1	OPEN DATE
Nov. 8	ST. LOUIS 12:01
Nov. 15	**at Detroit 8:20**
Nov. 22	at Atlanta 1:01
Nov. 29	TAMPA BAY 12:01
Dec. 6	**at Minnesota 7:20**
Dec. 13	at Green Bay 12:01
Dec. 20	BALTIMORE 12:01
Dec. 27	GREEN BAY 12:01

Nationally Televised Games in **Bold**/All times local

COACHING STAFF

Head Coach—Dave Wannstedt; Assistant Coaches—Keith Armstrong, Joe Brodsky, Clarence Brooks, Matt Cavanaugh, Ivan Fears, Carlos Mainord, Tom Rossley, Greg Schiano, Bob Slowik, Tony Wise.

1998 SCOUTING REPORT

In 1997, Chicago played the toughest schedule in the NFL (opponents had a combined winning percentage of .553) and it showed. The Bears suffered through one of their worst seasons, finishing 4-12.

With the fifth overall pick in the 1998 NFL draft, Chicago selected Penn State running back Curtis Enis, whom the Bears hope can step in immediately and put a charge in an offense that finished seventeenth in the league last season. The Bears also will need big years from quarterback Erik Kramer, re-signed in the offseason, and wide receiver Curtis Conway. Chicago was 3-0 last year when Conway recorded 100 or more receiving yards, but he missed nine games because of injuries in 1997. In the seven games he played, the Bears averaged 239.7 passing yards per game, compared to 174 without Conway.

1998 DRAFT CHOICES

RD. NAME	POS.	COLLEGE	RD. NAME	POS.	COLLEGE
1. Curtis Enis	RB	Penn St.	6a. Chris Draft	LB	Stanford
2. Tony Parrish	S	Washington	6b. Patrick Mannelly	T	Duke
3. Olin Kreutz	C	Washington	7a. Chad Overhauser	T	UCLA
4. Alonzo Mayes	TE	Oklahoma St.	7b. Moses Moreno	QB	Colorado St.

Enis will provide Bears' offense with power and speed and is expected to carry heavy load. He also has good hands and will be used as receiver out of backfield...Parrish is tenacious safety who is good at blitzing...Kreutz bench presses more than 500 pounds...Mayes could become one of top tight ends in NFL.

KEY ACQUISITIONS

NAME	POS.	PREVIOUS NFL TEAM	NAME	POS.	PREVIOUS NFL TEAM
Edgar Bennett (FA)	RB	Packers	Mike Wells (FA)	DT	Lions
Hallock (FA)	RB	Jaguars	Mike Zandofsky (FA)	G	Eagles

KEY LOSSES

NAME	POS.	NEW NFL TEAM	NAME	POS.	NEW NFL TEAM
Todd Burger (FA)	G	Jets	Anthony Peterson (Trade)	LB	49ers
Tony Carter (FA)	RB	Patriots	Ricky Proehl (FA)	WR	Rams
Chris Gray (FA)	G	Seahawks			

(FA) = Free Agent

1997 STATISTICAL LEADERS

SCORING
PLAYER	TD	PAT	FG	PTS.
Jaeger	0	20/20	21/26	83
R. Harris	10	0/0	0/0	60
Proehl	7	0/0	0/0	44
Penn	3	0/0	0/0	18
Engram	2	0/0	0/0	14
Kramer	2	0/0	0/0	12
Autry	1	0/0	0/0	8
Mirer	1	0/0	0/0	8
Conway	1	0/0	0/0	6
Wetnight	1	0/0	0/0	6
Flanigan	0	0/0	0/0	2
Bears	28	20/20	21/26	263
Opponents	50	45/45	24/32	421

2-Point conversions: Bears 5-8, Opponents 2-5

RUSHING
PLAYER	ATT.	YDS.	AVG.	TD
R. Harris	275	1,033	3.8	10
Autry	112	319	2.8	1
Salaam	31	112	3.6	0
Kramer	27	83	3.1	2
Mirer	20	78	3.9	1
Ton. Carter	9	56	6.2	0
Harmon	2	6	3.0	0
Conway	3	17	5.7	0
Hicks	4	14	3.5	0
Smith	1	12	12.0	0
Sauerbrun	2	8	4.0	0
Bears	490	1,746	3.6	14
Opponents	421	1,858	4.4	18

INTERCEPTIONS
PLAYER	NO.	YDS.	AVG.	TD
W. Harris	5	30	6.0	0
Tom Carter	3	12	4.0	0
Mangum	2	4	2.0	0
Bears	13	60	4.6	0
Opponents	22	328	14.9	1

RECEIVING
PLAYER	ATT.	YDS.	AVG.	TD
Proehl	58	753	13.0	7
Penn	47	576	12.3	3
Wetnight	46	464	10.1	1
Engram	45	399	8.9	2
Conway	30	476	15.9	1
R. Harris	28	115	4.1	0
Ton. Carter	24	152	6.3	0
Jennings	14	164	11.7	0
Bownes	12	146	12.2	0
Autry	9	59	6.6	0
Allred	8	70	8.8	0
Hughes	8	68	8.5	0
Harmon	2	8	4.0	0
Smith	2	22	11.0	0
Salaam	2	20	10.0	0
T. Allen	1	9	9.0	0
Bears	336	3,501	10.4	14
Opponents	273	3,289	12.0	25

KICKOFF RETURNS
PLAYER	NO.	YDS.	AVG.	TD
Hughes	43	1,008	23.4	0
Bownes	19	396	20.8	0
Smith	10	196	19.6	0
Bears	79	1,694	21.4	0
Opponents	52	1,237	23.8	0

PUNT RETURNS
PLAYER	NO.	YDS.	AVG.	TD
Hughes	36	258	7.2	0
Proehl	8	59	7.4	0
Bears	46	321	7.0	0
Opponents	52	727	14.0	2

PUNTING
PLAYER	NO.	YDS.	AVG.
Sauerbrun	95	4,059	42.7
Jaeger	1	18	18.0
Bears	96	4,077	42.5
Opponents	81	3,526	43.5

PASSING
PLAYER	ATT.	COMP.	YDS.	PCT.	TD	INT.	RAT.
Kramer	477	275	3,011	57.7	14	14	74.0
Mirer	103	53	420	51.5	0	6	37.7
Stenstrom	14	8	70	57.1	0	2	31.0
Conway	1	0	0	0.0	0	0	39.6
Bears	595	336	3,501	56.5	14	22	66.1
Opponents	476	273	3,289	57.4	25	13	84.8

SACKS: Flanigan 6.0, Minter 6.0, B. Cox 5.0, Bears 38.0, Opponents 43.0

(All individuals may not be represented.)

RECORD HOLDERS

INDIVIDUAL RECORDS—CAREER

CATEGORY	NAME	PERFORMANCE
Rushing (Yds.)	Walter Payton, 1975-1987	*16,726
Passing (Yds.)	Sid Luckman, 1939-1950	14,686
Passing (TDs)	Sid Luckman, 1939-1950	137
Receiving (No.)	Walter Payton, 1975-1987	492
Receiving (Yds.)	Johnny Morris, 1958-1967	5,059
Interceptions	Gary Fencik, 1976-1987	38
Punting (Avg.)	George Gulyanics, 1947-1952	44.5
Punt Return (Avg.)	Ray (Scooter) McLean, 1940-47	14.8
Kickoff Return (Avg.)	Gale Sayers, 1965-1971	30.6
Field Goals	Kevin Butler, 1985-1995	243
Touchdowns (Tot.)	Walter Payton, 1975-1987	125
Points	Kevin Butler, 1985-1995	1,116

INDIVIDUAL RECORDS—SINGLE SEASON

CATEGORY	NAME	PERFORMANCE
Rushing (Yds.)	Walter Payton, 1977	1,852
Passing (Yds.)	Erik Kramer, 1995	3,838
Passing (TDs)	Erik Kramer, 1995	29
Receiving (No.)	Johnny Morris, 1964	93
Receiving (Yds.)	Jeff Graham, 1995	1,301
Interceptions	Mark Carrier, 1990	10
Punting (Avg.)	Bobby Joe Green, 1963	46.5
Punt Return (Avg.)	Harry Clark, 1943	15.8
Kickoff Return (Avg.)	Gale Sayers, 1967	37.7
Field Goals	Kevin Butler, 1985	31
Touchdowns (Tot.)	Gale Sayers, 1965	22
Points	Kevin Butler, 1985	144

INDIVIDUAL RECORDS—SINGLE GAME

CATEGORY	NAME	PERFORMANCE
Rushing (Yds.)	Walter Payton, 11-20-77	*275
Passing (Yds.)	Johnny Lujack, 12-11-49	468
Passing (TDs)	Sid Luckman, 11-14-43	*7
Receiving (No.)	Jim Keane, 10-23-49	14
Receiving (Yds.)	Harlon Hill, 10-31-54	214
Interceptions	Many times.	3
	Last time by Mark Carrier, 12-9-90	
Field Goals	Roger LeClerc, 12-3-61	5
	Mac Percival, 10-20-68	5
Touchdowns (Tot.)	Gale Sayers, 12-12-65	*6
Points	Gale Sayers, 12-12-65	36

*NFL Record

CINCINNATI BENGALS

One Bengals Drive
Cincinnati, Ohio 45204
Telephone: (513) 621-3550
Website: nfl.com

Team Colors: Black, Orange, and White

1997 Regular-Season Attendance:
Home: 439,831 Away: 463,944
Playing Surface: AstroTurf-8
Training Camp:
Georgetown College
Georgetown, Kentucky 40324

AFC Central
1997 Record 7-9
Home: 6-2
Away: 1-7
Stadium: Cinergy Field
Capacity: 60,389

1997 RESULTS

DATE	RESULT	OPPONENT	ATT.
8/31	W 24-21	ARIZONA	53,644
9/7	L 10-23	at Baltimore	52,968
9/21	L 20-38	at Denver	73,871
9/28	L 14-31	NEW YORK JETS	57,209
10/5	L 13-21	at Jacksonville	67,128
10/12	L 7-30	at Tennessee	17,071
10/19	L 10-26	PITTSBURGH	60,020
10/26	L 27-29	at N.Y. Giants	72,584
11/2	W 38-31	SAN DIEGO	53,754
11/9	W 28-13	at Ind.	58,473
11/16	L 3-20	at Pittsburgh	55,226
11/23	W 31-26	JACKSONVILLE	55,158
11/30	L 42-44	at Phil.	66,623
12/4	W 41-14	TENNESSEE	49,086
12/14	W 31-24	DALLAS	60,043
12/21	W 16-14	BALTIMORE	50,917

1998 SCHEDULE

REGULAR SEASON

Sept. 6	TENNESSEE	1:01
Sept. 13	at Detroit	1:01
Sept. 20	GREEN BAY	1:01
Sept. 27	**at Baltimore**	**8:20**
Oct. 4	OPEN DATE	
Oct. 11	PITTSBURGH	1:01
Oct. 18	at Tennessee	12:01
Oct. 25	at Oakland	1:15
Nov. 1	DENVER	1:01
Nov. 8	at Jacksonville	1:01
Nov. 15	at Minnesota	12:01
Nov. 22	BALTIMORE	4:15
Nov. 29	JACKSONVILLE	1:01
Dec. 6	BUFFALO	1:01
Dec. 13	at Indianapolis	1:01
Dec. 20	at Pittsburgh	1:01
Dec. 27	TAMPA BAY	1:01

*Nationally Televised Games in **Bold**/All times local*

COACHING STAFF
Head Coach— Bruce Coslet; Assistant Coaches—Paul Alexander, Jim Anderson, Ken Anderson, Louie Cioffi, Mark Duffner, John Garrett, Ray Horton, Tim Krumrie, Dick LeBeau, Al Roberts, Kim Wood, Bob Wylie.

1998 SCOUTING REPORT

The Bengals are looking to play well at the start of the 1998 season. The past two years, Cincinnati struggled in the beginning (1-6 in 1996 and 1-7 in '97), but finished strong (7-2 and 6-2, respectively). It should help that three of the Bengals' first five games are at home, where Cincinnati is 11-2 since Bruce Coslet became head coach midway through the 1996 season.

Quarterback Jeff Blake, a Pro Bowl player in 1996, was benched in week 13 last year in favor of veteran Boomer Esiason. Esiason retired to go into broadcasting, so Blake gets another chance at rebuilding his once-promising career.

Corey Dillon, a second-round draft choice out of Washington in 1997, has superstar potential. He finished ninth in the league with 1,129 rushing yards, including 246 against the Oilers, most ever by a rookie.

1998 DRAFT CHOICES

RD. NAME	POS.	COLLEGE	RD. NAME	POS.	COLLEGE
1a. Takeo Spikes	LB	Auburn	4. Glen Steele	DT	Michigan
1b. Brian Simmons	LB	North Carolina	6. Jason Tucker	WR	Texas Christian
2. Artrell Hawkins	CB	Cincinnati	7a. Marcus Parker	RB	Virginia Tech
3a. Steve Foley	LB	N.E. Louisiana	7b. Damian Vaughn	TE	Miami (OH)
3b. Mike Goff	G	Iowa			

Spikes and Simmons are just who defensive coordinator Dick Lebeau needs to make his 3-4 defensive scheme work. Both linebackers have speed to cover from sideline to sideline and also are effective in pass coverage...Hawkins has excellent coverage skills and can play safety.

KEY ACQUISITIONS

NAME	POS.	PREVIOUS NFL TEAM	NAME	POS.	PREVIOUS NFL TEAM
...hael Bankston (FA)	DT	Cardinals	Thomas Randolph (FA)	CB	Giants
...Justin (Trade)	QB	Colts	Ray Seals (FA)	DT	Panthers

KEY LOSSES

NAME	POS.	NEW NFL TEAM	NAME	POS.	NEW NFL TEAM
Gerald Dixon (FA)	LB	Chargers	Dan Wilkinson (Trade)	DT	Redskins
Boomer Esiason (Retired)	QB	None			

(FA) = Free Agent

1997 STATISTICAL LEADERS

SCORING
PLAYER	TD	PAT	FG	PTS.
Pelfrey	0	41/43	12/16	77
Dillon	10	0/0	0/0	60
Carter	7	0/0	0/0	42
McGee	6	0/0	0/0	38
Pickens	5	0/0	0/0	30
Scott	5	0/0	0/0	30
Blake	3	0/0	0/0	18
Bieniemy	2	0/0	0/0	12
Dunn	2	0/0	0/0	12
Hundon	2	0/0	0/0	12
Milne	2	0/0	0/0	12
Battaglia	1	0/0	0/0	6
Copeland	1	0/0	0/0	6
Bengals	46	41/43	12/16	355
Opponents	48	45/45	24/29	405

2-Point conversions: Bengals 1-3, Opponents 0-3

RUSHING
PLAYER	ATT.	YDS.	AVG.	TD
Dillon	233	1,129	4.8	10
Carter	128	464	3.6	7
Blake	45	234	5.2	3
Bieniemy	21	97	4.6	1
Milne	13	32	2.5	2
Esiason	8	11	1.4	0
Scott	1	6	6.0	0
Johnson	1	0	0.0	0
Graham	1	-1	-1.0	0
Pickens	1	-6	-6.0	0
Bengals	452	1,966	4.3	23
Opponents	514	2,223	4.3	15

INTERCEPTIONS
PLAYER	NO.	YDS.	AVG.	TD
Sawyer	4	44	11.0	0
Ambrose	3	56	18.7	0
Mack	1	29	29.0	0
Bengals	13	183	14.1	0
Opponents	9	26	2.9	0

RECEIVING
PLAYER	ATT.	YDS.	AVG.	TD
Scott	54	797	14.8	5
Pickens	52	695	13.4	5
McGee	34	414	12.2	6
Bieniemy	31	249	8.0	0
Dunn	27	414	15.3	2
Dillon	27	259	9.6	0
Milne	23	138	6.0	0
Carter	21	157	7.5	0
Hundon	16	285	17.8	2
Battaglia	12	149	12.4	1
Twyner	4	45	11.3	0
Graham	1	1	1.0	0
Bengals	302	3,603	11.9	21
Opponents	309	3,668	11.9	30

KICKOFF RETURNS
PLAYER	NO.	YDS.	AVG.	TD
Bieniemy	34	789	23.2	1
Dunn	19	487	25.6	0
Hundon	10	169	16.9	0
Dillon	6	182	30.3	0
Twyner	4	72	18.0	0
Carter	1	9	9.0	0
Bengals	74	1,708	23.1	1
Opponents	67	1,406	21.0	0

PUNT RETURNS
PLAYER	NO.	YDS.	AVG.	TD
Myers	26	201	7.7	0
Bengals	26	201	7.7	0
Opponents	35	407	11.6	2

PUNTING
PLAYER	NO.	YDS.	AVG.
Johnson	81	3,471	42.9
Bengals	81	3,471	42.9
Opponents	69	3,082	44.7

PASSING
PLAYER	ATT.	COMP.	YDS.	PCT.	TD	INT.	RAT.
Blake	317	184	2,125	58.0	8	7	77.6
Esiason	186	118	1,478	63.4	13	2	106.9
Carter	1	0	0	0	0	0	39.6
Bengals	504	302	3,603	59.9	21	9	88.3
Opponents	542	309	3,668	57.0	30	13	86.2

SACKS: Dixon 8.5, Wilkinson 5.0, Shade 4.0, Bengals 35.0, Opponents 46.0

(All individuals may not be represented.)

RECORD HOLDERS

INDIVIDUAL RECORDS—CAREER

CATEGORY	NAME	PERFORMANCE
Rushing (Yds.)	James Brooks, 1984-1991	6,447
Passing (Yds.)	Ken Anderson, 1971-1986	32,838
Passing (TDs)	Ken Anderson, 1971-1986	197
Receiving (No.)	Cris Collinsworth, 1981-88	417
Receiving (Yds.)	Isaac Curtis, 1973-1984	7,101
Interceptions	Ken Riley, 1969-1983	65
Punting (Avg.)	Dave Lewis, 1970-73	43.9
Punt Return (Avg.)	Mitchell Price, 1990-92	10.4
Kickoff Return (Avg.)	Lemar Parrish, 1970-77	24.7
Field Goals	Jim Breech, 1980-1992	225
Touchdowns (Tot.)	Pete Johnson, 1977-1983	70
Points	Jim Breech, 1980-1992	1,151

INDIVIDUAL RECORDS—SINGLE SEASON

CATEGORY	NAME	PERFORMANCE
Rushing (Yds.)	James Brooks, 1989	1,239
Passing (Yds.)	Boomer Esiason, 1986	3,959
Passing (TDs)	Ken Anderson, 1981	29
Receiving (No.)	Carl Pickens, 1996	100
Receiving (Yds.)	Eddie Brown, 1988	1,273
Interceptions	Ken Riley, 1976	9
Punting (Avg.)	Dave Lewis, 1970	46.2
Punt Return (Avg.)	Mike Martin, 1984	15.7
Kickoff Return (Avg.)	Lemar Parrish, 1970	30.2
Field Goals	Doug Pelfrey, 1995	29
Touchdowns (Tot.)	Carl Pickens, 1995	17
Points	Doug Pelfrey, 1995	121

INDIVIDUAL RECORDS—SINGLE GAME

CATEGORY	NAME	PERFORMANCE
Rushing (Yds.)	Corey Dillon, 12-4-97	246
Passing (Yds.)	Boomer Esiason, 10-7-90	490
Passing (TDs)	Boomer Esiason, 12-21-86, 10-29-89	5
Receiving (No.)	James Brooks, 12-25-89	12
	Carl Pickens, 11-10-96	12
Receiving (Yds.)	Eddie Brown, 11-6-88	216
Interceptions	Many times; last time by David Fulcher, 12-17-89	3
Field Goals	Doug Pelfrey, 11-6-94	6
Touchdowns (Tot.)	Larry Kinnebrew, 10-28-84	4
	Corey Dillon, 12-4-97	4
Points	Larry Kinnebrew, 10-28-84	24
	Corey Dillon, 12-4-97	24

DALLAS COWBOYS

Cowboys Center
One Cowboys Parkway
Irving, Texas 75063
Telephone: (972) 556-9900
Website: nfl.com

Team Colors: Royal Blue, Silver, Blue, and White

1997 Regular-Season Attendance:
Home: 511,767 Away: 541,187
Playing Surface: Sportfield Turf
Training Camp: Midwestern State University Wichita Falls, Texas 76308

NFC East
1997 Record 6-10
Home: 5-3
Away: 1-7
Stadium: Texas Stadium
Capacity: 65,675

1997 RESULTS

DATE	RESULT	OPPONENT	ATT.
8/31	W 37-7	at Pittsburgh	60,396
9/7	L 22-25*	at Arizona	71,578
9/15	W 21-20	PHILADELPHIA	63,942
9/28	W 27-3	CHICAGO	64,082
10/5	L 17-20	at N.Y. Giants	77,137
10/13	L 16-21	at Washington	76,159
10/19	W 26-22	JACKSONVILLE	64,464
10/26	L 12-13	at Phil.	67,106
11/2	L 10-17	at S.F.	68,657
11/9	W 24-6	ARIZONA	64,302
11/16	W 17-14	WASHINGTON	64,559
11/23	L 17-45	at Green Bay	60,111
11/27	L 14-27	TENNESSEE	63,421
12/8	L 13-23	CAROLINA	63,251
12/14	L 24-31	at Cincinnati	60,043
12/21	L 7-20	N.Y. GIANTS	63,746

*Overtime

1998 SCHEDULE

REGULAR SEASON

Sept. 6	ARIZONA 3:05
Sept. 13	**at Denver 2:15**
Sept. 21	**at N.Y. Giants (Mon.) . . 8:20**
Sept. 27	OAKLAND 12:01
Oct. 4	at Washington 1:01
Oct. 11	CAROLINA 12:01
Oct. 18	**at Chicago 3:15**
Oct. 25	OPEN DATE
Nov. 2	**at Phila. (Mon.) 8:20**
Nov. 8	NEW YORK GIANTS 12:01
Nov. 15	at Arizona 2:15
Nov. 22	SEATTLE 12:01
Nov. 26	**MINNESOTA (Thurs.) . 3:05**
Dec. 6	at New Orleans 12:01
Dec. 13	**at Kansas City 3:15**
Dec. 20	**PHILADELPHIA 3:15**
Dec. 27	**WASHINGTON 7:20**

Nationally Televised Games in **Bold**/All times local

COACHING STAFF

Head Coach—Chan Gailey; Assistant Coaches—Joe Avezzano, Jim Bates, Dave Campo, George Edwards, Wayne (Buddy) Geis, Steve Hoffman, Hudson Houck, Joe Juraszek, Les Miles, Dwain Painter, Clancy Pendergast, Tommie Robinson, Clarence Shelmon, Mike Zimmer.

1998 SCOUTING REPORT

Barry Switzer is out, and former Pittsburgh Steelers offensive coordinator Chan Gailey is in as head coach of the Cowboys. Gailey brings a new offensive system and a fresh outlook to a team that lost five consecutive games at the end of the 1997 season.

The first item on Gailey's agenda is helping Troy Aikman, Emmitt Smith, Michael Irvin, and the rest of the Dallas offense rediscover the end zone. In 1997, the Cowboys finished twentieth in the NFL in total offense and struggled to cross the goal line. Dallas converted only 35.2 percent of its drives inside its opponents' 20-yard line into touchdowns, the worst percentage in the NFC.

Defense kept Dallas in most of its games. The Cowboys led the NFL in pass defense and were second in total defense. However, Dallas's defense recorded the fewest takeaways in the league (19).

1998 DRAFT CHOICES

RD.	NAME	POS.	COLLEGE
1.	Greg Ellis	DE	North Carolina
2.	Flozell Adams	T	Michigan St.
4.	Michael Myers	DT	Alabama
5a.	Darren Hambrick	LB	South Carolina
5b.	Oliver Ross	T	Iowa St.
6.	Izell Reese	DB	Ala.-Birmingham
7a.	Tarik Smith	RB	California
7b.	Antonio Fleming	G	Georgia
7c.	Rodrick Monroe	TE	Cincinnati

Cowboys hope Ellis fits into the mold of Charles Haley. Ellis has size (6-4, 281) and motor to be dominating pass rusher that team sorely needs...Adams does fine job at both run and pass blocking...Myers can be disruptive force if he's blocked one-on-one.

KEY ACQUISITIONS

NAME	POS.	PREVIOUS NFL TEAM
Everett McIver (FA)	G	Dolphins
Ernie Mills (FA)	WR	Panthers
Chris Warren (FA)	RB	Seahawks

KEY LOSSES

NAME	POS.	NEW NFL TEAM
John Flannery (FA)	C	Rams
George Hegamin (FA)	T	Eagles
Brock Marion (FA)	S	Dolphins

(FA) = Free Agent

1997 STATISTICAL LEADERS

SCORING

PLAYER	TD	PAT	FG	PTS.
Cunningham	0	24/24	*34/37	126
Irvin	9	0/0	0/0	54
E. Smith	4	0/0	0/0	26
Miller	4	0/0	0/0	24
LaFleur	2	0/0	0/0	12
Sanders	2	0/0	0/0	12
Walker	2	0/0	0/0	12
Sh. Williams	2	0/0	0/0	12
Coakley	1	0/0	0/0	6
Hennings	1	0/0	0/0	6
Johnston	1	0/0	0/0	6
St. Williams	1	0/0	0/0	6
Bjornson	0	0/0	0/0	2
Gowin	0	0/0	0/1	0
Cowboys	29	24/24	34/38	304
Opponents	36	34/34	20/27	314

2-Point conversions: Cowboys 2-5, Opponents 2-2

RUSHING

PLAYER	ATT.	YDS.	AVG.	TD
E. Smith	261	1,074	4.1	4
Sh. Williams	121	468	3.9	2
Aikman	25	79	3.2	0
Walker	6	20	3.3	0
Miller	1	6	6.0	0
Johnston	2	3	1.5	0
Wilson	6	-2	-.3	0
Sanders	1	-11	-11.0	0
Cowboys	423	1,637	3.9	6
Opponents	511	1,994	3.9	12

INTERCEPTIONS

PLAYER	NO.	YDS.	AVG.	TD
Sanders	2	81	40.5	1
Stoutmire	2	8	4.0	0
K. Smith	1	21	21.0	0
Woodson	1	14	14.0	0
Cowboys	7	130	18.6	1
Opponents	12	211	17.6	1

RECEIVING

PLAYER	ATT.	YDS.	AVG.	TD
Irvin	75	1,180	15.7	9
Bjornson	47	442	9.4	0
Miller	46	645	14.0	4
E. Smith	40	234	5.9	0
St. Williams	30	308	10.3	1
Sh. Williams	21	159	7.6	0
Johnston	18	166	9.2	1
LaFleur	18	122	6.8	2
Walker	14	149	10.6	2
B. Davis	3	33	11.0	0
Galbraith	2	16	8.0	0
Sanders	0	0	—	0
Cowboys	314	3,454	11.0	19
Opponents	253	2,717	10.7	20

KICKOFF RETURNS

PLAYER	NO.	YDS.	AVG.	TD
Walker	50	1,167	23.3	0
Marion	10	311	31.1	0
Galbraith	2	24	12.0	0
Sanders	1	18	18.0	0
Cowboys	63	1,520	24.1	0
Opponents	65	1,172	18.0	0

PUNT RETURNS

PLAYER	NO.	YDS.	AVG.	TD
Sanders	33	407	12.3	1
Mathis	11	91	8.3	0
St. Williams	2	14	7.0	0
Pittman	1	0	0.0	0
Cowboys	47	512	10.9	1
Opponents	40	365	9.1	0

PUNTING

PLAYER	NO.	YDS.	AVG.
Gowin	86	3,592	41.8
Cowboys	86	3,592	41.8
Opponents	95	4,142	43.6

PASSING

PLAYER	ATT.	COMP.	YDS.	PCT.	TD	INT.	RAT.
Aikman	518	292	3,283	56.4	19	12	78.0
Wilson	21	12	115	57.1	0	0	72.5
Garrett	14	10	56	71.4	0	0	78.3
Cowboys	553	314	3,454	56.8	19	12	77.8
Opponents	473	253	2,717	53.5	20	7	78.5

SACKS: Carver 6.0, Tolbert 5.0, Hennings 4.5, Cowboys 38.0, Opponents 39.0

*League Leader   (All individuals may not be represented.)

RECORD HOLDERS

INDIVIDUAL RECORDS—CAREER

CATEGORY	NAME	PERFORMANCE
Rushing (Yds.)	Tony Dorsett, 1977-1987	12,036
Passing (Yds.)	Troy Aikman, 1989-1997	26,016
Passing (TDs)	Danny White, 1976-1988	155
Receiving (No.)	Michael Irvin, 1988-1997	666
Receiving (Yds.)	Michael Irvin, 1988-1997	10,680
Interceptions	Mel Renfro, 1964-1977	52
Punting (Avg.)	Mike Saxon, 1985-1992	41.5
Punt Return (Avg.)	Bob Hayes, 1965-1974	11.1
Kickoff Return (Avg.)	Mel Renfro, 1964-1977	26.4
Field Goals	Rafael Septien, 1978-1986	162
Touchdowns (Tot.)	Emmitt Smith, 1990-97	119
Points	Rafael Septien, 1978-1986	874

INDIVIDUAL RECORDS—SINGLE SEASON

CATEGORY	NAME	PERFORMANCE
Rushing (Yds.)	Emmitt Smith, 1995	1,773
Passing (Yds.)	Danny White, 1983	3,980
Passing (TDs)	Danny White, 1983	29
Receiving (No.)	Michael Irvin, 1995	111
Receiving (Yds.)	Michael Irvin, 1995	1,603
Interceptions	Everson Walls, 1981	11
Punting (Avg.)	Sam Baker, 1962	45.4
Punt Return (Avg.)	Bob Hayes, 1968	20.8
Kickoff Return (Avg.)	Mel Renfro, 1965	30.0
Field Goals	Richie Cunningham, 1997	34
Touchdowns (Tot.)	Emmitt Smith, 1995	*25
Points	Emmitt Smith, 1995	150

INDIVIDUAL RECORDS—SINGLE GAME

CATEGORY	NAME	PERFORMANCE
Rushing (Yds.)	Emmitt Smith, 10-31-93	237
Passing (Yds.)	Don Meredith, 11-10-63	460
Passing (TDs)	Many times; last time by Danny White, 10-30-83	5
Receiving (No.)	Lance Rentzel, 11-19-67	13
Receiving (Yds.)	Bob Hayes, 11-13-66	246
Interceptions	Herb Adderley, 9-26-71; Lee Roy Jordan, 11-4-73;	3
	Dennis Thurman, 12-13-81	3
Field Goals	Chris Boniol, 11-18-96	*7
Touchdowns (Tot.)	Many times.	4
	Last time by Emmitt Smith, 9-4-95	
Points	Many times.	24
	Last time by Emmitt Smith, 9-4-95	

*NFL Record

DENVER BRONCOS

13655 Broncos Parkway
Englewood, Colorado 80112
Telephone: (303) 649-9000
Website: nfl.com

Team Colors: Orange, Navy Blue, and White

1997 Regular-Season Attendance:
Home: 590,189 Away: 499,942
Playing Surface: Grass (PAT)
Training Camp: University of Northern Colorado
Greeley, Colorado 80639

AFC West
1997 Record 12-4
Home: 8-0 **Away:** 4-4
Stadium: Denver Mile High Stadium
Capacity: 76,082

1997 RESULTS

DATE	RESULT	OPPONENT	ATT.
8/31	W 19-3	Kansas City	75,600
9/7	W 35-14	at Seattle	55,859
9/14	W 35-14	St. Louis	74,338
9/21	W 38-20	Cincinnati	73,871
9/28	W 29-21	at Atlanta	48,211
10/6	W 34-13	New England	75,821
10/19	L 25-28	at Oakland	57,006
10/26	W 23-20*	at Buffalo	78,458
11/2	W 30-27	Seattle	74,212
11/9	W 34-0	Carolina	71,408
11/16	L 22-24	at Kansas City	77,963
11/24	W 31-3	Oakland	75,307
11/30	W 38-28	at San Diego	54,245
12/7	L 24-35	at Pittsburgh	59,739
12/15	L 17-34	at S.F.	68,461
12/21	W 38-3	San Diego	69,632
POSTSEASON			
12/27	W 42-17	Jacksonville	74,481
1/4	W 14-10	at Kansas City	76,965
1/11	W 24-21	at Pittsburgh	61,382
1/25	W 31-24	Green Bay, Super Bowl XXXII	68,912

*Overtime

1998 SCHEDULE

REGULAR SEASON

Sept. 7	**NEW ENGLAND (Mon.).**	**6:20**
Sept. 13	**DALLAS**	**2:15**
Sept. 20	**at Oakland**	**1:15**
Sept. 27	at Washington	1:01
Oct. 4	**PHILADELPHIA**	**2:15**
Oct. 11	**at Seattle**	**1:15**
Oct. 18	OPEN DATE	
Oct. 25	**JACKSONVILLE**	**2:15**
Nov. 1	at Cincinnati	1:01
Nov. 8	**SAN DIEGO**	**2:15**
Nov. 16	**at Kansas City (Mon.)**	**7:20**
Nov. 22	**OAKLAND**	**2:15**
Nov. 29	**at San Diego**	**5:20**
Dec. 6	**KANSAS CITY**	**2:15**
Dec. 13	at New York Giants	1:01
Dec. 21	**at Miami (Mon.)**	**8:20**
Dec. 27	**SEATTLE**	**2:15**

Nationally Televised Games in **Bold**/All times local

COACHING STAFF

Head Coach—Mike Shanahan; Assistant Coaches—Frank Bush, Barney Chavous, Rick Dennison, Ed Donatell, George Dyer, Alex Gibbs, Mike Heimerdinger, Gary Kubiak, Brian Pariani, Ricky Porter, Greg Robinson, Greg Saporta, Rick Smith, John Teerlinck, Bobby Turner, Rich Tuten.

1998 SCOUTING REPORT

Nothing short of a return trip to the Super Bowl will do for Denver in 1998. Winning back-to-back NFL titles won't be easy, but it's certainly within the grasp of the Broncos, who return almost their entire roster from last season.

The most notable player to return in 1998 is quarterback John Elway, who, after 15 NFL seasons, had contemplated retirement. Pro Bowl tackle Gary Zimmerman, who retired before the 1997 season but changed his mind, also should be back again in '98.

Last year, the Broncos became the first team since the 1979 Steelers to lead the AFC in total offense and defense. Denver was only the second team in NFL history to have a 3,000-yard passer (Elway), a 1,500-yard rusher (Super Bowl XXXII MVP Terrell Davis), and two 1,000-yard receivers (Rod Smith and tight end Shannon Sharpe).

1998 DRAFT CHOICES

RD. NAME	POS.	COLLEGE	RD. NAME	POS.	COLLEGE
1. Marcus Nash	WR	Tennessee	5. Chris Howard	RB	Michigan
2. Eric Brown	S	Mississippi St.	7a. Trey Teague	T	Tennessee
3. Brian Griese	QB	Michigan	7b. Nate Wayne	LB	Mississippi
4. Curtis Alexander	RB	Alabama			

Nash is big receiver and very dangerous in open field after catch...Brown is hard-hitting strong safety who'll provide solid run support...Griese is competent leader who has poise and other intagibles that will help him succeed in NFL...Teague is versatile enough to play guard, center, and handle long-snapping duties.

KEY ACQUISITIONS

NAME	POS.	PREVIOUS NFL TEAM	NAME	POS.	PREVIOUS NFL TEAM
Justin Armour (FA)	WR	49ers	Doug Nussmeier (FA)	QB	Saints
Carl Kidd (FA)	CB	Raiders	Marvin Washington (FA)	DE	49ers

KEY LOSSES

NAME	POS.	NEW NFL TEAM	NAME	POS.	NEW NFL TEAM
Allen Aldridge (FA)	LB	Lions	Brian Habib (FA)	G	Seahawks
Jamie Brown (Trade)	T	49ers			

(FA) = Free Agent

1997 STATISTICAL LEADERS

SCORING

PLAYER	TD	PAT	FG	PTS.
Elam	0	46/46	26/36	124
Davis	15	0/0	0/0	96
R. Smith	12	0/0	0/0	72
McCaffrey	8	0/0	0/0	48
Gordon	4	0/0	0/0	24
Sharpe	3	0/0	0/0	20
Green	2	0/0	0/0	12
Bentley	0	4/4	2/3	10
Atwater	1	0/0	0/0	6
Braxton	1	0/0	0/0	6
Carswell	1	0/0	0/0	6
Elway	1	0/0	0/0	6
Hebron	1	0/0	0/0	6
Johnson	1	0/0	0/0	6
Loville	1	0/0	0/0	6
Broncos	55	50/50	28/39	472
Opponents	35	35/35	14/19	287

2-Point conversions: Broncos 4-5, Opponents: 0-0

RUSHING

PLAYER	ATT.	YDS.	AVG.	TD
Davis	369	1,750	4.7	*15
Hebron	49	222	4.5	1
Elway	50	218	4.4	1
Loville	25	124	5.0	1
Griffith	9	34	3.8	0
R. Smith	5	16	3.2	0
D. Smith	4	10	2.5	0
Brister	4	2	0.5	0
Broncos	520	2,378	4.6	18
Opponents	381	1,803	4.7	10

INTERCEPTIONS

PLAYER	NO.	YDS.	AVG.	TD
Braxton	4	113	28.3	1
Gordon	4	64	16.0	0
Crockett	4	18	4.5	0
Broncos	18	319	17.7	5
Opponents	11	193	17.5	1

RECEIVING

PLAYER	ATT.	YDS.	AVG.	TD
Sharpe	72	1,107	15.4	3
R. Smith	70	1,180	16.9	12
McCaffrey	45	590	13.1	8
Davis	42	287	6.8	0
Green	19	240	12.6	2
Carswell	12	96	8.0	1
Griffith	11	55	5.0	0
D. Smith	4	41	10.3	1
Hebron	3	36	12.0	0
Jeffers	3	24	8.0	0
Chamberlain	2	18	9.0	0
Loville	2	10	5.0	0
Lynn	1	21	21.0	0
Nalen	1	-1	-1.0	0
Broncos	287	3,704	12.9	27
Opponents	290	3,166	10.9	20

KICKOFF RETURNS

PLAYER	NO.	YDS.	AVG.	TD
Hebron	43	1,009	23.5	0
Loville	5	136	27.2	0
Burns	4	45	11.3	0
Chamberlain	1	13	13.0	0
D. Smith	1	0	0.0	0
Broncos	54	1,203	22.3	0
Opponents	89	1,827	20.5	0

PUNT RETURNS

PLAYER	NO.	YDS.	AVG.	TD
Gordon	40	543	13.6	3
R. Smith	1	12	12.0	0
Broncos	41	555	13.5	3
Opponents	26	235	9.0	1

PUNTING

PLAYER	NO.	YDS.	AVG.
Rouen	60	2,598	43.3
Broncos	60	2,598	43.3
Opponents	94	4,091	43.5

PASSING

PLAYER	ATT.	COMP.	YDS.	PCT.	TD	INT.	RAT.
Elway	502	280	3,635	55.8	27	11	87.5
Brister	9	6	48	66.7	0	0	79.9
Lewis	2	1	21	50.0	0	0	87.5
Broncos	513	287	3,704	55.9	27	11	87.4
Opponents	526	290	3,166	55.1	20	18	71.5

SACKS: N. Smith 8.5, Tanuvasa 8.5, Williams 8.5, Broncos 44.0, Opponents 35.0

*League Leader   (All individuals may not be represented.)

RECORD HOLDERS

INDIVIDUAL RECORDS—CAREER

CATEGORY	NAME	PERFORMANCE
Rushing (Yds.)	Floyd Little, 1967-1975	6,323
Passing (Yds.)	John Elway, 1983-1997	48,669
Passing (TDs)	John Elway, 1983-1997	278
Receiving (No.)	Lionel Taylor, 1960-66	543
Receiving (Yds.)	Lionel Taylor, 1960-66	6,872
Interceptions	Steve Foley, 1976-1986	44
Punting (Avg.)	Jim Fraser, 1962-64	45.2
Punt Return (Avg.)	Darrien Gordon, 1997	13.6
Kickoff Return (Avg.)	Abner Haynes, 1965-66	26.3
Field Goals	Jim Turner, 1971-79	151
Touchdowns (Tot.)	Floyd Little, 1967-1975	54
Points	Jim Turner, 1971-79	742

INDIVIDUAL RECORDS—SINGLE SEASON

CATEGORY	NAME	PERFORMANCE
Rushing (Yds.)	Terrell Davis, 1997	1,750
Passing (Yds.)	John Elway, 1993	4,030
Passing (TDs)	John Elway, 1997	27
Receiving (No.)	Lionel Taylor, 1961	100
Receiving (Yds.)	Steve Watson, 1981	1,244
Interceptions	Goose Gonsoulin, 1960	11
Punting (Avg.)	Jim Fraser, 1963	46.1
Punt Return (Avg.)	Floyd Little, 1967	16.9
Kickoff Return (Avg.)	Bill Thompson, 1969	28.5
Field Goals	Jason Elam, 1995	31
Touchdowns (Tot.)	Terrell Davis, 1996, 1997	15
Points	Gene Mingo, 1962	137

INDIVIDUAL RECORDS—SINGLE GAME

CATEGORY	NAME	PERFORMANCE
Rushing (Yds.)	Terrell Davis, 9-21-97	215
Passing (Yds.)	Frank Tripucka, 9-15-62	447
Passing (TDs)	Frank Tripucka, 10-28-62; John Elway, 11-18-84	5
Receiving (No.)	Lionel Taylor, 11-29-64; Bobby Anderson, 9-30-73	13
Receiving (Yds.)	Lionel Taylor, 11-27-60	199
Interceptions	Goose Gonsoulin, 9-18-60; Willie Brown, 11-15-64	*4
Field Goals	Gene Mingo, 10-6-63	5
	Rich Karlis, 11-20-83	5
	Jason Elam, 9-3-95	5
Touchdowns (Tot.)	Many times	3
	Last time by Terrell Davis, 11-24-97	
Points	Gene Mingo, 12-10-60	21

*NFL Record

DETROIT LIONS

Pontiac Silverdome
1200 Featherstone Road
Pontiac, Michigan 48342
Telephone: (248) 335-4131
Website: nfl.com

Team Colors: Honolulu Blue and Silver
NFC Central
1997 Record 9-7
Home: 6-2
Away: 3-5
Stadium: Pontiac Silverdome
Capacity: 80,368

1997 Regular-Season Attendance:
Home: 554,898 Away: 527,918
Playing Surface: AstroTurf
Training Camp: Saginaw Valley State College University Center, MI 48710

1997 RESULTS

DATE	RESULT	OPPONENT	ATT.
8/31	W 28-17	Atlanta	61,244
9/7	L 17-24	Tampa Bay	58,234
9/14	W 32-7	at Chicago	59,147
9/21	L 17-35	at N.O.	50,016
9/28	W 26-15	Green Bay	78,110
10/5	L 13-22	at Buffalo	78,025
10/12	W 27-9	at Tampa Bay	72,095
10/19	L 20-26*	N.Y. Giants	70,069
11/2	L 10-20	at Green Bay	60,126
11/9	L 7-30	at Washington	75,261
11/16	W 38-15	Minnesota	68,910
11/23	W 32-10	Indianapolis	62,803
11/27	W 55-20	Chicago	77,904
12/7	L 30-33	at Miami	72,266
12/14	W 14-13	at Minnesota	60,982
12/21	W 13-10	New York Jets	77,624

POSTSEASON

12/28	L 10-20	at Tampa Bay	73,361

*Overtime

1998 SCHEDULE

REGULAR SEASON

Sept. 6	at Green Bay	12:01
Sept. 13	CINCINNATI	1:01
Sept. 20	at Minnesota	12:01
Sept. 28	TAMPA BAY (Mon.)	8:20
Oct. 4	at Chicago	12:01
Oct. 11	OPEN DATE	
Oct. 15	**GREEN BAY (Thurs.)**	**8:20**
Oct. 25	MINNESOTA	1:01
Nov. 1	ARIZONA	1:01
Nov. 8	at Philadelphia	1:01
Nov. 15	**CHICAGO**	**8:20**
Nov. 22	at Tampa Bay	1:01
Nov. 26	**PITTS. (Thurs.)**	**12:35**
Dec. 6	at Jacksonville	1:01
Dec. 14	**at S.F. (Mon.)**	**5:20**
Dec. 20	ATLANTA	1:01
Dec. 27	at Baltimore	1:01

Nationally Televised Games in **Bold**/All times local

COACHING STAFF
Head Coach—Bobby Ross; Assistant Coaches—Brian Baker, Don Clemons, Sylvester Croom, Frank Falks, Jack Henry, Bert Hill, Stan Kwan, John Misciagna, Gary Moeller, Dennis Murphy, Bob Palcic, Larry Peccatiello, Chuck Priefer, Richard Selcer, Jerry Sullivan, Jim Zorn.

1998 SCOUTING REPORT

By hiring former Seahawks quarterback Jim Zorn, a left-hander who played 10 seasons in the NFL, as their new quarterbacks coach, the Lions gave a clear indication that the key to their success is more consistent play from their left-handed quarterback Scott Mitchell.

Detroit has offensive weapons in wide receiver Herman Moore, who tied for the league lead with 104 receptions in 1997, and Barry Sanders, who rushed for 2,053 yards, second-best single-season total in NFL history. But the perennial Pro Bowl players need a more polished performance from Mitchell. Although Detroit's offense ranked second in the league in 1997, it was hot and cold, scoring 30 or more points in five games and 14 or fewer points in five games.

1998 DRAFT CHOICES

RD. NAME	POS.	COLLEGE	RD. NAME	POS.	COLLEGE
1. Terry Fair	CB	Tennessee	6. Jamaal Alexander	S	So. Mississippi
2a. Germane Crowell	WR	Virginia	7. Chris Liwienski	T	Indiana
2b. Charlie Batch	QB	E. Michigan			

Fair is ball-hawking cornerback who excels in man-for-man coverage. He doesn't possess blazing speed, but is a dangerous kick returner...Crowell has outstanding size (6-4, 210) and will frustrate smaller defensive backs. He'll learn from veteran Herman Moore how to use his size and shield defenders...Batch has strong arm and is dangerous when flushed out of pocket...Alexander displays good range and closes well on ball.

KEY ACQUISITIONS

NAME	POS.	PREVIOUS NFL TEAM	NAME	POS.	PREVIOUS NFL TEAM
Allen Aldridge (FA)	LB	Broncos	Dan Owens (FA)	DT	Falcons
Rob Fredrickson (Trade)	LB	Raiders	Jim Pyne (FA)	C	Buccaneers
Jim Miller (FA)	QB	Steelers			

KEY LOSSES

NAME	POS.	NEW NFL TEAM	NAME	POS.	NEW NFL TEAM
Reggie Brown (Retired)	LB	None	Van Malone (FA)	S	Cardinals
Kevin Glover (FA)	C	Seahawks	Glyn Milburn (Trade)	RB	Packers
Antonio London (FA)	LB	Packers	Mike Wells (FA)	DT	Bears

(FA) = Free Agent

1997 STATISTICAL LEADERS

SCORING

PLAYER	TD	PAT	FG	PTS.
Hanson	0	39/40	26/29	117
Sanders	14	0/0	0/0	84
Moore	8	0/0	0/0	50
Morton	6	0/0	0/0	36
Vardell	6	0/0	0/0	36
Brown	2	0/0	0/0	12
Scroggins	1	0/0	0/0	8
S. Boyd	1	0/0	0/0	6
Chryplewicz	1	0/0	0/0	6
Mitchell	1	0/0	0/0	6
Rivers	1	0/0	0/0	6
Schlesinger	1	0/0	0/0	6
Westbrook	1	0/0	0/0	6
Lions	43	39/40	26/29	379
Opponents	33	29/30	25/32	306

2-Point conversions: Lions 1-3, Opponents 1-2

RUSHING

PLAYER	ATT.	YDS.	AVG.	TD
Sanders	335	*2,053	6.1	11
Rivers	29	166	5.7	1
Vardell	32	122	3.8	6
Mitchell	37	83	2.2	1
Morton	3	33	11.0	0
Schlesinger	7	11	1.6	0
Reich	4	-4	-1.0	0
Lions	447	2,464	5.5	19
Opponents	471	1,833	3.9	15

INTERCEPTIONS

PLAYER	NO.	YDS.	AVG.	TD
Carrier	5	94	18.8	0
Brown	2	83	41.5	2
Westbrook	2	64	32.0	1
Abrams	1	29	29.0	0
Rice	1	18	18.0	0
Raymond	1	17	17.0	0
Lions	17	309	18.2	3
Opponents	17	191	11.2	2

RECEIVING

PLAYER	ATT.	YDS.	AVG.	TD
Moore	*104	1,293	12.4	8
Morton	80	1,057	13.2	6
Sanders	33	305	9.2	3
Sloan	29	264	9.1	0
Metzelaars	17	144	8.5	0
Vardell	16	218	13.6	0
T. Boyd	10	142	14.2	0
Milburn	5	77	15.4	0
Schlesinger	5	69	13.8	1
Chryplewicz	3	27	9.0	1
McCorvey	2	9	4.5	0
Mitchell	0	0	—	0
Lions	304	3,605	11.9	19
Opponents	281	3,401	12.1	15

KICKOFF RETURNS

PLAYER	NO.	YDS.	AVG.	TD
Milburn	55	1,315	23.9	0
Rivers	2	34	17.0	0
Russell	1	0	0.0	0
Vardell	1	15	15.0	0
Lions	59	1,364	23.1	0
Opponents	61	1,269	20.8	0

PUNT RETURNS

PLAYER	NO.	YDS.	AVG.	TD
Milburn	47	433	9.2	0
Carrier	1	0	0.0	0
Lions	48	433	9.0	0
Opponents	51	434	8.5	1

PUNTING

PLAYER	NO.	YDS.	AVG.
Jett	84	3,576	35.6
Lions	86	3,576	35.6
Opponents	97	4,296	38.4

PASSING

PLAYER	ATT.	COMP.	YDS.	PCT.	TD	INT.	RAT.
Mitchell	509	293	3,484	57.6	19	14	79.6
Reich	30	11	121	36.7	0	2	21.7
Blundin	1	0	0	0.0	0	1	0.0
Lions	540	304	3,605	56.3	19	17	75.4
Opponents	507	281	3,401	55.4	15	17	72.1

SACKS: Porcher 12.5, Elliss 8.5, Scroggins 7.5, Lions 43.0, Opponents 41.0

*League Leaders (All individuals may not be represented.)

RECORD HOLDERS

INDIVIDUAL RECORDS—CAREER

CATEGORY	NAME	PERFORMANCE
Rushing (Yds.)	Barry Sanders, 1989-1997	13,778
Passing (Yds.)	Bobby Layne, 1950-58	15,710
Passing (TDs)	Bobby Layne, 1950-58	118
Receiving (No.)	Herman Moore, 1991-97	528
Receiving (Yds.)	Herman Moore, 1991-97	7,484
Interceptions	Dick LeBeau, 1959-1972.	62
Punting (Avg.)	Yale Lary, 1952-53, 1956-1964	44.3
Punt Return (Avg.)	Jack Christiansen, 1951-58	12.8
Kickoff Return (Avg.)	Pat Studstill, 1961-67	25.7
Field Goals	Eddie Murray, 1980-1991	243
Touchdowns (Tot.)	Barry Sanders, 1989-1997	105
Points	Eddie Murray, 1980-1991	1,113

INDIVIDUAL RECORDS—SINGLE SEASON

CATEGORY	NAME	PERFORMANCE
Rushing (Yds.)	Barry Sanders, 1997	2,053
Passing (Yds.)	Scott Mitchell, 1995	4,338
Passing (TDs)	Scott Mitchell, 1995	32
Receiving (No.)	Herman Moore, 1995	*123
Receiving (Yds.)	Herman Moore, 1995	1,686
Interceptions	Don Doll, 1950	12
	Jack Christiansen, 1953	12
Punting (Avg.)	Yale Lary, 1963	48.9
Punt Return (Avg.)	Jack Christiansen, 1952	21.5
Kickoff Return (Avg.)	Tom Watkins, 1965	34.4
Field Goals	Jason Hanson, 1993	34
Touchdowns (Tot.)	Barry Sanders, 1991	17
Points	Jason Hanson, 1995	132

INDIVIDUAL RECORDS—SINGLE GAME

CATEGORY	NAME	PERFORMANCE
Rushing (Yds.)	Barry Sanders, 11-13-94	237
Passing (Yds.)	Scott Mitchell, 11-23-95	410
Passing (TDs)	Gary Danielson, 12-9-78	5
Receiving (No.)	Herman Moore, 12-4-95	14
Receiving (Yds.)	Cloyce Box, 12-3-50	302
Interceptions	Don Doll, 10-23-49	*4
Field Goals	Garo Yepremian, 11-13-66	6
Touchdowns (Tot.)	Dutch Clark, 10-22-34; Cloyce Box, 12-3-50;	4
	Barry Sanders, 11-24-91	4
Points	Dutch Clark, 10-22-34; Cloyce Box, 12-3-50;	24
	Barry Sanders, 11-24-91	24

*NFL Record

GREEN BAY PACKERS

1265 Lombardi Avenue
Green Bay, Wisconsin 54304
Telephone: (920) 496-5700
Website: www.packers.com

Team Colors: Dark Green, Gold, and White

1997 Regular-Season Attendance:
Home: 481,494 Away: 536,436
Playing Surface: Grass
Training Camp:
St. Norbert College
De Pere, Wisconsin 54115

NFC Central
1997 Record 13-3
Home: 8-0
Away: 5-3
Stadium: Lambeau Field
Capacity: 60,790

1997 RESULTS

DATE	RESULT	OPPONENT	ATT.
9/1	W 38-24	Chicago	60,766
9/7	L 9-10	at Phil.	66,803
9/14	W 23-18	Miami	60,075
9/21	W 38-32	Minnesota	60,115
9/28	L 15-26	at Detroit	78,110
10/5	W 21-16	Tampa Bay	60,100
10/12	W 24-23	at Chicago	62,212
10/27	W 28-10	at N.E.	59,972
11/2	W 20-10	Detroit	60,126
11/9	W 17-7	St. Louis	60,093
11/16	L 38-41	at Ind.	60,928
11/23	W 45-17	Dallas	60,111
12/1	W 27-11	at Minnesota	64,001
12/7	W 17-6	at Tampa Bay	73,523
12/14	W 31-10	at Carolina	70,887
12/20	W 31-21	Buffalo	60,108

POSTSEASON

1/4	W 21-7	Tampa Bay	60,327
1/11	W 23-10	at S.F.	68,987
1/25	L 24-31	Denver, Super Bowl XXXII	68,912

1998 SCHEDULE

REGULAR SEASON

Sept. 6 DETROIT............12:01
Sept. 13 TAMPA BAY.........12:01
Sept. 20 at Cincinnati...........1:01
Sept. 27 at Carolina............1:01
Oct. 5 MINNESOTA (Mon.)...7:20
Oct. 11 OPEN DATE
Oct. 15 at Detroit (Thurs.)...8:20
Oct. 25 BALTIMORE.........12:01
Nov. 1 SAN FRANCISCO......3:15
Nov. 9 at Pittsburgh (Mon.)..8:20
Nov. 15 at New York Giants....4:15
Nov. 22 at Minnesota..........12:01
Nov. 29 PHILADELPHIA......3:15
Dec. 7 at Tampa Bay (Mon.)..8:20
Dec. 13 CHICAGO...........12:01
Dec. 20 TENNESSEE.........12:01
Dec. 27 at Chicago............12:01

*Nationally Televised Games in **Bold**/All times local*

COACHING STAFF

Head Coach—Mike Holmgren; Assistant Coaches—Larry Brooks, Nolan Cromwell, Ken Flajole, Johnny Holland, Kent Johnston, Sherman Lewis, Jim Lind, Tom Lovat, Andy Reid, Gary Reynolds, Mike Sherman, Fritz Shurmur, Harry Sydney, Bob Valesente.

1998 SCOUTING REPORT

Everybody wants a piece of the teams that are on top, and Green Bay found that out the hard way in 1997. First the Packers surrendered their NFL crown to Denver in Super Bowl XXXII, then they lost a slew of key players to free agency in the offseason. At least Reggie White changed his mind and decided to return for another season.

Despite the losses, Green Bay still will contend for the NFL title in 1998. The Packers have posted the best overall record (37-11) in the past three years, and they still have Pro Bowl quarterback Brett Favre, who has passed for more than 3,000 yards and 30 touchdowns each of the last four years. Green Bay also has dangerous wide receivers Antonio Freeman and Robert Brooks.

1998 DRAFT CHOICES

RD.	NAME	POS.	COLLEGE
1.	Vonnie Holliday	DT	North Carolina
3.	Jonathan Brown	DE	Tennessee
4.	Roosevelt Blackmon	CB	Morris Brown
5.	Corey Bradford	WR	Jackson St.
6a.	Scott McGarrahan	S	New Mexico
6b.	Matt Hasselbeck	QB	Boston College
7.	Edwin Watson	RB	Purdue

Packers needed depth on defensive line and got plenty of it with selections of Holliday and Brown. Holliday is relentless and is good at getting into backfield. Brown is excellent pass rusher…Blackmon is rangy cornerback whose man-for-man coverage skills belie fact he played against lesser competition at small college…Bradford has great speed.

KEY ACQUISITIONS

NAME	POS.	PREVIOUS NFL TEAM
Eric Curry (FA)	DE	Buccaneers
Roger Harper (FA)	S	Cowboys
Sean Landeta (FA)	P	Buccaneers
Antonio London (FA)	LB	Lions
Glyn Milburn (Trade)	RB	Lions

KEY LOSSES

NAME	POS.	NEW NFL TEAM
Edgar Bennett (FA)	RB	Bears
Steve Bono (Trade)	QB	Rams
Doug Evans (FA)	CB	Panthers
Craig Hentrich (FA)	P	Oilers
Terry Mickens (FA)	WR	Raiders
Eugene Robinson (FA)	S	Falcons
Aaron Taylor (FA)	G	Chargers
Gabe Wilkins (FA)	DE	49ers

(FA) = Free Agent

1997 STATISTICAL LEADERS

SCORING

PLAYER	TD	PAT	FG	PTS.
Longwell	0	*48/48	24/30	120
Levens	12	0/0	0/0	74
Freeman	12	0/0	0/0	72
R. Brooks	7	0/0	0/0	42
Chmura	6	0/0	0/0	36
Sharper	3	0/0	0/0	18
T. Davis	2	0/0	0/0	12
Wilkins	2	0/0	0/0	12
Favre	1	0/0	0/0	6
Hayden	1	0/0	0/0	6
Henderson	1	0/0	0/0	6
Mickens	1	0/0	0/0	6
Schroeder	1	0/0	0/0	6
Thomason	1	0/0	0/0	6
Packers	50	48/48	24/30	422
Opponents	30	18/18	24/30	282

2-Point conversions: Packers 1-2, Opponents 6-12

RUSHING

PLAYER	ATT.	YDS.	AVG.	TD
Levens	329	1,435	4.4	7
Favre	58	187	3.2	1
Hayden	32	148	4.6	1
Henderson	31	113	3.6	0
R. Brooks	2	19	9.5	0
Freeman	1	14	14.0	0
Bono	3	-3	-1.0	0
Pederson	3	-4	-1.3	0
Packers	459	1,909	4.2	9
Opponents	443	1,876	4.2	16

INTERCEPTIONS

PLAYER	NO.	YDS.	AVG.	TD
Butler	5	4	0.8	0
Prior	4	72	18.0	0
Evans	3	33	11.0	0
Sharper	2	70	35.0	2
B. Williams	2	30	15.0	0
Packers	21	329	15.7	3
Opponents	16	305	19.1	3

RECEIVING

PLAYER	ATT.	YDS.	AVG.	TD
Freeman	81	1,243	15.3	12
R. Brooks	60	1,010	16.8	7
Levens	53	370	7.0	5
Henderson	41	367	9.0	1
Chmura	38	417	11.0	6
Mayes	18	290	16.1	0
Thomason	9	115	12.8	1
Beebe	2	28	14.0	0
T. Davis	2	28	14.0	1
Schroeder	2	15	7.5	1
Hayden	2	11	5.5	0
Mickens	1	2	2.0	1
Packers	309	3,896	12.6	35
Opponents	288	3,225	11.2	10

KICKOFF RETURNS

PLAYER	NO.	YDS.	AVG.	TD
Schroeder	24	562	23.4	0
Preston	7	211	30.1	0
Beebe	6	134	22.3	0
Hayden	6	141	23.5	0
Darkins	4	68	17.0	0
Mickens	1	0	0.0	0
Sharper	1	3	3.0	0
Packers	49	1,119	22.8	0
Opponents	78	1,599	20.5	0

PUNT RETURNS

PLAYER	NO.	YDS.	AVG.	TD
Schroeder	33	342	10.4	0
Mayes	14	141	10.1	0
Sharper	7	32	4.6	0
Preston	1	0	0	0
Prior	1	0	0.0	0
Packers	56	515	9.2	0
Opponents	32	255	8.0	0

PUNTING

PLAYER	NO.	YDS.	AVG.
Hentrich	75	3,378	45.0
Packers	75	3,378	45.0
Opponents	90	3,828	42.5

PASSING

PLAYER	ATT.	COMP.	YDS.	PCT.	TD	INT.	RAT.
Favre	513	304	3,867	59.3	*35	16	92.6
Bono	10	5	29	50.0	0	0	56.3
Packers	523	309	3,896	59.1	35	16	91.9
Opponents	563	288	3,225	51.2	10	21	59.0

SACKS: White 11.0, S. Dotson 5.5, Wilkins 5.5, Packers 41.0, Opponents 26.0

*League Leaders   (All individuals may not be represented.)

RECORD HOLDERS

INDIVIDUAL RECORDS—CAREER

CATEGORY	NAME	PERFORMANCE
Rushing (Yds.)	Jim Taylor, 1958-1966	8,207
Passing (Yds.)	Bart Starr, 1956-1971	24,718
Passing (TDs)	Brett Favre, 1992-97	182
Receiving (No.)	Sterling Sharpe, 1988-1994	595
Receiving (Yds.)	James Lofton, 1978-1986	9,656
Interceptions	Bobby Dillon, 1952-59	52
Punting (Avg.)	Craig Hentrich, 1994-97	42.8
Punt Return (Avg.)	Desmond Howard 1996	15.1
Kickoff Return (Avg.)	Travis Williams, 1967-1970	26.7
Field Goals	Chris Jacke, 1989-1996	173
Touchdowns (Tot.)	Don Hutson, 1935-1945	105
Points	Don Hutson, 1935-1945	823

INDIVIDUAL RECORDS—SINGLE SEASON

CATEGORY	NAME	PERFORMANCE
Rushing (Yds.)	Jim Taylor, 1962	1,474
Passing (Yds.)	Lynn Dickey, 1983	4,458
Passing (TDs)	Brett Favre, 1996	39
Receiving (No.)	Sterling Sharpe, 1993	112
Receiving (Yds.)	Robert Brooks, 1995	1,497
Interceptions	Irv Comp, 1943	10
Punting (Avg.)	Craig Hentrich, 1997	45.0
Punt Return (Avg.)	Billy Grimes, 1950	19.1
Kickoff Return (Avg.)	Travis Williams, 1967	*41.1
Field Goals	Chester Marcol, 1972	33
Touchdowns (Tot.)	Jim Taylor, 1962	19
Points	Paul Hornung, 1960	*176

INDIVIDUAL RECORDS—SINGLE GAME

CATEGORY	NAME	PERFORMANCE
Rushing (Yds.)	Dorsey Levens, 11-23-97	190
Passing (Yds.)	Lynn Dickey, 10-12-80	418
Passing (TDs)	Many times. Last time by Brett Favre, 9-21-97	5
Receiving (No.)	Don Hutson, 11-22-42	14
Receiving (Yds.)	Bill Howton, 10-21-56	257
Interceptions	Bobby Dillon, 11-26-53	*4
	Willie Buchanon, 9-24-78	*4
Field Goals	Chris Jacke, 11-11-90, 10-14-96	5
Touchdowns (Tot.)	Paul Hornung, 12-12-65	5
Points	Paul Hornung, 10-8-61	33

*NFL Record

INDIANAPOLIS COLTS

P.O. Box 535000
Indianapolis, Indiana 46253
Telephone: (317) 297-2658
Website: nfl.com

Team Colors: Royal Blue and White

1997 Regular-Season Attendance:
Home: 451,455 Away: 483,840
Playing Surface: AstroTurf
Training Camp:
Anderson University
Anderson, Indiana 46011

AFC East
1997 Record 3-13
Home: 2-6
Away: 1-7
Stadium: RCA Dome
Capacity: 60,567

1997 RESULTS

DATE	RESULT	OPPONENT	ATT.
8/31	L 10-16	at Miami	70,813
9/7	L 6-31	NEW ENGLAND	53,632
9/14	L 3-31	SEATTLE	49,194
9/21	L 35-37	at Buffalo	55,340
10/5	L 12-16	NEW YORK JETS	48,295
10/12	L 22-24	at Pittsburgh	57,925
10/20	L 6-9	BUFFALO	61,139
10/26	L 19-35	at San Diego	63,177
11/2	L 28-31	TAMPA BAY	58,512
11/9	L 13-28	CINCINNATI	58,473
11/16	W 41-38	GREEN BAY	60,928
11/23	L 10-32	at Detroit	62,803
11/30	L 17-20	at N.E.	58,507
12/7	W 22-14	at N.Y. Jets	61,168
12/14	W 41-0	MIAMI	61,282
12/21	L 28-39	at Minnesota	54,107

1998 SCHEDULE

REGULAR SEASON

Sept. 6	MIAMI	3:15
Sept. 13	**at New England**	**8:20**
Sept. 20	at New York Jets	1:01
Sept. 27	NEW ORLEANS	12:01
Oct. 4	SAN DIEGO	12:01
Oct. 11	BUFFALO	12:01
Oct. 18	at San Francisco	1:05
Oct. 25	OPEN DATE	
Nov. 1	NEW ENGLAND	1:01
Nov. 8	at Miami	1:01
Nov. 15	NEW YORK JETS	1:01
Nov. 22	at Buffalo	1:01
Nov. 29	at Baltimore	1:01
Dec. 6	at Atlanta	1:01
Dec. 13	CINCINNATI	1:01
Dec. 20	at Seattle	1:05
Dec. 27	CAROLINA	1:01

*Nationally Televised Games in **Bold**/All times local*

COACHING STAFF

Head Coach—Jim Mora; Assistant Coaches—Bruce Arians, Greg Blache, George Catavolos, Gene Huey, Tony Marciano, Tom Moore, Howard Mudd, Mike Murphy, Jay Norvell, John Pagano, Kevin Spencer, Rusty Tillman, Jon Torine, Tom Zupancic.

1998 SCOUTING REPORT

Three years ago, Indianapolis came within an eyelash of representing the AFC in Super Bowl XXX. Last year, the Colts had the poorest record in the NFL. To get Indianapolis back on the right track, owner Jim Irsay hired one of the league's most respected administrators, Bill Polian, away from the Carolina Panthers to serve as the Colts' president and general manger.

Polian hired Jim Mora, who compiled a 93-78 record with the Saints from 1986-1996, as Indianapolis's new head coach. With the first overall choice in the 1998 NFL draft, the Colts selected quarterback Peyton Manning, who won the Maxwell Award as the nation's best player as a senior at Tennessee. To improve in 1998, Indianapolis is banking on a solid showing from Manning, increased production from running back Marshall Faulk, and a tougher offensive line (the Colts allowed the most sacks, 62, in the AFC in 1997).

1998 DRAFT CHOICES

RD.	NAME	POS.	COLLEGE
1.	Peyton Manning	QB	Tennessee
2.	Jerome Pathon	WR	Washington
3.	E.G. Green	WR	Florida St.
4.	Steve McKinney	G	Texas A&M
5.	Antony Jordon	LB	Vanderbilt
7a.	Aaron Taylor	G	Nebraska
7b.	Corey Gaines	CB	Tennessee

Manning should not have problem making transition from college to NFL and will start immediately. He is intelligent, confident, and natural leader…Pathon can make difficult catches look easy…Green should give Manning reliable possession receiver…McKinney could start as rookie on offensive line…Gaines played free safety in college.

KEY ACQUISITIONS

NAME	POS.	PREVIOUS NFL TEAM
Jeff Burris (FA)	CB	Bills
Jeff Herrod (FA)	LB	Eagles
Tom Myslinski (FA)	G	Steelers
Torrance Small (FA)	WR	Rams

KEY LOSSES

NAME	POS.	NEW NFL TEAM
Jim Harbaugh (Trade)	QB	Ravens
Paul Justin (Trade)	QB	Bengals
Dedric Mathis (FA)	CB	Bears
Brian Stablein (FA)	WR	Patriots

(FA) = Free Agent

1997 STATISTICAL LEADERS

SCORING

PLAYER	TD	PAT	FG	PTS.
Blanchard	0	21/21	32/*41	117
Faulk	8	0/0	0/0	48
Harrison	6	0/0	0/0	40
Bailey	3	0/0	0/0	18
Dilger	3	0/0	0/0	18
Dawkins	2	0/0	0/0	12
Warren	2	0/0	0/0	12
Stablein	1	0/0	0/0	8
Alexander	1	0/0	0/0	6
Belser	1	0/0	0/0	6
Blackmon	1	0/0	0/0	6
Crockett	1	0/0	0/0	6
Fontenot	1	0/0	0/0	6
McElroy	1	0/0	0/0	6
Colts	31	21/21	32/41	313
Opponents	46	42/44	27/31	401

2-Point conversions: Colts 4-10, Opponents: 0-2

RUSHING

PLAYER	ATT.	YDS.	AVG.	TD
Faulk	264	1,054	4.0	7
Crockett	95	300	3.2	1
Harbaugh	36	206	5.7	0
Warren	28	80	2.9	2
Groce	10	66	6.6	0
Bailey	3	20	6.7	0
Holcomb	5	5	1.0	0
Justin	6	2	0.3	0
Colts	450	1,727	3.8	10
Opponents	438	2,034	4.6	18

INTERCEPTIONS

PLAYER	NO.	YDS.	AVG.	TD
Belser	2	121	60.5	1
Coryatt	2	3	1.5	0
C. Gray	2	0	0.0	0
Team	12	234	19.5	2
Opponents	17	285	16.8	0

RECEIVING

PLAYER	ATT.	YDS.	AVG.	TD
Harrison	73	866	11.9	6
Dawkins	68	804	11.8	2
Faulk	47	471	10.0	1
Dilger	27	380	14.1	3
Bailey	26	329	12.7	3
Stablein	25	253	10.1	1
Warren	20	192	9.6	0
Crockett	15	112	7.5	0
Pollard	10	116	11.6	0
Slutzker	3	22	7.3	0
Doering	2	12	6.0	0
Glenn	1	3	3.0	0
Colts	317	3,560	11.2	16
Opponents	261	3,067	11.8	26

KICKOFF RETURNS

PLAYER	NO.	YDS.	AVG.	TD
Bailey	55	1,206	21.9	0
Jacquet	8	156	19.5	0
Hetherington	2	23	11.5	0
Groce	1	15	15.0	0
Neal	1	23	23.0	0
Warren	1	19	19.0	0
Colts	68	1,442	21.2	0
Opponents	64	1,544	24.1	1

PUNT RETURNS

PLAYER	NO.	YDS.	AVG.	TD
Stablein	17	133	7.8	0
Jacquet	13	96	7.4	0
Bailey	1	19	19.0	0
Harrison	0	0	—	0
Colts	31	248	8.0	0
Opponents	43	491	11.4	0

PUNTING

PLAYER	NO.	YDS.	AVG.
Gardocki	67	3,034	45.3
Colts	67	3,034	45.3
Opponents	64	2,948	46.1

PASSING

PLAYER	ATT.	COMP.	YDS.	PCT.	TD	INT.	RAT.
Harbaugh	309	189	2,060	61.2	10	4	86.2
Justin	140	83	1,046	59.3	5	5	79.6
Holcomb	73	45	454	61.6	1	8	44.3
Warren	1	0	0	0	0	0	39.6
Colts	523	317	3,560	60.6	16	17	77.6
Opponents	453	261	3,067	57.6	26	12	86.4

SACKS: Footman 10.5, Fontenot 4.5, E. Johnson 4.5, Colts 37.0, Opponents 62.0

*League Leader   (All individuals may not be represented.)

RECORD HOLDERS

INDIVIDUAL RECORDS—CAREER

CATEGORY	NAME	PERFORMANCE
Rushing (Yds.)	Lydell Mitchell, 1972-77	5,487
Passing (Yds.)	Johnny Unitas, 1956-1972	39,768
Passing (TDs)	Johnny Unitas, 1956-1972	287
Receiving (No.)	Raymond Berry, 1955-1967	631
Receiving (Yds.)	Raymond Berry, 1955-1967	9,275
Interceptions	Bob Boyd, 1960-68	57
Punting (Avg.)	Rohn Stark, 1982-1994	43.8
Punt Return (Avg.)	Wendell Harris, 1964	12.6
Kickoff Return (Avg.)	Jim Duncan, 1969-1971	32.5
Field Goals	Dean Biasucci, 1984, 1986-1994	176
Touchdowns (Tot.)	Lenny Moore, 1956-1967	113
Points	Dean Biasucci, 1984, 1986-1994	783

INDIVIDUAL RECORDS—SINGLE SEASON

CATEGORY	NAME	PERFORMANCE
Rushing (Yds.)	Eric Dickerson, 1988	1,659
Passing (Yds.)	Johnny Unitas, 1963	3,481
Passing (TDs)	Johnny Unitas, 1959	32
Receiving (No.)	Reggie Langhorne, 1993	85
Receiving (Yds.)	Raymond Berry, 1960	1,298
Interceptions	Tom Keane, 1953	11
Punting (Avg.)	Rohn Stark, 1985	45.9
Punt Return (Avg.)	Clarence Verdin, 1989	12.9
Kickoff Return (Avg.)	Jim Duncan, 1970	35.4
Field Goals	Cary Blanchard, 1996	36
Touchdowns (Tot.)	Lenny Moore, 1964	20
Points	Cary Blanchard, 1996	135

INDIVIDUAL RECORDS—SINGLE GAME

CATEGORY	NAME	PERFORMANCE
Rushing (Yds.)	Norm Bulaich, 9-19-71	198
Passing (Yds.)	Johnny Unitas, 9-17-67	401
Passing (TDs)	Gary Cuozzo, 11-14-65; Gary Hogeboom, 10-4-87	5
Receiving (No.)	Lydell Mitchell, 12-15-74; Joe Washington, 9-2-79	13
Receiving (Yds.)	Raymond Berry, 11-10-57	224
Interceptions	Many times. Last time by Mike Prior, 12-20-92	3
Field Goals	Many times. Last time by Cary Blanchard, 9-21-97	5
Touchdowns (Tot.)	Many times. Last time by Eric Dickerson, 10-31-88	4
Points	Many times, last time by Eric Dickerson, 10-31-88	24

JACKSONVILLE JAGUARS

ALLTEL Stadium
One ALLTEL Stadium Place
Jacksonville, Florida 32202
Telephone: (904) 633-6000
Website: nfl.com

Team Colors: Teal, Black, and Gold
AFC Central

1997 Regular-Season Attendance:
Home: 557,547 Away: 420,543
Playing Surface: Grass
Training Camp:
ALLTEL Stadium
Jacksonville, Florida 32202

1997 Record 11-5
Home: 7-1
Away: 4-4
Stadium: ALLTEL Stadium
Capacity: 73,000

1997 RESULTS

DATE	RESULT	OPPONENT	ATT.
8/31	W 28-27	at Baltimore	61,018
9/7	W 40-13	N.Y. GIANTS	70,581
9/22	W 30-21	PITTSBURGH	73,016
9/28	L 12-24	at Washington	74,421
10/5	W 21-13	CINCINNATI	67,128
10/12	W 38-21	PHILADELPHIA	69,150
10/19	L 22-26	at Dallas	64,464
10/26	L 17-23*	at Pittsburgh	57,011
11/2	W 30-24	at Tennessee	27,208
11/9	W 24-10	KANSAS CITY	70,464
11/16	W 17-9	TENNESSEE	70,070
11/23	L 26-31	at Cincinnati	55,158
11/30	W 29-27	BALTIMORE	63,712
12/7	L 20-26	NEW ENGLAND	73,446
12/14	W 20-14	at Buffalo	41,231
12/21	W 20-9	at Oakland	40,032

POSTSEASON

12/27	L 17-42	at Denver	74,481

*Overtime

COACHING STAFF

Head Coach—Tom Coughlin; Assistant Coaches—Joe Baker, Pete Carmichael, Perry Fewell, Greg Finnegan, Fred Hoaglin, Jerald Ingram, Dick Jauron, Mike Maser, Chris Palmer, Jerry Palmieri, Larry Pasquale, John Pease, Lucious Selmon, Steve Szabo.

1998 SCHEDULE

REGULAR SEASON

Sept. 6	at Chicago	12:01
Sept. 13	KANSAS CITY	1:01
Sept. 20	BALTIMORE	4:15
Sept. 27	at Tennessee	12:01
Oct. 4	OPEN DATE	
Oct. 12	**MIAMI (Mon.)**	**8:20**
Oct. 18	at Buffalo	1:01
Oct. 25	**at Denver**	**2:15**
Nov. 1	at Baltimore	1:01
Nov. 8	CINCINNATI	1:01
Nov. 15	TAMPA BAY	4:15
Nov. 22	at Pittsburgh	1:01
Nov. 29	at Cincinnati	1:01
Dec. 6	DETROIT	1:01
Dec. 13	TENNESSEE	1:01
Dec. 20	**at Minnesota**	**7:20**
Dec. 28	**PITTSBURGH (Mon.)**	**8:20**

Nationally Televised Games in **Bold**/All times local

1998 SCOUTING REPORT

The Jaguars made the playoffs for the second consecutive year in 1997. They finished with a franchise-best 11-5 record but lost to eventual Super Bowl-champion Denver in a wild-card playoff game.

Jacksonville went that far despite losing Pro Bowl quarterback Mark Brunell for the first two games because of a knee injury. Although Brunell's mobility was limited last year—in 1996, he rushed for 396 yards and in 1997, only 257—he started the final 14 games of the season and still finished first in the AFC and third in the NFL with a 91.2 passer rating.

Jaguars coach Tom Coughlin addressed the team's biggest need in the offseason by signing pass-rush specialist Bryce Paup, a Pro Bowl linebacker with Buffalo and the 1995 NFL defensive player of the year. Paup will give a big boost to Jacksonville's pass defense, which finished twenty-fourth in the NFL last year.

1998 DRAFT CHOICES

RD. NAME	POS.	COLLEGE	RD. NAME	POS.	COLLEGE
1a. Fred Taylor	RB	Florida	5. John Wade	C	Marshall
1b. Donovin Darius	S	Syracuse	6a. Lamanzer Williams	DE	Minnesota
2. Cordell Taylor	CB	Hampton	6b. Kevin McLeod	RB	Auburn
3. Jonathan Quinn	QB	Middle Tenn. St.	7a. Alvis Whitted	WR	N. Carolina St.
4a. Tavian Banks	RB	Iowa	7b. Brandon Tolbert	LB	Georgia
4b. Harry Deligianis	DT	Youngstown			

Taylor will help fill void made by departure of Means in Jaguars' backfield...Darius has linebacker's mentality and is aggressive against both run and pass...Taylor is physical cornerback.

KEY ACQUISITIONS

NAME	POS.	PREVIOUS NFL TEAM	NAME	POS.	PREVIOUS NFL TEAM
Jamie Martin (FA)	QB	Redskins	Bryce Paup (FA)	LB	Bills
Quentin Neujahr (FA)	C	Ravens			

KEY LOSSES

NAME	POS.	NEW NFL TEAM	NAME	POS.	NEW NFL TEAM
Dana Hall (FA)	S	Unsigned	Rob Johnson (Trade)	QB	Bills
Ty Hallock (FA)	RB	Bears	Natrone Means (FA)	RB	Chargers

(FA) = Free Agent

1997 STATISTICAL LEADERS

SCORING
PLAYER	TD	PAT	FG	PTS.
Hollis	0	41/41	31/36	*134
Means	9	0/0	00	54
Stewart	9	0/0	00	54
McCardell	5	0/0	00	30
Mitchell	4	0/0	00	24
Smith	4	0/0	00	24
Jackson	2	0/0	00	14
Brunell	2	0/0	00	12
Hudson	2	0/0	00	12
Jones	2	0/0	00	12
Barlow	1	0/0	00	6
Brown	1	0/0	00	6
Hallock	1	0/0	00	6
Jaguars	43	41/41	31/36	394
Opponents	39	31/32	17/25	318

2-Point conversions: Jaguars 1-2, Opponents: 1-6

RUSHING
PLAYER	ATT.	YDS.	AVG.	TD
Means	244	823	3.4	9
Stewart	136	555	4.1	8
Brunell	48	257	5.4	2
Johnson	10	34	3.4	1
Hallock	4	21	5.3	0
Jackson	3	14	4.7	0
Matthews	1	10	10.0	0
Shelton	6	4	0.7	0
Jordan	1	2	2.0	0
Jaguars	454	1,720	3.8	20
Opponents	455	1,734	3.8	12

INTERCEPTIONS
PLAYER	NO.	YDS.	AVG.	TD
Figures	5	48	9.6	0
Hudson	3	26	8.7	0
Thomas	2	34	17.0	0
Jaguars	14	145	10.4	0
Opponents	9	184	20.4	2

RECEIVING
PLAYER	ATT.	YDS.	AVG.	TD
McCardell	85	1,164	13.7	5
Smith	82	1,324	16.1	4
Stewart	41	336	8.2	1
Mitchell	35	380	10.9	4
Hallock	18	131	7.3	1
Jackson	17	206	12.1	2
Means	15	104	6.9	0
Brown	8	84	10.5	1
Jones	5	87	17.4	2
Barlow	5	74	14.8	0
Hall	1	22	22.0	0
Moore	1	10	10.0	0
Jaguars	313	3,922	12.5	20
Opponents	320	3,835	12.0	24

KICKOFF RETURNS
PLAYER	NO.	YDS.	AVG.	TD
Jackson	32	653	20.4	0
Barlow	10	267	26.7	1
Logan	10	236	23.6	0
Mitchell	2	17	8.5	0
Davis	1	9	9.0	0
Hallock	1	6	6.0	0
Moore	1	36	36.0	0
C. Parker	1	9	9.0	0
Jaguars	58	1,233	21.3	1
Opponents	77	1,730	22.5	0

PUNT RETURNS
PLAYER	NO.	YDS.	AVG.	TD
Barlow	36	412	11.4	0
Jaguars	36	412	11.4	0
Opponents	29	241	8.3	0

PUNTING
PLAYER	NO.	YDS.	AVG.
Barker	66	2,964	44.9
Jaguars	66	2,964	44.9
Opponents	73	3,060	41.9

PASSING
PLAYER	ATT.	COMP.	YDS.	PCT.	TD	INT.	RAT.
Brunell	435	264	3,281	60.7	18	7	91.2
Matthews	40	26	275	65.0	0	0	84.9
Johnson	28	22	344	78.6	2	2	111.9
Barker	1	1	22	100.0	0	0	118.8
Jaguars	504	313	3,922	62.1	20	9	92.0
Opponents	532	320	3,835	60.2	24	14	86.3

SACKS: Simmons 8.5, Brackens 7.0, Smeenge 6.5, Jaguars 48.0, Opponents 40.0

*League Leader   (All individuals may not be represented.)

RECORD HOLDERS

INDIVIDUAL RECORDS—CAREER

CATEGORY	NAME	PERFORMANCE
Rushing (Yds.)	James Stewart, 1995-97	1,803
Passing (Yds.)	Mark Brunell, 1995-97	9,816
Passing (TDs)	Mark Brunell, 1995-97	52
Receiving (No.)	Jimmy Smith, 1995-97	187
Receiving (Yds.)	Jimmy Smith, 1995-97	2,856
Interceptions	Deon Figures, 1997	5
	Chris Hudson 1996-97	5
Punting (Avg.)	Bryan Barker, 1995-97	44.1
Punt Return (Avg.)	Reggie Barlow, 1997	11.4
Kickoff Return (Avg.)	Jimmy Smith, 1995-97	22.7
Field Goals	Mike Hollis, 1995-97	81
Touchdowns (Tot.)	James Stewart, 1995-97	22
Points	Mike Hollis, 1995-97	338

INDIVIDUAL RECORDS—SINGLE SEASON

CATEGORY	NAME	PERFORMANCE
Rushing (Yds.)	Natrone Means, 1997	823
Passing (Yds.)	Mark Brunell, 1996	4,367
Passing (TDs)	Mark Brunell, 1996	19
Receiving (No.)	Keenan McCardell, 1996 & 1997	85
Receiving (Yds.)	Jimmy Smith, 1997	1,324
Interceptions	Deon Figures, 1997	5
Punting (Avg.)	Bryan Barker, 1997	44.9
Punt Return (Avg.)	Reggie Barlow, 1997	11.4
Kickoff Return (Avg.)	Bucky Brooks, 1996	24.2
Field Goals	Mike Hollis, 1997	31
Touchdowns (Tot.)	James Stewart, 1996	10
Points	Mike Hollis, 1997	134

INDIVIDUAL RECORDS—SINGLE GAME

CATEGORY	NAME	PERFORMANCE
Rushing (Yds.)	James Stewart, 10-20-96	112
Passing (Yds.)	Mark Brunell, 9-22-96	432
Passing (TDs)	Mark Brunell, 10-15-95, 12-10-95, 9-22-96, 10-5-97, 10-19-97	3
Receiving (No.)	Keenan McCardell, 10-20-96	16
Receiving (Yds.)	Keenan McCardell, 10-20-96	232
Interceptions	Deon Figures, 8-31-97	2
Field Goals	Mike Hollis, 12-1-96, 11-30-97	5
Touchdowns (Tot.)	James Stewart, 10-12-97	5
Points	James Stewart, 10-12-97	30

KANSAS CITY CHIEFS

One Arrowhead Drive
Kansas City, Missouri 64129
Telephone: (816) 924-9300
Website: www.kcchiefs.com

Team Colors: Red, Gold, and White

1997 Regular-Season Attendance:
Home: 610,192 Away: 532,248
Playing Surface: Grass
Training Camp: University of Wisconsin-River Falls, River Falls, Wisconsin 54022

AFC West
1997 Record 13-3
Home: 8-0
Away: 5-3
Stadium: Arrowhead Stadium
Capacity: 79,409

1997 RESULTS

DATE	RESULT	OPPONENT	ATT.
8/31	L 3-19	at Denver	75,600
9/8	W 28-27	at Oakland	61,523
9/14	W 22-16	BUFFALO	78,169
9/21	W 35-14	at Carolina	67,402
9/28	W 20-17*	SEATTLE	77,877
10/5	L 14-17	at Miami	71,794
10/16	W 31-3	SAN DIEGO	77,196
10/26	W 28-20	at St. Louis	64,864
11/3	W 13-10	PITTSBURGH	78,301
11/9	L 10-24	at Jacksonville	70,444
11/16	W 24-22	DENVER	77,963
11/23	W 19-14	at Seattle	66,264
11/30	W 44-9	SAN FRANCISCO	77,535
12/7	W 30-0	OAKLAND	76,379
12/14	W 29-7	at San Diego	54,594
12/21	W 25-13	NEW ORLEANS	66,772

POSTSEASON

1/4	L 10-14	DENVER	76,965

*Overtime

1998 SCHEDULE

REGULAR SEASON

Sept. 6	**OAKLAND**	**7:20**
Sept. 13	at Jacksonville	1:01
Sept. 20	SAN DIEGO	12:01
Sept. 27	at Philadelphia	1:01
Oct. 4	**SEATTLE**	**7:20**
Oct. 11	at New England	1:01
Oct. 18	OPEN DATE	
Oct. 26	**PITTSBURGH (Mon.)**	**7:20**
Nov. 1	NEW YORK JETS	3:05
Nov. 8	at Seattle	1:15
Nov. 16	**DENVER (Mon.)**	**7:20**
Nov. 22	at San Diego	1:15
Nov. 29	ARIZONA	12:01
Dec. 6	**at Denver**	**2:15**
Dec. 13	**DALLAS**	**3:15**
Dec. 20	at N. Y. Giants	1:01
Dec. 26	**at Oakland (Sat.)**	**1:05**

Nationally Televised Games in **Bold**/All times local

COACHING STAFF

Head Coach—Marty Schottenheimer; Assistant Coaches—Russ Ball, Gunther Cunningham, Jim Erkenbeck, Jeff Hurd, Lionel James, Bob Karmelowicz, Woodrow Lowe, Mike McCarthy, Roberto Parker, Jimmy Raye, Al Saunders, Brian Schottenheimer, Kurt Schottenheimer, Mike Solari, Mike Stock, Darvin Wallis.

1998 SCOUTING REPORT

Winning in the regular season hasn't been a problem for Kansas City. The Chiefs are the only NFL team to have finished in either first or second place in its division each of the last nine seasons, and they've been to the playoffs seven of the past eight years. However, winning in the playoffs has been a problem—Kansas City has advanced past the divisional playoffs only once in its previous seven postseason appearances.

Offense has been a big reason the Chiefs have struggled in the postseason. Last year, they signed free-agent quarterback Elvis Grbac, and he proved to be a big improvement until a broken collarbone caused him to miss six games. The offense should benefit from a healthy Grbac and the addition of wide receiver Derrick Alexander to go with 1997 standout Andre Rison, but the running game remains a question.

1998 DRAFT CHOICES

RD. NAME	POS.	COLLEGE	RD. NAME	POS.	COLLEGE
1. Victor Riley	T	Auburn	6. Derrick Ransom	DT	Cincinnati
3. Rashaan Shehee	RB	Washington	7a. Eric Warfield	CB	Nebraska
4. Greg Favors	LB	Mississippi St.	7b. Ernest Blackwell	RB	Missouri
5. Robert Williams	CB	North Carolina			

Riley has good body control and quick feet for 320-pound player. He has played every position on offensive line except center and could be dominant force for Chiefs…If Shehee can stay healthy, he is big play threat who will help strengthen running game weakened by loss of Marcus Allen and Greg Hill…Favors has excellent pass-rushing skills.

KEY ACQUISITIONS

NAME	POS.	PREVIOUS NFL TEAM	NAME	POS.	PREVIOUS NFL TEAM
Derrick Alexander (FA)	WR	Ravens	Chester McGlockton (FA)	DT	Raiders
Kevin Johnson (Trade)	S	Buccaneers	Leslie O'Neal (FA)	DE	Rams

KEY LOSSES

NAME	POS.	NEW NFL TEAM	NAME	POS.	NEW NFL TEAM
Marcus Allen (Retired)	RB	None	Joe Phillips (Retired)	DT	None
Greg Hill (FA)	RB	Unsigned	Derrick Walker (FA)	TE	Unsigned

(FA) = Free Agent

1997 STATISTICAL LEADERS

SCORING

PLAYER	TD	PAT	FG	PTS.
Stoyanovich	0	35/36	26/27	113
Allen	11	0/0	0/0	66
Rison	7	0/0	0/0	42
Hughes	3	0/0	0/0	18
McMillian	3	0/0	0/0	18
Richardson	3	0/0	0/0	18
Gonzalez	2	0/0	0/0	14
Vanover	2	0/0	0/0	14
Anders	2	0/0	0/0	12
Dawson	2	0/0	0/0	12
Gannon	2	0/0	0/0	12
Popson	2	0/0	0/0	12
Anderson	1	0/0	0/0	6
Chiefs	42	35/36	26/27	375
Opponents	23	22/22	24/33	232

2-Point conversions: Chiefs 2-6, Opponents: 0-1

RUSHING

PLAYER	ATT.	YDS.	AVG.	TD
Hill	157	550	3.5	0
Allen	124	505	4.1	11
Anders	79	397	5.0	2
Bennett	94	369	3.9	1
Grbac	30	168	5.6	1
Gannon	33	109	3.3	2
Vanover	5	50	10.0	0
Aguiar	2	11	5.5	0
Richardson	2	11	5.5	0
Chiefs	529	2,171	4.1	15
Opponents	413	1,621	3.9	8

INTERCEPTIONS

PLAYER	NO.	YDS.	AVG.	TD
McMillian	8	274	34.3	3
Woods	4	57	14.3	0
Chiefs	21	432	20.6	4
Opponents	10	148	14.8	0

RECEIVING

PLAYER	ATT.	YDS.	AVG.	TD
Rison	72	1,092	15.2	7
Anders	59	453	7.7	2
Popson	35	320	9.1	2
Gonzalez	33	368	11.2	2
Dawson	21	273	13.0	2
Hill	12	126	10.5	0
Allen	11	86	7.8	0
Vanover	7	92	13.1	0
Hughes	7	65	9.3	2
Bennett	7	5	0.7	0
Perriman	6	83	13.8	0
Walker	5	60	12.0	0
Richardson	3	6	2.0	3
Horn	2	65	32.5	0
Lockett	1	35	35.0	0
Chiefs	281	3,129	11.1	20
Opponents	271	3,618	13.4	15

KICKOFF RETURNS

PLAYER	NO.	YDS.	AVG.	TD
Vanover	51	1,308	25.6	1
Anders	1	0	0.0	0
Hughes	1	21	21.0	0
Manusky	1	16	16.0	0
Chiefs	54	1,345	24.9	1
Opponents	80	1,672	20.9	0

PUNT RETURNS

PLAYER	NO.	YDS.	AVG.	TD
Vanover	35	383	10.9	1
Chiefs	35	383	10.9	1
Opponents	39	255	6.5	0

PUNTING

PLAYER	NO.	YDS.	AVG.
Aguiar	82	3,465	42.3
Stoyanovich	1	24	24.0
Chiefs	83	3,489	42.0
Opponents	84	3,468	41.3

PASSING

PLAYER	ATT.	COMP.	YDS.	PCT.	TD	INT.	RAT.
Grbac	314	179	1,943	57.0	11	6	79.1
Gannon	175	98	1,144	56.0	7	4	79.8
Tolliver	1	1	-8	100.0	0	0	79.2
Allen	2	2	15	100.0	2	0	137.5
Aguiar	1	1	35	100.0	0	0	118.8
Chiefs	493	281	3,129	57.0	20	10	81.1
Opponents	507	271	3,618	53.5	15	21	69.0

SACKS: Williams 10.5, Thomas 9.5, Booker 4.0, Chiefs 54.0, Opponents 32.0

(All individuals may not be represented.)

RECORD HOLDERS

INDIVIDUAL RECORDS—CAREER

CATEGORY	NAME	PERFORMANCE
Rushing (Yds.)	Christian Okoye, 1987-1992	4,897
Passing (Yds.)	Len Dawson, 1962-1975	28,507
Passing (TDs)	Len Dawson, 1962-1975	237
Receiving (No.)	Henry Marshall, 1976-1987	416
Receiving (Yds.)	Otis Taylor, 1965-1975	7,306
Interceptions	Emmitt Thomas, 1966-1978	58
Punting (Avg.)	Jerrel Wilson, 1963-1977	43.5
Punt Return (Avg.)	J.T. Smith, 1979-1984	10.6
Kickoff Return (Avg.)	Noland Smith, 1967-69	26.8
Field Goals	Nick Lowery, 1980-1993	329
Touchdowns (Tot.)	Otis Taylor, 1965-1975	60
Points	Nick Lowery, 1980-1993	1,466

INDIVIDUAL RECORDS—SINGLE SEASON

CATEGORY	NAME	PERFORMANCE
Rushing (Yds.)	Christian Okoye, 1989	1,480
Passing (Yds.)	Bill Kenney, 1983	4,348
Passing (TDs)	Len Dawson, 1964	30
Receiving (No.)	Carlos Carson, 1983	80
Receiving (Yds.)	Carlos Carson, 1983	1,351
Interceptions	Emmitt Thomas, 1974	12
Punting (Avg.)	Jerrel Wilson, 1965	46.0
Punt Return (Avg.)	Abner Haynes, 1960	15.4
Kickoff Return (Avg.)	Dave Grayson, 1962	29.7
Field Goals	Nick Lowery, 1990	34
Touchdowns (Tot.)	Abner Haynes, 1962	19
Points	Nick Lowery, 1990	139

INDIVIDUAL RECORDS—SINGLE GAME

CATEGORY	NAME	PERFORMANCE
Rushing (Yds.)	Barry Word, 10-14-90	200
Passing (Yds.)	Len Dawson, 11-1-64	435
Passing (TDs)	Len Dawson, 11-1-64	6
Receiving (No.)	Ed Podolak, 10-7-73	12
Receiving (Yds.)	Stephone Paige, 12-22-85	309
Interceptions	Bobby Ply, 12-16-62	*4
	Bobby Hunt, 12-4-64	*4
	Deron Cherry, 9-29-85	*4
Field Goals	Many times. Last time by Nick Lowery, 9-20-93	5
Touchdowns (Tot.)	Abner Haynes, 11-26-61	5
Points	Abner Haynes, 11-26-61	30

*NFL Record

MIAMI DOLPHINS

7500 S.W. 30th Street
Davie, Florida 33314
Telephone: (954) 452-7000
Websites: nfl.com and
http://pwr.com/dolphins

Team Colors: Aqua, Coral, Blue, and White
AFC East

1997 Regular-Season Attendance:
Home: 574,811 Away: 522,208
Playing Surface: Grass (PAT)
Training Camp:
Nova University
Davie, Florida 33314

1997 Record 9-7
Home: 6-2
Away: 3-5
Stadium: Pro Player Stadium
Capacity: 75,192

1997 RESULTS

DATE	RESULT	OPPONENT	ATT.
8/31	W 16-10	INDIANAPOLIS	70,813
9/7	W 16-13*	TENNESSEE	64,439
9/14	L 18-23	at Green Bay	60,075
9/21	L 21-31	at Tampa Bay	73,314
10/5	W 17-14	KANSAS CITY	71,794
10/12	W 31-20	at N.Y. Jets	75,601
10/19	W 24-13	at Baltimore	64,354
10/27	L 33-36*	CHICAGO	73,156
11/2	L 6-9	at Buffalo	78,011
11/09	W 24-17	NEW YORK JETS	73,809
11/17	W 30-13	BUFFALO	74,155
11/23	L 24-27	at N.E.	59,002
11/30	W 34-16	at Oakland	50,569
12/7	W 33-30	DETROIT	72,266
12/14	L 0-41	at Ind.	61,282
12/22	L 12-14	NEW ENGLAND	74,379

POSTSEASON

| 12/28 | L 3-17 | at N.E. | 60,041 |

*Overtime

1998 SCHEDULE

REGULAR SEASON

Sept. 6 at Indianapolis 3:15
Sept. 13 BUFFALO. 1:01
Sept. 20 PITTSBURGH. 1:01
Sept. 27 OPEN DATE
Oct. 4 at New York Jets. 1:01
Oct. 12 at Jacksonville (Mon.) . 8:20
Oct. 18 ST. LOUIS 4:15
Oct. 25 NEW ENGLAND 1:01
Nov. 1 at Buffalo 1:01
Nov. 8 INDIANAPOLIS. 1:01
Nov. 15 at Carolina 1:01
Nov. 23 at New England (Mon.) 8:20
Nov. 29 NEW ORLEANS 1:01
Dec. 6 at Oakland 1:15
Dec. 13 NEW YORK JETS. 8:20
Dec. 21 DENVER (Mon.) 8:20
Dec. 27 at Atlanta. 1:01

Nationally Televised Games in Bold/All times local

COACHING STAFF

Head Coach—Jimmy Johnson; Assistant Coaches—Larry Beightol, Doug Blevins, Kippy Brown, Joel Collier, John Gamble, Cary Godette, George Hill, Pat Jones, Bill Lewis, Rich McGeorge, Mel Phillips, Brad Roll, Larry Seiple, Mike Westhoff.

1998 SCOUTING REPORT

Dan Marino, the most prolific passer in NFL history, has yet to win a Super Bowl, and time is running out for the 15-year veteran. Broncos quarterback John Elway, who was drafted in the same year as Marino (1983), finally won an NFL title last year.

In order to get to Super Bowl XXXIII (which will be played in Miami), Dolphins head coach Jimmy Johnson knows that Marino has to pass less and the team has to run more.

In 1997, Miami finished last in the AFC in rushing and averaged only 3.1 yards per carry, the poorest mark in club history. The Dolphins hope Lawrence Phillips, the Rams' first-round draft choice in 1996 who struggled off the field and eventually was waived by St. Louis, can fulfill his potential. Pass-oriented offensive coordinator Gary Stevens was replaced by running backs coach Kippy Brown.

1998 DRAFT CHOICES

RD. NAME	POS.	COLLEGE	RD. NAME	POS.	COLLEGE
1. John Avery	RB	Mississippi	4. Lorenzo Bromell	DE	Clemson
2a. Patrick Surtain	CB	So. Mississippi	5. Scott Shaw	G	Michigan St.
2b. Kenny Mixon	DE	Louisiana St.	6a. Nathan Strikwerda	C	Northwestern
3a. Brad Jackson	LB	Cincinnati	6b. John Dutton	QB	Nevada
3b. Larry Shannon	WR	East Carolina	7. Jim Bundren	G	Clemson

Avery gives Dolphins double threat. He explodes through holes as runner and is excellent receiver out of backfield...Surtain is wily defender...Mixon is talented pass rusher who also is effective against run...Jackson will play weakside linebacker.

KEY ACQUISITIONS

NAME	POS.	PREVIOUS NFL TEAM	NAME	POS.	PREVIOUS NFL TEAM
Alexander (FA)	WR	Giants	Brock Marion (FA)	S	Cowboys
Donnalley (FA)	G	Oilers	Stan White (FA)	QB	Giants

KEY LOSSES

NAME	POS.	NEW NFL TEAM	NAME	POS.	NEW NFL TEAM
Qadry Ismail (FA)	WR	Saints	Roosevelt Potts (FA)	RB	Ravens
Everett McIver (FA)	G	Cowboys	George Teague (FA)	S	Unsigned

(FA) = Free Agent

1997 STATISTICAL LEADERS

SCORING

PLAYER	TD	PAT	FG	PTS.
Mare	0	33/33	28/36	117
Abdul-Jabbar	*16	0/0	0/0	96
Drayton	4	0/0	0/0	24
Jordan	3	0/0	0/0	18
McDuffie	2	0/0	0/0	12
McPhail	2	0/0	0/0	12
Spikes	2	0/0	0/0	12
L. Thomas	2	0/0	0/0	12
Barnett	1	0/0	0/0	6
Bowens	1	0/0	0/0	6
Buckley	1	0/0	0/0	6
Parmalee	1	0/0	0/0	6
Perriman	1	0/0	0/0	6
Dolphins	37	33/33	28/36	339
Opponents	36	30/32	25/35	327

2-Point conversions: Dolphins 0-4, Opponents: 2-4

RUSHING

PLAYER	ATT.	YDS.	AVG.	TD
Abdul-Jabbar	283	892	3.2	*15
Phillips	18	44	2.4	0
Spikes	63	180	2.9	2
McPhail	17	146	8.6	1
Parmalee	18	59	3.3	0
Jordan	3	12	4.0	0
Erickson	4	8	2.0	0
Pritchett	3	7	2.3	0
Kidd	1	4	4.0	0
Potts	1	3	3.0	0
Nealy	1	2	2.0	0
Marino	18	-14	-.8	0
Dolphins	430	1,343	3.1	18
Opponents	443	1,813	4.1	9

INTERCEPTIONS

PLAYER	NO.	YDS.	AVG.	TD
Buckley	4	26	6.5	0
Teague	2	25	12.5	0
Dolphins	10	92	9.2	0
Opponents	12	307	25.6	4

RECEIVING

PLAYER	ATT.	YDS.	AVG.	TD
McDuffie	76	943	12.4	1
Drayton	39	558	14.3	4
McPhail	34	262	7.7	1
Abdul-Jabbar	29	261	9.0	1
L. Thomas	28	402	14.4	2
Parmalee	28	301	10.8	1
Jordan	27	471	17.4	3
Perriman	19	309	16.3	1
Barnett	17	166	9.8	1
Perry	11	45	4.1	1
Manning	7	85	12.1	0
Spikes	7	70	10.0	0
Pritchett	5	35	7.0	0
Potts	3	27	9.0	0
Phillips	1	6	6.0	0
Dotson	1	4	4.0	0
Dolphins	332	3,945	11.9	16
Opponents	329	3,782	11.5	23

KICKOFF RETURNS

PLAYER	NO.	YDS.	AVG.	TD
Spikes	24	565	23.5	0
McPhail	15	314	20.9	0
C. Harris	11	224	20.4	0
Ismail	8	166	20.8	0
A. Harris	1	0	0.0	0
Dolphins	63	1,298	20.6	0
Opponents	53	1,018	19.2	0

PUNT RETURNS

PLAYER	NO.	YDS.	AVG.	TD
Jordan	26	273	10.5	0
Buckley	4	58	14.5	0
Dolphins	32	335	10.5	0
Opponents	43	323	7.5	0

PUNTING

PLAYER	NO.	YDS.	AVG.
Kidd	52	2,247	43.2
Richardson	11	480	43.6
Dolphins	68	2,962	43.6
Opponents	63	2,679	42.5

PASSING

PLAYER	ATT.	COMP.	YDS.	PCT.	TD	INT.	RAT.
Marino	*548	*319	3,780	58.2	16	11	80.7
Erickson	28	13	165	46.4	0	1	50.4
Dolphins	576	332	3,945	57.6	16	12	79.2
Opponents	530	329	3,782	62.1	23	10	90.1

SACKS: Armstrong 5.5, Bowens 5.0, Rodgers 5.0, Dolphins 31.0, Opponents 22.0

*League Leaders   (All individuals may not be represented.)

RECORD HOLDERS

INDIVIDUAL RECORDS—CAREER

CATEGORY	NAME	PERFORMANCE
Rushing (Yds.)	Larry Csonka, 1968-1974, 1979	6,737
Passing (Yds.)	Dan Marino, 1983-1997	*55,416
Passing (TDs)	Dan Marino, 1983-1997	*385
Receiving (No.)	Mark Clayton, 1983-1992	550
Receiving (Yds.)	Mark Duper, 1982-1992	8,869
Interceptions	Jake Scott, 1970-75	35
Punting (Avg.)	John Kidd, 1994-97	44.2
Punt Return (Avg.)	Freddie Solomon, 1975-77	11.4
Kickoff Return (Avg.)	Mercury Morris, 1969-1975	26.5
Field Goals	Pete Stoyanovich, 1989-1995	176
Touchdowns (Tot.)	Mark Clayton, 1983-1992	82
Points	Garo Yepremian, 1970-78	830

INDIVIDUAL RECORDS—SINGLE SEASON

CATEGORY	NAME	PERFORMANCE
Rushing (Yds.)	Delvin Williams, 1978	1,258
Passing (Yds.)	Dan Marino, 1984	*5,084
Passing (TDs)	Dan Marino, 1984	*48
Receiving (No.)	Mark Clayton, 1988	86
Receiving (Yds.)	Mark Clayton, 1984	1,389
Interceptions	Dick Westmoreland, 1967	10
Punting (Avg.)	John Kidd, 1996	46.3
Punt Return (Avg.)	Freddie Solomon, 1975	12.3
Kickoff Return (Avg.)	Duriel Harris, 1976	32.9
Field Goals	Pete Stoyanovich, 1991	31
Touchdowns (Tot.)	Mark Clayton, 1984	18
Points	Pete Stoyanovich, 1992	124

INDIVIDUAL RECORDS—SINGLE GAME

CATEGORY	NAME	PERFORMANCE
Rushing (Yds.)	Mercury Morris, 9-30-73	197
Passing (Yds.)	Dan Marino, 10-23-88	521
Passing (TDs)	Bob Griese, 11-24-77	6
	Dan Marino, 9-21-86	6
Receiving (No.)	Jim Jensen, 11-6-88	12
Receiving (Yds.)	Mark Duper, 11-10-85	217
Interceptions	Dick Anderson, 12-3-73	*4
Field Goals	Garo Yepremian, 9-26-71	5
Touchdowns (Tot.)	Paul Warfield, 12-15-73	4
	Mark Ingram, 11-27-94	4
Points	Paul Warfield, 12-15-73	24
	Mark Ingram, 11-27-94	24

*NFL Record

MINNESOTA VIKINGS

9520 Viking Drive
Eden Prairie, MN 55344
Telephone: (612) 828-6500
Website: nfl.com

Team Colors: Purple, Gold, and White

1997 Regular-Season Attendance:
Home: 486,921 Away: 505,684
Playing Surface: AstroTurf
Training Camp:
Mankato State University
Mankato, Minnesota 56001

NFC Central
1997 Record 9-7
Home: 5-3 **Away:** 4-4
Stadium: Hubert H. Humphrey Metrodome
Capacity: 64,182

1997 RESULTS

DATE	RESULT	OPPONENT	ATT.
8/31	W 34-13	at Buffalo	79,139
9/7	W 27-24	at Chicago	59,263
9/14	L 14-28	TAMPA BAY	63,697
9/21	L 32-38	at Green Bay	60,115
9/28	W 28-19	PHILADELPHIA	55,149
10/5	W 20-19	at Arizona	45,550
10/12	W 21-14	CAROLINA	62,625
10/26	W 10-6	at Tampa Bay	66,815
11/2	W 23-18	NEW ENGLAND	62,917
11/9	W 29-22	CHICAGO	63,443
11/16	L 15-38	at Detroit	68,910
11/23	L 21-23	at N.Y. Jets	70,131
12/1	L 11-27	GREEN BAY	64,001
12/7	L 17-28	at S.F.	55,761
12/14	L 13-14	DETROIT	60,982
12/21	W 39-28	INDIANAPOLIS	54,107

POSTSEASON

12/27	W 23-22	at N.Y. Giants	77,710
1/3	L 22-38	at S.F.	65,018

1998 SCHEDULE

REGULAR SEASON

Sept. 6	TAMPA BAY 12:01
Sept. 13	at St. Louis 12:01
Sept. 20	DETROIT................ 12:01
Sept. 27	**at Chicago 3:15**
Oct. 5	**at Green Bay (Mon.) .. 7:20**
Oct. 11	OPEN DATE
Oct. 18	WASHINGTON 12:01
Oct. 25	at Detroit................ 1:01
Nov. 1	at Tampa Bay 1:01
Nov. 8	NEW ORLEANS 12:01
Nov. 15	CINCINNATI 12:01
Nov. 22	GREEN BAY 12:01
Nov. 26	**at Dallas (Thurs.) ... 3:05**
Dec. 6	**CHICAGO............ 7:20**
Dec. 13	at Baltimore 4:15
Dec. 20	**JACKSONVILLE....... 7:20**
Dec. 26	**at Tenn. (Sat.) ... 11:35 A.M.**

Nationally Televised Games in **Bold**/All times local

COACHING STAFF

Head Coach—Dennis Green; Assistant Coaches—Hubbard Alexander, Dave Atkins, Brian Billick, Foge Fazio, Jeff Friday, Carl Hargrave, Wade Harman, Chip Myers, Tom Olivadotti, Andre Patterson, Richard Solomon, Mike Tice, Trent Walters, Steve Wetzel, Gary Zauner.

1998 SCOUTING REPORT

Entering the 1998 NFL season, Minnesota might have the league's most explosive offense.

Brad Johnson, who threw 20 touchdown passes and had an 84.5 passer rating in 1997, enters his third season as the team's starting quarterback.

Wide receivers Cris Carter (89 receptions for 1,069 yards and a league-high 13 touchdown receptions) and Jake Reed (68 for 1,138 and 6) are back along with running back Robert Smith, who finished third in the NFC with 1,266 yards and averaged 5.5 yards per carry in 1997.

There also is a key addition: 6-foot 5-inch, 211-pound Randy Moss, a fast and potentially unstoppable receiver. Moss, the Vikings' first-round draft choice, won the Fred Biletnikoff Award as the nation's best collegiate receiver last year and was considered one of the top players in the draft, but he fell to the Vikings, who had the twenty-first selection.

1998 DRAFT CHOICES

RD. NAME	POS.	COLLEGE	RD. NAME	POS.	COLLEGE
1. Randy Moss	WR	Marshall	5. Kerry Cooks	S	Iowa
2. Kailee Wong	LB	Stanford	6. Matt Birk	T	Harvard
3. Ramos McDonald	S	New Mexico	7a. Chester Burnett	LB	Arizona
4. Kivuusama Mays	LB	North Carolina	7b. Tony Darden	CB	Texas Tech

Moss has all tools to become great NFL receiver. He caught 90 passes for 1,647 yards and 25 touchdowns as senior at Marshall...Wong likely will line up at right end where he can take advantage of speed and athleticism...McDonald played cornerback in college but is projected as free safety...Cooks will provide solid run support.

KEY ACQUISITIONS

NAME	POS.	PREVIOUS NFL TEAM	NAME	POS.	PREVIOUS NFL TEAM
Gary Anderson (FA)	K	49ers	Jimmy Hitchcock (Trade)	CB	New England

KEY LOSSES

NAME	POS.	NEW NFL TEAM	NAME	POS.	NEW NFL TEAM
Dewayne Washington (FA)	CB	Steelers	Leonard Wheeler (FA)	CB	Panthers

(FA) = Free Agent

1997 STATISTICAL LEADERS

SCORING
PLAYER	TD	PAT	FG	PTS.
Carter	13	0/0	0/0	84
Murray	0	23/24	12/17	59
R. Smith	7	0/0	0/0	42
Reed	6	0/0	0/0	36
Davis	0	10/10	7/10	31
Hoard	4	0/0	0/0	24
Glover	3	0/0	0/0	18
Evans	2	0/0	0/0	14
Palmer	2	0/0	0/0	12
Johnson	1	0/0	0/0	10
Brady	1	0/0	0/0	6
Thomas	1	0/0	0/0	6
Walsh	1	0/0	0/0	6
M. Williams	1	0/0	0/0	6
Vikings	42	33/34	19/27	354
Opponents	42	36/37	23/30	359

2-Point conversions: Vikings 6-8, Opponents 1-5

RUSHING
PLAYER	ATT.	YDS.	AVG.	TD
R. Smith	232	1,266	5.5	6
Hoard	80	235	2.9	4
Evans	43	157	3.7	2
Johnson	35	139	4.0	0
Cunningham	19	127	6.7	0
M. Williams	22	59	2.7	1
Palmer	11	36	3.3	1
Green	6	22	3.7	0
Berger	1	0	0.0	0
Vikings	449	2,041	4.5	14
Opponents	442	1,983	4.5	13

INTERCEPTIONS
PLAYER	NO.	YDS.	AVG.	TD
Washington	4	71	17.8	0
Griffith	2	26	13.0	0
Fuller	2	24	12.0	0
Thomas	2	1	0.5	0
Vikings	12	141	11.8	0
Opponents	16	166	10.4	0

RECEIVING
PLAYER	ATT.	YDS.	AVG.	TD
Carter	89	1,069	12.0	*13
Reed	68	1,138	16.7	6
R. Smith	37	197	5.3	1
Glover	32	378	11.8	3
Palmer	26	193	7.4	1
Evans	21	152	7.2	0
Walsh	11	114	10.4	1
Hoard	11	84	7.6	0
DeLong	8	75	9.4	0
Goodwin	7	61	8.7	0
M. Williams	4	14	3.5	0
Hatchette	3	54	18.0	0
Green	1	5	5.0	0
Johnson	1	3	3.0	1
Vikings	319	3,537	11.1	26
Opponents	336	3,957	11.8	28

KICKOFF RETURNS
PLAYER	NO.	YDS.	AVG.	TD
Palmer	32	711	22.2	0
M. Williams	16	388	24.3	0
Tate	10	196	19.6	0
Morrow	5	99	19.8	0
George	1	10	10.0	0
Walsh	1	10	10.0	0
Vikings	65	1,414	21.8	0
Opponents	67	1,398	20.9	0

PUNT RETURNS
PLAYER	NO.	YDS.	AVG.	TD
Palmer	34	444	13.1	0
Vikings	34	444	13.1	0
Opponents	49	566	11.6	1

PUNTING
PLAYER	NO.	YDS.	AVG.
Berger	73	3,133	42.9
Cunningham	8	274	34.3
Vikings	81	3,407	42.1
Opponents	70	2,932	41.9

PASSING
PLAYER	ATT.	COMP.	YDS.	PCT.	TD	INT.	RAT.
Johnson	452	275	3,036	60.8	20	12	84.5
Cunningham	88	44	501	50.0	6	4	71.3
Vikings	540	319	3,537	59.1	26	16	82.3
Opponents	542	336	3,957	62.0	28	12	92.2

SACKS: Randle *15.5, Clemons 7.0, Rudd 5.0, Vikings 44.0, Opponents 33.0

*League Leaders   (All individuals may not be represented.)

RECORD HOLDERS

INDIVIDUAL RECORDS—CAREER

CATEGORY	NAME	PERFORMANCE
Rushing (Yds.)	Chuck Foreman, 1973-79	5,879
Passing (Yds.)	Fran Tarkenton, 1961-66, 1972-78	33,098
Passing (TDs)	Fran Tarkenton, 1961-66, 1972-78	239
Receiving (No.)	Cris Carter, 1990-97	667
Receiving (Yds.)	Cris Carter, 1990-97	7,986
Interceptions	Paul Krause, 1968-1979	53
Punting (Avg.)	Harry Newsome, 1990-93	43.8
Punt Return (Avg.)	David Palmer, 1994-97	10.7
Kickoff Return (Avg.)	Charlie West, 1968-1973	25.5
Field Goals	Fred Cox, 1963-1977	282
Touchdowns (Tot.)	Bill Brown, 1962-1974	76
Points	Fred Cox, 1963-1977	1,365

INDIVIDUAL RECORDS—SINGLE SEASON

CATEGORY	NAME	PERFORMANCE
Rushing (Yds.)	Robert Smith, 1997	1,266
Passing (Yds.)	Warren Moon, 1994	4,264
Passing (TDs)	Warren Moon, 1995	33
Receiving (No.)	Cris Carter, 1994, 1995	122
Receiving (Yds.)	Cris Carter, 1995	1,371
Interceptions	Paul Krause, 1975	10
Punting (Avg.)	Bobby Walden, 1964	46.4
Punt Return (Avg.)	David Palmer, 1995	13.2
Kickoff Return (Avg.)	John Gilliam, 1972	26.3
Field Goals	Fuad Reveiz, 1994	34
Touchdowns (Tot.)	Chuck Foreman, 1975	22
Points	Chuck Foreman, 1975	132
	Fuad Reveiz, 1994	132

INDIVIDUAL RECORDS—SINGLE GAME

CATEGORY	NAME	PERFORMANCE
Rushing (Yds.)	Chuck Foreman, 10-24-76	200
Passing (Yds.)	Tommy Kramer, 11-2-86	490
Passing (TDs)	Joe Kapp, 9-28-69	*7
Receiving (No.)	Rickey Young, 12-16-79	15
Receiving (Yds.)	Sammy White, 11-7-76	210
Interceptions	Many times, last time by Jack Del Rio, 12-5-93	3
Field Goals	Rich Karlis, 11-5-89	*7
Touchdowns (Tot.)	Chuck Foreman, 12-20-75	4
	Ahmad Rashad, 9-2-79	4
Points	Chuck Foreman, 12-20-75	24
	Ahmad Rashad, 9-2-79	24

*NFL Record

NEW ENGLAND PATRIOTS

Foxboro Stadium
60 Washington Street
Foxboro, MA 02035
Telephone: (508) 543-8200
Website: nfl.com

Team Colors: Blue, Red, Silver, and White

AFC East

1997 Regular-Season Attendance:
Home: 477,431 Away: 547,518
Playing Surface: Grass
Training Camp:
Bryant College
Smithfield, Rhode Island 02917

1997 Record 10-6
Home: 6-2
Away: 4-4
Stadium: Foxboro Stadium
Capacity: 60,292

1997 RESULTS

DATE	RESULT	OPPONENT	ATT.
8/31	W 41-7	SAN DIEGO	60,190
9/7	W 31-6	at Ind.	53,632
9/14	W 27-24*	N.Y. JETS	60,072
9/21	W 31-3	CHICAGO	59,873
10/6	L 13-34	at Denver	75,821
10/12	W 33-6	BUFFALO	59,802
10/19	L 19-24	at N.Y. Jets	71,061
10/27	L 10-28	GREEN BAY	59,972
11/2	L 18-23	at Minnesota	62,917
11/9	W 31-10	at Buffalo	65,783
11/16	L 7-27	at Tampa Bay	70,479
11/23	W 27-24	MIAMI	59,002
11/30	W 20-17	INDIANAPOLIS	58,507
12/7	W 26-20	at Jacksonville	73,446
12/13	L 21-24*	PITTSBURGH	60,013
12/22	W 14-12	at Miami	74,379

POSTSEASON

12/28	W 17-3	MIAMI	60,041
1/3	L 6-7	at Pittsburgh	61,228

*Overtime

1998 SCHEDULE

REGULAR SEASON

Sept. 7	at Denver (Mon.)	6:20
Sept. 13	**INDIANAPOLIS**	**8:20**
Sept. 20	TENNESSEE	1:01
Sept. 27	OPEN DATE	
Oct. 4	at New Orleans	12:01
Oct. 11	KANSAS CITY	1:01
Oct. 19	**NEW YORK JETS (Mon.)**	**8:20**
Oct. 25	at Miami	1:01
Nov. 1	at Indianapolis	1:01
Nov. 8	ATLANTA	1:01
Nov. 15	at Buffalo	1:01
Nov. 23	**MIAMI (Mon.)**	**8:20**
Nov. 29	BUFFALO	4:05
Dec. 6	at Pittsburgh	1:01
Dec. 13	at St. Louis	12:01
Dec. 20	SAN FRANCISCO	1:01
Dec. 27	at New York Jets	1:01

Nationally Televised Games in **Bold**/All times local

COACHING STAFF

Head Coach—Pete Carroll; Assistant Coaches—Paul Boudreau, Jeff Davidson, Ray Hamilton, Ron Lynn, Johnny Parker, Bo Pelini, Jack Reilly, Dante Scarnecchia, Steve Sidwell, Carl Smith, DeWayne Walker, Steve Walters, Kirby Wilson, Ernie Zampese.

1998 SCOUTING REPORT

In 1997, first-year head coach Pete Carroll proved the Patriots could win without Bill Parcells, who left to coach the Jets after guiding New England to Super Bowl XXXI. The Patriots finished 10-6 and won the AFC East last year.

In 1998, New England has another hurdle to clear. The Patriots have to prove they can win without Pro Bowl running back Curtis Martin, who rushed for more than 1,000 yards each of the past three years, and fullback Keith Byars. Both players joined the Jets as free agents. That left unproven Sedrick Shaw, a 1997 rookie, as the team's best back. Robert Edwards, New England's first-round draft choice this year, should have an immediate impact. New offensive co-ordinator Ernie Zampese will build his attack around Pro Bowl quarterback Drew Bledsoe, who finished third in the NFL in touchdown passes.

1998 DRAFT CHOICES

RD. NAME	POS.	COLLEGE	RD. NAME	POS.	COLLEGE
1a. Robert Edwards	RB	Georgia	3b. Greg Spires	DE	Florida St.
1b. Tebucky Jones	S	Syracuse	4. Leonta Rheams	DT	Houston
2a. Tony Simmons	WR	Wisconsin	5. Ron Merkerson	LB	Colorado
2b. Rod Rutledge	TE	Alabama	6. Harold Shaw	RB	So. Mississippi
3a. Chris Floyd	RB	Michigan	7. Jason Anderson	C	Brigham Young

Edwards had history of injury problems in college, but if he can stay healthy could contend for rookie-of-year honors. He is elusive, big-play runner with good body control...Jones played on defense for only one year in college, but should make big impact for Patriots.

KEY ACQUISITIONS

NAME	POS.	PREVIOUS NFL TEAM	NAME	POS.	PREVIOUS NFL TEAM
Tony Carter (FA)	RB	Bears	Brian Stablein (FA)	WR	Colts

KEY LOSSES

NAME	POS.	NEW NFL TEAM	NAME	POS.	NEW NFL TEAM
Keith Byars (FA)	RB	Jets	Jimmy Hitchcock (Trade)	CB	Vikings
Sam Gash (FA)	RB	Bills	Curtis Martin (FA)	RB	Jets
Mike Gisler (FA)	C	Jets			

(FA) = Free Agent

1997 STATISTICAL LEADERS

SCORING

PLAYER	TD	PAT	FG	PTS.
Vinatieri	0	40/40	25/29	115
Coates	8	0/0	0/0	48
T. Brown	6	0/0	0/0	36
Martin	5	0/0	0/0	30
Byars	3	0/0	0/0	18
Gash	3	0/0	0/0	18
Purnell	3	0/0	0/0	18
Brisby	2	0/0	0/0	12
Glenn	2	0/0	0/0	12
Jefferson	2	0/0	0/0	12
Meggett	2	0/0	0/0	12
Clay	1	0/0	0/0	6
Cullors	1	0/0	0/0	6
Grier	1	0/0	0/0	6
Patriots	42	40/40	25/29	369
Opponents	33	29/29	20/29	289

2-Point conversions: Patriots 0-2, Opponents: 1-4

RUSHING

PLAYER	ATT.	YDS.	AVG.	TD
Martin	274	1,160	4.2	4
Cullors	22	101	4.6	0
Grier	33	75	2.3	1
Meggett	20	60	3.0	1
Bledsoe	28	55	2.0	0
Byars	11	24	2.2	0
Gash	6	10	1.7	0
Zolak	3	-3	-1.0	0
Patriots	398	1,464	3.7	6
Opponents	436	1,616	3.7	16

INTERCEPTIONS

PLAYER	NO.	YDS.	AVG.	TD
Clay	6	109	18.2	1
Law	3	70	23.3	0
Milloy	3	15	5.0	0
Hitchcock	2	104	52.0	1
Patriots	19	366	19.3	4
Opponents	15	213	14.2	2

RECEIVING

PLAYER	ATT.	YDS.	AVG.	TD
Coates	66	737	11.2	8
Jefferson	54	841	15.6	2
T. Brown	41	607	14.8	6
Martin	41	296	7.2	1
Glenn	27	431	16.0	2
Brisby	23	276	12.0	2
Gash	22	154	7.0	3
Byars	20	189	9.5	3
Meggett	19	203	10.7	1
Purnell	5	57	11.4	3
Cullors	2	8	4.0	0
Jells	1	9	9.0	0
Patriots	321	3,808	11.9	31
Opponents	368	3,772	10.3	14

KICKOFF RETURNS

PLAYER	NO.	YDS.	AVG.	TD
Meggett	33	816	24.7	0
Cullors	15	386	25.7	1
Canty	4	115	28.8	0
Coates	1	20	20.0	0
Patriots	53	1,337	25.2	1
Opponents	75	1,651	22.0	1

PUNT RETURNS

PLAYER	NO.	YDS.	AVG.	TD
Meggett	45	467	10.4	0
Patriots	45	467	10.4	0
Opponents	38	437	11.5	0

PUNTING

PLAYER	NO.	YDS.	AVG.
Tupa	78	3,569	45.8
Patriots	79	3,569	45.2
Opponents	74	3,288	44.4

PASSING

PLAYER	ATT.	COMP.	YDS.	PCT.	TD	INT.	RAT.
Bledsoe	522	314	3,706	60.2	28	15	87.7
Zolak	9	6	67	66.7	2	0	128.2
Meggett	1	1	35	100.0	1	0	158.3
Patriots	532	321	3,808	60.3	31	15	89.9
Opponents	619	368	3,772	59.5	14	19	71.8

SACKS: Slade 9.0, Thomas 7.0, Bruschi 4.0, Patriots 45.0, Opponents 30.0

(All individuals may not be represented.)

RECORD HOLDERS

INDIVIDUAL RECORDS—CAREER

CATEGORY	NAME	PERFORMANCE
Rushing (Yds.)	Sam Cunningham, 1973-79, 1981-82	5,453
Passing (Yds.)	Steve Grogan, 1975-1990	26,886
Passing (TDs)	Steve Grogan, 1975-1990	182
Receiving (No.)	Stanley Morgan, 1977-1989	534
Receiving (Yds.)	Stanley Morgan, 1977-1989	10,352
Interceptions	Raymond Clayborn, 1977-1989	36
Punting (Avg.)	Tom Tupa, 1996-97	44.7
Punt Return (Avg.)	Mack Herron, 1973-75	12.0
Kickoff Return (Avg.)	Allen Carter, 1975-76	27.2
Field Goals	Gino Cappelletti, 1960-1970	176
Touchdowns (Tot.)	Stanley Morgan, 1977-1989	68
Points	Gino Cappelletti, 1960-1970	1,130

INDIVIDUAL RECORDS—SINGLE SEASON

CATEGORY	NAME	PERFORMANCE
Rushing (Yds.)	Curtis Martin, 1995	1,487
Passing (Yds.)	Drew Bledsoe, 1994	4,555
Passing (TDs)	Vito (Babe) Parilli, 1964	31
Receiving (No.)	Ben Coates, 1994	96
Receiving (Yds.)	Stanley Morgan, 1986	1,491
Interceptions	Ron Hall, 1964	11
Punting (Avg.)	Tom Tupa, 1997	45.8
Punt Return (Avg.)	Mack Herron, 1974	14.8
Kickoff Return (Avg.)	Raymond Clayborn, 1977	31.0
Field Goals	Tony Franklin, 1986	32
Touchdowns (Tot.)	Curtis Martin, 1996	17
Points	Gino Cappelletti, 1964	155

INDIVIDUAL RECORDS—SINGLE GAME

CATEGORY	NAME	PERFORMANCE
Rushing (Yds.)	Tony Collins, 9-18-83	212
Passing (Yds.)	Drew Bledsoe, 11-13-94	426
Passing (TDs)	Vito (Babe) Parilli, 11-15-64, 10-15-67	5
	Steve Grogan, 9-9-79	5
Receiving (No.)	Ben Coates, 11-27-94	12
Receiving (Yds.)	Stanley Morgan, 11-8-81	182
Interceptions	Many times	3
	Last time by Roland James, 10-23-83	
Field Goals	Gino Cappelletti, 10-4-64	6
Touchdowns (Tot.)	Many times	3
	Last time by Curtis Martin, 11-3-96	
Points	Gino Cappelletti, 12-18-65	28

NEW ORLEANS SAINTS

5800 Airline Highway
Metairie, Louisiana 70003
Telephone: (504) 733-0255
Website: nfl.com

Team Colors: Old Gold, Black, and White

1997 Regular-Season Attendance:
Home: 443,614 Away: 467,609
Playing Surface: AstroTurf
Training Camp: University of Wisconsin-La Crosse
La Crosse, Wisconsin 54601

NFC West
1997 Record 6-10
Home: 3-5
Away: 3-5
Stadium: Louisiana Superdome
Capacity: 69,029

1997 RESULTS

DATE	RESULT	OPPONENT	ATT.
8/31	L 24-38	at St. Louis	64,575
9/7	L 6-20	SAN DIEGO	65,760
9/14	L 7-33	at S.F.	61,838
9/21	W 35-17	DETROIT	50,016
9/28	L 9-14	at N.Y. Giants	68,891
10/5	W 20-17	at Chicago	58,865
10/12	L 17-23	ATLANTA	65,619
10/19	L 0-13	CAROLINA	50,963
10/26	L 0-23	SAN FRANCISCO	60,443
11/9	W 13-10	at Oakland	40,091
11/16	W 20-17*	SEATTLE	50,493
11/23	L 3-20	at Atlanta	48,620
11/30	W 16-13	at Carolina	57,957
12/7	L 27-34	ST. LOUIS	54,803
12/14	W 27-10	ARIZONA	45,517
12/21	L 13-25	at Kansas City	66,772

*Overtime

1998 SCHEDULE

REGULAR SEASON

Sept. 6	at St. Louis	12:01
Sept. 13	CAROLINA	12:01
Sept. 20	OPEN DATE	
Sept. 27	at Indianapolis	12:01
Oct. 4	NEW ENGLAND	12:01
Oct. 11	SAN FRANCISCO	12:01
Oct. 18	at Atlanta	1:01
Oct. 25	TAMPA BAY	12:01
Nov. 1	at Carolina	1:01
Nov. 8	at Minnesota	12:01
Nov. 15	ST. LOUIS	12:01
Nov. 22	**at San Francisco**	**5:20**
Nov. 29	at Miami	1:01
Dec. 6	DALLAS	12:01
Dec. 13	ATLANTA	12:01
Dec. 20	at Arizona	2:15
Dec. 27	BUFFALO	12:01

Nationally Televised Games in **Bold**/All times local

COACHING STAFF
Head Coach—Mike Ditka; Assistant Coaches—Danny Abramowicz, Bobby April, Tom Clements, Walt Corey, Jack Del Rio, Judd Garrett, Harold Jackson, Ned James, Lary Kuharich, Dan Neal, Markus Paul, Dick Stanfel, Rick Venturi, Mike Woicik, Zaven Yaralian.

1998 SCOUTING REPORT

Despite finishing last in the NFL in total offense and scoring, New Orleans still managed to win six games, a testament to the iron will of head coach Mike Ditka and the fierce play of its defense, which ranked fourth overall in the league.

Quarterback is the Saints' most unsettled position. Heath Shuler, Billy Joe Hobert, and Danny Wuerffel will compete for the job, but Hobert has the advantage after starting the final four games of the 1997 season and showing some promise. Hobert was signed by New Orleans after being released by Buffalo in November. The Saints hope Seattle free-agent Lamar Smith and 1997 rookie Troy Davis will provide some consistency at running back.

1998 DRAFT CHOICES

RD. NAME	POS.	COLLEGE	RD. NAME	POS.	COLLEGE
1. Kyle Turley	T	San Diego St.	5. Wilmont Perry	RB	Livingstone
2. Cameron Cleeland	TE	Washington	6. Chris Bordano	LB	So. Methodist
4a. Fred Weary	CB	Florida	7a. Andy McCullough	WR	Tennessee
4b. Julian Pittman	DE	Florida St.	7b. Ron Warner	LB	Kansas

Expect Turley to step in and start right away at right tackle. He's very versatile and plays with tenacity that is typical of players Ditka loves to coach…Cleeland is big target (6-4, 272) and should help fill void left by departure of Irv Smith…Weary is tough in man-for-man coverage and will punish receivers…Pittman is most effective against run.

KEY ACQUISITIONS

NAME	POS.	PREVIOUS NFL TEAM	NAME	POS.	PREVIOUS NFL TEAM
Chad Cota (FA)	S	Panthers	Qadry Ismail (FA)	WR	Dolphins
Aaron Craver (FA)	RB	Chargers	Kevin Mitchell (FA)	LB	49ers
Sean Dawkins (FA)	WR	Colts	Andre Royal (FA)	LB	Panthers
Tyronne Drakeford (FA)	CB	49ers	Lamar Smith (FA)	RB	Seahawks

KEY LOSSES

NAME	POS.	NEW NFL TEAM	NAME	POS.	NEW NFL TEAM
Eric Allen (Trade)	CB	Raiders	Doug Nussmeier (QB)	QB	Broncos
Mario Bates (FA)	RB	Cardinals	Irv Smith (FA)	TE	49ers
Ernest Dixon (FA)	LB	Panthers	Winfred Tubbs (FA)	LB	49ers
Anthony Newman (FA)	S	Raiders	Ricky Whittle (FA)	RB	Oilers

(FA) = Free Agent

1997 STATISTICAL LEADERS

SCORING
PLAYER	TD	PAT	FG	PTS.
Brien	0	22/22	23/27	91
Hastings	5	0/0	0/0	32
Bates	4	0/0	0/0	24
Zellars	4	0/0	0/0	24
Guliford	2	0/0	0/0	12
Hill	2	0/0	0/0	12
Poole	2	0/0	0/0	12
Farquhar	1	0/0	0/0	6
Fields	1	0/0	0/0	6
Hobbs	1	0/0	0/0	6
Shuler	1	0/0	0/0	6
I. Smith	1	0/0	0/0	6
Saints	24	22/22	23/27	237
Opponents	35	33/33	28/36	327

2-Point conversions: Saints 1-2, Opponents 0-2.

RUSHING
PLAYER	ATT.	YDS.	AVG.	TD
Zellars	156	552	3.5	4
Bates	119	440	3.7	4
T. Davis	75	271	3.6	0
Hobert	12	36	3.0	0
Shuler	22	38	1.7	1
Hastings	4	35	8.8	0
Nussmeier	8	30	3.8	0
Wuerffel	6	26	4.3	0
McCrary	8	15	1.9	0
Hill	1	11	11.0	0
Saints	417	1,461	3.5	9
Opponents	496	1,764	3.6	11

INTERCEPTIONS
PLAYER	NO.	YDS.	AVG.	TD
Knight	5	75	15.0	0
Newman	3	19	6.3	0
Washington	2	30	15.0	0
Allen	2	27	13.5	0
Saints	16	194	12.1	0
Opponents	33	342	10.4	1

RECEIVING
PLAYER	ATT.	YDS.	AVG.	TD
Hill	55	761	13.8	2
Hastings	48	722	15.0	5
Zellars	31	263	8.5	0
Guliford	27	362	13.4	1
Farquhar	17	253	14.9	1
I. Smith	17	180	10.6	1
T. Davis	13	85	6.5	0
Bates	5	42	8.4	0
Poole	4	98	24.5	2
McCrary	4	17	4.3	0
Bech	3	50	16.7	0
Hobbs	2	41	20.5	1
Savoie	1	14	14.0	0
T. Johnson	1	13	13.0	0
Saints	228	2901	12.7	13
Opponents	293	3289	11.2	21

KICKOFF RETURNS
PLAYER	NO.	YDS.	AVG.	TD
Guliford	43	1,128	26.2	1
T. Davis	9	173	19.2	0
Bech	3	47	15.7	0
McCrary	2	26	13.0	0
Saints	58	1,374	23.7	1
Opponents	51	1,139	22.3	0

PUNT RETURNS
PLAYER	NO.	YDS.	AVG.	TD
Guliford	47	498	10.6	0
Hastings	1	-2	-2.0	0
Saints	48	496	10.3	0
Opponents	50	706	14.1	1

PUNTING
PLAYER	NO.	YDS.	AVG.
Royals	88	4,038	*45.9
Saints	88	4,038	45.9
Opponents	92	3,668	39.9

PASSING
PLAYER	ATT.	COMP.	YDS.	PCT.	TD	INT.	RAT.
Shuler	203	106	1,288	52.2	2	14	46.6
Hobert	131	61	891	46.6	6	8	59.0
Wuerffel	91	42	518	46.2	4	8	42.3
Saints	458	228	2,901	49.8	13	33	49.4
Opponents	518	293	3,289	56.6	21	16	76.3

SACKS: Martin 10.5; J. Johnson 8.5; Fields 8.0; Saints 59.0; Opponents 50.0

*League Leader (All individuals may not be represented.)

RECORD HOLDERS

INDIVIDUAL RECORDS—CAREER

CATEGORY	NAME	PERFORMANCE
Rushing (Yds.)	George Rogers, 1981-84	4,267
Passing (Yds.)	Archie Manning, 1971-1982	21,734
Passing (TDs)	Archie Manning, 1971-1982	115
Receiving (No.)	Eric Martin, 1985-1993	532
Receiving (Yds.)	Eric Martin, 1985-1993	7,854
Interceptions	Dave Waymer, 1980-89	37
Punting (Avg.)	Mark Royals, 1997	45.9
Punt Return (Avg.)	Mel Gray, 1986-88	13.4
Kickoff Return (Avg.)	Walter Roberts, 1967	26.3
Field Goals	Morten Andersen, 1982-1994	302
Touchdowns (Tot.)	Dalton Hilliard, 1986-1993	53
Points	Morten Andersen, 1982-1994	1,318

INDIVIDUAL RECORDS—SINGLE SEASON

CATEGORY	NAME	PERFORMANCE
Rushing (Yds.)	George Rogers, 1981	1,674
Passing (Yds.)	Jim Everett, 1995	3,970
Passing (TDs)	Jim Everett, 1995	26
Receiving (No.)	Eric Martin, 1988	85
Receiving (Yds.)	Eric Martin, 1989	1,090
Interceptions	Dave Whitsell, 1967	10
Punting (Avg.)	Mark Royals, 1997	45.9
Punt Return (Avg.)	Mel Gray, 1987	14.7
Kickoff Return (Avg.)	Don Shy, 1969	27.9
	Mel Gray, 1986	27.9
Field Goals	Morten Andersen, 1985	31
Touchdowns (Tot.)	Dalton Hilliard, 1989	18
Points	Morten Andersen, 1987	121

INDIVIDUAL RECORDS—SINGLE GAME

CATEGORY	NAME	PERFORMANCE
Rushing (Yds.)	George Rogers, 9-4-83	206
Passing (Yds.)	Archie Manning, 12-7-80	377
Passing (TDs)	Billy Kilmer, 11-2-69	6
Receiving (No.)	Tony Galbreath, 9-10-78	14
Receiving (Yds.)	Wes Chandler, 9-2-79	205
Interceptions	Tommy Myers, 9-3-78; Dave Waymer, 10-6-85	3
	Reggie Sutton, 10-18-87; Gene Atkins, 12-22-91	3
Field Goals	Many times	5
	Last time by Morten Andersen, 12-11-94	
Touchdowns (Tot.)	Many times, last time by Mario Bates, 12-4-94	3
Points	Many times, last time by Mario Bates, 12-4-94	18

NEW YORK GIANTS

Giants Stadium
East Rutherford, NJ 07073
Telephone: (201) 935-8111
Website: www.giants.com

Team Colors: Blue, Red, and White

1997 Regular-Season Attendance:
Home: 573,241 Away: 477,528
Playing Surface: AstroTurf
Training Camp:
University at Albany
Albany, N.Y. 12222

NFC East
1997 Record 10-5-1
Home: 6-2
Away: 4-3-1
Stadium: Giants Stadium
Capacity: 78,148

1997 RESULTS

DATE	RESULT	OPPONENT	ATT.
8/31	W 31-17	PHILADELPHIA	70,296
9/7	L 13-40	at Jacksonville	70,581
9/14	L 23-24	BALTIMORE	69,768
9/21	L 3-13	at St. Louis	64,642
9/28	W 14-9	NEW ORLEANS	68,891
10/5	W 20-17	DALLAS	77,137
10/12	W 27-13	at Arizona	38,959
10/19	W 26-20*	at Detroit	70,069
10/26	W 29-27	CINCINNATI	72,584
11/9	L 6-10	at Tennessee	26,744
11/16	W 19-10	ARIZONA	68,316
11/23	T 7-7*	at Washington	75,703
11/30	L 8-20	TAMPA BAY	68,678
12/7	W 31-21	at Phil.	67,084
12/13	W 30-10	WASHINGTON	77,571
12/21	W 20-7	at Dallas	63,746

POSTSEASON

12/27	L 22-33	MINNESOTA	77,710

*Overtime

1998 SCHEDULE

REGULAR SEASON

Sept. 6	WASHINGTON	1:01
Sept. 13	at Oakland	1:15
Sept. 21	**DALLAS (Mon.)**	**8:20**
Sept. 27	at San Diego	1:15
Oct. 4	at Tampa Bay	4:15
Oct. 11	ATLANTA	8:20
Oct. 18	**ARIZONA**	**1:01**
Oct. 25	OPEN DATE	
Nov. 1	at Washington	1:01
Nov. 8	at Dallas	12:01
Nov. 15	**GREEN BAY**	**4:15**
Nov. 22	PHILADELPHIA	1:01
Nov. 30	**at San Francisco (Mon.)**	**5:20**
Dec. 6	at Arizona	2:05
Dec. 13	DENVER	1:01
Dec. 20	KANSAS CITY	1:01
Dec. 27	at Philadelphia	4:05

Nationally Televised Games in **Bold**/All times local

COACHING STAFF

Head Coach—Jim Fassel; Assistant Coaches—Dave Brazil, Rod Dowhower, John Dunn, John Fox, Mike Gillhamer, Mike Haluchak, Johnnie Lynn, Larry MacDuff, Denny Marcin, John Matsko, Dick Rehbein, Jimmy Robinson, Jim Skipper, Craig Stoddard.

1998 SCOUTING REPORT

Jim Fassel became an NFL head coach for the first time in 1997, and all he did was lead the Giants to the NFC East championship. The Giants became the first NFC East team to finish undefeated within its division, and New York did it with one of the youngest teams in the league (22 players on its roster had less than two years of NFL experience).

The Giants should be even better this year. Quarterback Danny Kanell enters the 1998 season as the starter. Although he directed a relatively mistake-free offense (New York committed the fewest turnovers in the league with 19), he'll have to improve on his 70.7 passer rating and 11 touchdown passes.

The defense, which forced an NFL-high 44 turnovers in 1997, is led by two Pro Bowl players, linebacker Jessie Armstead and defensive end Michael Strahan.

1998 DRAFT CHOICES

RD. NAME	POS.	COLLEGE	RD. NAME	POS.	COLLEGE
1. Shaun Williams	S	UCLA	5. Toby Myles	T	Jackson St.
2. Joe Jurevicius	WR	Penn State	6. Todd Pollack	TE	Boston College
3. Brian Alford	WR	Purdue	7. Ben Fricke	C	Houston

Williams is powerful hitter who projects as strong safety. Giants already have three young safeties in Tito Wooten, Sam Garnes, and Percy Ellsworth, but expect Williams, who's also capable of playing cornerback, to play right away...Jurevicius is prototypical possession receiver...Alford runs precise routes and has good hands.

KEY ACQUISITIONS

NAME	POS.	PREVIOUS NFL TEAM	NAME	POS.	PREVIOUS NFL TEAM
Gary Brown (FA)	RB	Chargers	LeShon Johnson (FA)	RB	Cardinals
Kent Graham (FA)	QB	Cardinals			

KEY LOSSES

NAME	POS.	NEW NFL TEAM	NAME	POS.	NEW NFL TEAM
Ray Agnew (FA)	DT	Rams	Brian Kozlowski (FA)	TE	Falcons
Kevin Alexander (FA)	WR	Dolphins	Thomas Randolph (FA)	CB	Bengals
Dave Brown (FA)	QB	Cardinals	Stan White (FA)	QB	Dolphins
Rodney Hampton (FA)	RB	Unsigned			

(FA) = Free Agent

1997 STATISTICAL LEADERS

SCORING
PLAYER	TD	PAT	FG	PTS.
Daluiso	0	27/29	22/32	93
Calloway	8	0/0	0/0	48
Way	5	0/0	0/0	30
Barber	4	0/0	0/0	26
Wheatley	4	0/0	0/0	24
Cross	2	0/0	0/0	12
Patten	2	0/0	0/0	12
Toomer	2	0/0	0/0	12
Alexander	1	0/0	0/0	6
Armstead	1	0/0	0/0	6
Brown	1	0/0	0/0	6
Garnes	1	0/0	0/0	6
Hampton	1	0/0	0/0	6
Pegram	1	0/0	0/0	6
Giants	35	27/29	22/32	307
Opponents	30	26/27	19/25	265

2-Point conversions: Giants 1-5, Opponents 1-3

RUSHING
PLAYER	ATT.	YDS.	AVG.	TD
Way	151	698	4.6	4
Wheatley	152	583	3.8	4
Barber	136	511	3.8	3
Pegram	19	72	3.8	1
Hampton	23	81	3.5	1
Brown	17	29	1.7	1
Lane	5	13	2.6	0
Kanell	15	2	0.1	0
Patten	1	2	2.0	0
Giants	521	1,988	3.8	14
Opponents	432	1,451	3.4	17

INTERCEPTIONS
PLAYER	NO.	YDS.	AVG.	TD
Sehorn	6	74	12.3	1
Wooten	5	146	29.2	1
Sparks	5	72	14.4	0
Ellsworth	4	40	10.0	0
Giants	27	503	18.6	4
Opponents	12	230	19.2	2

RECEIVING
PLAYER	ATT.	YDS.	AVG.	TD
Calloway	58	849	14.6	8
Way	37	304	8.2	1
Barber	34	299	8.8	1
Cross	21	150	7.1	2
Pegram	19	83	4.4	0
Alexander	18	276	15.3	1
Toomer	16	263	16.4	1
Wheatley	16	140	8.8	0
Patten	13	226	17.4	2
Pierce	10	47	4.7	0
Lewis	5	84	16.8	0
Hilliard	2	42	21.0	0
Giants	249	2,763	11.1	16
Opponents	325	3,957	12.2	10

KICKOFF RETURNS
PLAYER	NO.	YDS.	AVG.	TD
Pegram	22	382	17.4	0
Lewis	14	364	26.0	0
Patten	8	123	15.4	0
Alexander	3	30	10.0	0
Way	2	46	23.0	0
Pierce	1	10	10.0	0
Sparks	1	8	8.0	0
Giants	51	963	18.9	0
Opponents	49	1,163	23.7	1

PUNT RETURNS
PLAYER	NO.	YDS.	AVG.	TD
Toomer	47	455	9.7	1
Giants	47	455	9.7	1
Opponents	40	378	9.5	0

PUNTING
PLAYER	NO.	YDS.	AVG.
Maynard	*111	4,531	40.8
Giants	112	4,531	40.5
Opponents	89	3,748	42.1

PASSING
PLAYER	ATT.	COMP.	YDS.	PCT.	TD	INT.	RAT.
Kanell	294	156	1,740	53.1	11	9	70.7
Brown	180	93	1,023	51.7	5	3	71.1
Giants	474	249	2,763	52.5	16	12	70.9
Opponents	596	325	3,957	54.5	10	27	61.9

SACKS: Strahan 14.0, Harris 10.0, K. Hamilton 8.0, Giants 54.0, Opponents 32.0

*League Leader   (All individuals may not be represented.)

RECORD HOLDERS

INDIVIDUAL RECORDS—CAREER

CATEGORY	NAME	PERFORMANCE
Rushing (Yds.)	Rodney Hampton, 1990-97	6,897
Passing (Yds.)	Phil Simms, 1979-1993	33,462
Passing (TDs)	Phil Simms, 1979-1993	199
Receiving (No.)	Joe Morrison, 1959-1972	395
Receiving (Yds.)	Frank Gifford, 1952-1960, 1962-64	5,434
Interceptions	Emlen Tunnell, 1948-1958	74
Punting (Avg.)	Don Chandler, 1956-1964	43.8
Punt Return (Avg.)	David Meggett, 1989-1994	11.0
Kickoff Return (Avg.)	Rocky Thompson, 1971-72	27.2
Field Goals	Pete Gogolak, 1966-1974	126
Touchdowns (Tot.)	Frank Gifford, 1952-1960, 1962-64	78
Points	Pete Gogolak, 1966-1974	646

INDIVIDUAL RECORDS—SINGLE SEASON

CATEGORY	NAME	PERFORMANCE
Rushing (Yds.)	Joe Morris, 1986	1,516
Passing (Yds.)	Phil Simms, 1984	4,044
Passing (TDs)	Y.A. Tittle, 1963	36
Receiving (No.)	Earnest Gray, 1983	78
Receiving (Yds.)	Homer Jones, 1967	1,209
Interceptions	Otto Schnellbacher, 1951; Jim Patton, 1958	11
Punting (Avg.)	Don Chandler, 1959	46.6
Punt Return (Avg.)	Amani Toomer, 1996	16.6
Kickoff Return (Avg.)	John Salscheider, 1949	31.6
Field Goals	Ali Haji-Sheikh, 1983	35
Touchdowns (Tot.)	Joe Morris, 1985	21
Points	Ali Haji-Sheikh, 1983	127

INDIVIDUAL RECORDS—SINGLE GAME

CATEGORY	NAME	PERFORMANCE
Rushing (Yds.)	Gene Roberts, 11-12-50	218
Passing (Yds.)	Phil Simms, 10-13-85	513
Passing (TDs)	Y.A. Tittle, 10-28-62	*7
Receiving (No.)	Mark Bavaro, 10-13-85	12
Receiving (Yds.)	Del Shofner, 10-28-62	269
Interceptions	Many times. Last time by Terry Kinard, 9-27-87	3
Field Goals	Joe Danelo, 10-18-81	6
Touchdowns (Tot.)	Ron Johnson, 10-2-72; Earnest Gray, 9-7-80	4
	Rodney Hampton, 9-24-95	4
Points	Ron Johnson, 10-2-72; Earnest Gray, 9-7-80	24
	Rodney Hampton, 9-24-95	24

*NFL Record

NEW YORK JETS

1000 Fulton Avenue
Hempstead, New York 11550
Telephone: (516) 560-8100
Website: nfl.com

Team Colors: Green and White

1997 Regular-Season Attendance:
Home: 543,181 Away: 464,320
Playing Surface: AstroTurf
Training Camp:
1000 Fulton Avenue
Hempstead, New York 11550

AFC East
1997 Record 9-7
Home: 5-3
Away: 4-4
Stadium: Giants Stadium
Capacity: 78,803

1997 RESULTS

DATE	RESULT	OPPONENT	ATT.
8/31	W 41-3	at Seattle	53,893
9/7	L 22-28	BUFFALO	72,988
9/14	L 24-27*	at N.E.	60,072
9/21	W 23-22	OAKLAND	72,586
9/28	W 31-14	at Cincinnati	57,209
10/5	W 16-12	at Ind.	48,295
10/12	L 20-31	MIAMI	75,601
10/19	W 24-19	NEW ENGLAND	71,061
11/2	W 19-16*	BALTIMORE	59,524
11/9	L 17-24	at Miami	73,809
11/16	W 23-15	at Chicago	45,642
11/23	W 23-21	MINNESOTA	70,131
11/30	L 10-20	at Buffalo	47,776
12/7	L 14-22	INDIANAPOLIS	61,168
12/14	W 31-0	TAMPA BAY	60,122
12/21	L 10-13	at Detroit	77,624

*Overtime

1998 SCHEDULE

REGULAR SEASON

Sept. 6	**at San Francisco**	**1:15**
Sept. 13	BALTIMORE	1:01
Sept. 20	INDIANAPOLIS	1:01
Sept. 27	OPEN DATE	
Oct. 4	MIAMI	1:01
Oct. 11	at St. Louis	3:15
Oct. 19	**at N.E. (Mon.)**	**8:20**
Oct. 25	ATLANTA	1:01
Nov. 1	at Kansas City	3:05
Nov. 8	BUFFALO	4:15
Nov. 15	at Indianapolis	1:01
Nov. 22	at Tennessee	3:15
Nov. 29	CAROLINA	1:01
Dec. 6	SEATTLE	1:01
Dec. 13	**at Miami**	**8:20**
Dec. 19	**at Buffalo (Sat.)**	**12:35**
Dec. 27	NEW ENGLAND	1:01

Nationally Televised Games in **Bold**/All times local

COACHING STAFF
Head Coach— Bill Parcells; Assistant Coaches—Bill Belichick, Maurice Carthon, Romeo Crennel, Al Groh, Todd Haley, Dan Henning, Pat Hodgson, John Lott, Eric Mangini, Bill Muir, Charlie Weis.

1998 SCOUTING REPORT

In 1996, the Jets finished with a 1-15 record, the poorest in the NFL. They hired Bill Parcells as head coach before the 1997 season, and an amazing change took place. Parcells guided the Jets to a 9-7 record and third place in the AFC East.

The Jets will try to top last season's performance with a new starting quarterback, fifth-year player Glenn Foley. Foley was impressive when he played in 1997 (twice he came off the bench in the second half to lead the Jets to victory), but a knee injury sidelined him for the final five games of the season.

Foley will have help from Pro Bowl running back Curtis Martin, who signed as a free agent after rushing for more than 1,000 yards each of the past three years with the Patriots.

1998 DRAFT CHOICES

RD. NAME	POS.	COLLEGE	RD. NAME	POS.	COLLEGE
2. Dorian Boose	DE	Washington St.	5c. Blake Spence	TE	Oregon
3a. Scott Frost	S	Nebraska	5d. Eric Bateman	T	Brigham Young
3b. Kevin Williams	CB	Oklahoma St.	6a. Eric Ogbogu	DE	Maryland
4. Jason Fabini	T	Cincinnati	6b. Chris Brazzell	WR	Angelo St.
5a. Casey Dailey	LB	Northwestern	6c. Dustin Johnson	RB	Brigham Young
5b. Doug Karczewski	G	Virginia	7. Lawrence Hart	TE	Southern

Jets get active defensive lineman in Boose, who always seems to be around ball...Frost will quarterback secondary and has been compared to Buccaneers safety John Lynch.

KEY ACQUISITIONS

NAME	POS.	PREVIOUS NFL TEAM	NAME	POS.	PREVIOUS NFL TEAM
Todd Burger (FA)	G	Bears	Curtis Martin (FA)	RB	Patriots
Keith Byars (FA)	RB	Patriots	Kevin Mawae (FA)	C	Seahawks
Mike Gisler (FA)	C	Patriots	Anthony Pleasant (FA)	DE	Falcons

KEY LOSSES

NAME	POS.	NEW NFL TEAM	NAME	POS.	NEW NFL TEAM
Jon Clark (FA)	T	Cardinals	Jeff Graham (Trade)	WR	Eagles
Hugh Douglas (Trade)	DE	Eagles	Adrian Murrell (Trade)	RB	Cardinals
Roger Duffy (FA)	C	Steelers	Lorenzo Neal (Trade)	RB	Buccaneers

(FA) = Free Agent

1997 STATISTICAL LEADERS

SCORING
PLAYER	TD	PAT	FG	PTS.
Hall	0	36/36	28/41	120
Murrell	7	0/0	0/0	42
K. Johnson	5	0/0	0/0	30
L. Johnson	4	0/0	0/0	24
Baxter	3	0/0	0/0	18
Chrebet	3	0/0	0/0	18
Smith	3	0/0	0/0	18
Brady	2	0/0	0/0	12
Graham	2	0/0	0/0	12
Van Dyke	2	0/0	0/0	12
Anderson	1	0/0	0/0	6
Glenn	1	0/0	0/0	6
Lewis	1	0/0	0/0	6
Mickens	1	0/0	0/0	6
Jets	38	36/36	28/41	348
Opponents	33	27/28	18/27	287

2-Point conversions: Jets: 0-2, Opponents: 2-5

RUSHING
PLAYER	ATT.	YDS.	AVG.	TD
Murrell	300	1,086	3.6	7
L. Johnson	48	158	3.3	2
Anderson	21	70	3.3	0
Lucas	6	55	9.2	0
O'Donnell	32	36	1.1	1
Sowell	7	35	5.0	0
Neal	10	28	2.8	0
Jets	431	1,485	3.4	10
Opponents	470	1,899	4.0	5

INTERCEPTIONS
PLAYER	NO.	YDS.	AVG.	TD
Smith	6	158	26.3	3
Mickens	4	2	0.5	0
Green	3	89	29.7	0
Jets	18	379	21.1	4
Opponents	10	100	10.0	1

RECEIVING
PLAYER	ATT.	YDS.	AVG.	TD
K. Johnson	70	963	13.8	5
Chrebet	58	799	13.8	3
Graham	42	542	12.9	2
Baxter	27	276	10.2	3
Murrell	27	106	3.9	0
Anderson	26	150	5.8	1
Brady	22	238	10.8	2
Ward	18	212	11.8	1
L. Johnson	16	142	8.9	0
Neal	8	40	5.0	1
Van Dyke	3	53	17.7	2
Brown	1	26	26.0	0
Sowell	1	8	8.0	0
Jets	319	3,555	11.1	20
Opponents	304	3,663	12.0	23

KICKOFF RETURNS
PLAYER	NO.	YDS.	AVG.	TD
Glenn	28	741	26.5	1
L. Johnson	12	319	26.6	1
Van Dyke	6	138	23.0	0
Neal	2	22	11.0	0
Ward	2	10	5.0	0
Jets	54	1,236	22.9	2
Opponents	54	1,134	21.0	0

PUNT RETURNS
PLAYER	NO.	YDS.	AVG.	TD
L. Johnson	51	619	12.1	1
Ward	8	55	6.9	0
Jets	59	674	11.4	1
Opponents	47	459	9.8	0

PUNTING
PLAYER	NO.	YDS.	AVG.
Hansen	71	3,068	43.2
Hall	3	144	48.0
Jets	75	3,212	42.8
Opponents	92	3,862	42.0

PASSING
PLAYER	ATT.	COMP.	YDS.	PCT.	TD	INT.	RAT.
O'Donnell	460	259	2,796	56.3	17	7	80.3
Foley	97	56	705	57.7	3	1	86.5
Lucas	4	3	28	75.0	0	1	54.2
L. Johnson	2	0	0	0.0	0	1	0.0
Hansen	1	1	26	100.0	0	0	118.8
Jets	564	319	3,555	56.6	20	10	79.9
Opponents	558	304	3,663	54.5	23	18	75.1

SACKS: Lewis 8.0, Douglas 4.0, Ferguson 3.5, Jets 29.0, Opponents 48.0

(All individuals may not be represented.)

RECORD HOLDERS

INDIVIDUAL RECORDS—CAREER

CATEGORY	NAME	PERFORMANCE
Rushing (Yds.)	Freeman McNeil, 1981-1992	8,074
Passing (Yds.)	Joe Namath, 1965-1976	27,057
Passing (TDs)	Joe Namath, 1965-1976	170
Receiving (No.)	Don Maynard, 1960-1972	627
Receiving (Yds.)	Don Maynard, 1960-1972	11,732
Interceptions	Bill Baird, 1963-69	34
Punting (Avg.)	Curley Johnson, 1961-68	42.8
Punt Return (Avg.)	Dick Christy, 1961-63	16.2
Kickoff Return (Avg.)	Bobby Humphery, 1984-89	22.8
Field Goals	Pat Leahy, 1974-1991	304
Touchdowns (Tot.)	Don Maynard, 1960-1972	88
Points	Pat Leahy, 1974-1991	1,470

INDIVIDUAL RECORDS—SINGLE SEASON

CATEGORY	NAME	PERFORMANCE
Rushing (Yds.)	Freeman McNeil, 1985	1,331
Passing (Yds.)	Joe Namath, 1967	4,007
Passing (TDs)	Al Dorow, 1960	26
	Joe Namath, 1967	26
Receiving (No.)	Al Toon, 1988	93
Receiving (Yds.)	Don Maynard, 1967	1,434
Interceptions	Dainard Paulson, 1964	12
Punting (Avg.)	Curley Johnson, 1965	45.3
Punt Return (Avg.)	Dick Christy, 1961	21.3
Kickoff Return (Avg.)	Bobby Humphery, 1984	30.7
Field Goals	Jim Turner, 1968	34
Touchdowns (Tot.)	Art Powell, 1960	14
	Don Maynard, 1965	14
	Emerson Boozer, 1972	14
Points	Jim Turner, 1968	145

INDIVIDUAL RECORDS—SINGLE GAME

CATEGORY	NAME	PERFORMANCE
Rushing (Yds.)	Freeman McNeil, 9-15-85	192
Passing (Yds.)	Joe Namath, 9-24-72	496
Passing (TDs)	Joe Namath, 9-24-72	6
Receiving (No.)	Clark Gaines, 9-21-80	17
Receiving (Yds.)	Don Maynard, 11-17-68	228
Interceptions	Many times, last time by Marcus Turner, 11-20-94	3
Field Goals	Jim Turner, 11-3-68; Bobby Howfield, 12-3-72	6
Touchdowns (Tot.)	Wesley Walker, 9-21-86	4
Points	Wesley Walker, 9-21-86	24

OAKLAND RAIDERS

1220 Harbor Bay Parkway
Alameda, California 94502
Telephone: (510) 864-5000
Website: nfl.com
Team Colors: Silver and Black

1997 Regular-Season Attendance:
Home: 375,499 Away: 505,402
Playing Surface: Grass
Training Camp:
Napa Valley Marriott
Napa, California 94558

AFC West
1997 Record 4-12
Home: 2-6 **Away:** 2-6
Stadium: Oakland-Alameda County Coliseum
Capacity: 63,142

1997 RESULTS

DATE	RESULT	OPPONENT	ATT.
8/31	L 21-24*	at Tennessee	30,171
9/8	L 27-28	Kansas City	61,523
9/14	W 36-31	at Atlanta	47,922
9/21	L 22-23	at N.Y. Jets	72,586
9/28	W 35-17	St. Louis	42,506
10/5	L 10-25	San Diego	43,648
10/19	W 28-25	Denver	57,006
10/26	L 34-45	at Seattle	66,264
11/2	L 14-38	at Carolina	71,064
11/9	L 10-13	New Orleans	40,091
11/16	W 38-13	at San Diego	65,714
11/24	L 3-31	at Denver	75,307
11/30	L 16-34	Miami	50,569
12/7	L 0-30	at Kansas City	76,379
12/14	L 21-22	Seattle	40,124
12/21	L 9-20	Jacksonville	40,032

*Overtime

1998 SCHEDULE

REGULAR SEASON

Sept. 6	at Kansas City	**7:20**
Sept. 13	NEW YORK GIANTS	1:15
Sept. 20	**DENVER**	**1:15**
Sept. 27	at Dallas	12:01
Oct. 4	at Arizona	1:05
Oct. 11	SAN DIEGO	1:15
Oct. 18	OPEN DATE	
Oct. 25	CINCINNATI	1:15
Nov. 1	**at Seattle**	**5:20**
Nov. 8	at Baltimore	1:01
Nov. 15	SEATTLE	1:05
Nov. 22	**at Denver**	**2:15**
Nov. 29	WASHINGTON	1:15
Dec. 6	MIAMI	1:15
Dec. 13	at Buffalo	1:01
Dec. 20	at San Diego	1:05
Dec. 26	**KANSAS CITY (Sat.)**	**1:05**

Nationally Televised Games in **Bold**/All times local

COACHING STAFF

Head Coach—Jon Gruden; Assistant Coaches—Dave Adolph, Fred Biletnikoff, Chuck Bresnahan, Willie Brown, Bill Callahan, Frank Gansz, Jr., Garrett Giemont, Don Martin, John Morton, Skip Peete, Keith Rowen, David Shaw, Willie Shaw, Gary Stevens, Mike Waufle.

1998 SCOUTING REPORT

Consistency and better balance are two things new Raiders head coach Jon Gruden must bring to Oakland if it is going to better its 1997 record of 4-12, the club's poorest finish since 1962.

Quarterback Jeff George, who was one of the NFL's most prominent free-agent signings before the 1997 season, lived up to his billing by leading the AFC in passing yards and touchdown passes. Pro Bowl wide receiver Tim Brown tied for the NFL lead with a career-high 104 receptions, and running back Napoleon Kaufman was electrifying.

But despite big numbers, the Raiders' offense went cold at times in 1997. Combine that with a defense that finished last in the league against both the run and the pass, and it is easy to see how the Raiders lost eight of their last nine games. New cornerbacks Eric Allen and Charles Woodson should make a difference.

1998 DRAFT CHOICES

RD. NAME	POS.	COLLEGE	RD. NAME	POS.	COLLEGE
1a. Charles Woodson	CB	Michigan	5a. Jeremy Brigham	TE	Washington
1b. Mo Collins	T	Florida	5b. Travian Smith	LB	Oklahoma
2. Leon Bender	DT	Washington St.	7a. Vince Amey	DE	Arizona St.
3. Jon Ritchie	RB	Stanford	7b. David Sanders	DE	Arkansas
4. Gennaro DiNapoli	G	Virginia Tech			

Woodson is brilliant cornerback who believes every pass thrown in his direction belongs to him. If opponents test him too much, he has opportunity to play in Pro Bowl as rookie... Collins is exceptional pass blocker who can play both tackle positions and guard.

KEY ACQUISITIONS

NAME	POS.	PREVIOUS NFL TEAM	NAME	POS.	PREVIOUS NFL TEAM
Eric Allen (Trade)	CB	Saints	Anthony Newman (FA)	S	Saints
Terry Mickens (FA)	WR	Packers			

KEY LOSSES

NAME	POS.	NEW NFL TEAM	NAME	POS.	NEW NFL TEAM
Rob Fredrickson (Trade)	LB	Lions	Carl Kidd (FA)	CB	Broncos
Lester Holmes (FA)	G	Cardinals	Chester McGlockton (FA)	DT	Chiefs

(FA) = Free Agent

1997 STATISTICAL LEADERS

SCORING
PLAYER	TD	PAT	FG	PTS.
Ford	0	33/35	13/22	72
Jett	12	0/0	0/0	72
Kaufman	8	0/0	0/0	48
Dudley	7	0/0	0/0	42
T. Brown	5	0/0	0/0	32
Williams	5	0/0	0/0	32
Shedd	1	0/0	0/0	6
Truitt	1	0/0	0/0	6
Turner	1	0/0	0/0	6
Washington	1	0/0	0/0	6
Smith	0	0/0	0/0	2
Raiders	41	33/35	13/22	324
Opponents	44	37/37	38/43	419

2-Point conversions: Raiders 2-6, Opponents 2-7

RUSHING
PLAYER	ATT.	YDS.	AVG.	TD
Kaufman	272	1,294	4.8	6
Hall	23	120	5.2	0
Williams	18	70	3.9	3
George	17	44	2.6	0
Fenner	7	24	3.4	0
T. Brown	5	19	3.8	0
Aska	12	10	0.8	0
Davison	2	4	2.0	0
Levitt	2	3	1.5	0
Araguz	1	0	0.0	0
Klingler	1	0	0.0	0
Raiders	360	1,588	4.4	9
Opponents	525	2,246	4.3	19

INTERCEPTIONS
PLAYER	NO.	YDS.	AVG.	TD
Turner	2	45	22.5	0
Washington	2	44	22.0	1
Trapp	2	24	12.0	0
Lynch	2	6	3.0	0
Raiders	10	149	14.9	1
Opponents	10	192	19.2	2

RECEIVING
PLAYER	ATT.	YDS.	AVG.	TD
T. Brown	*104	1,408	13.5	5
Dudley	48	787	16.4	7
Jett	46	804	17.5	12
Kaufman	40	403	10.1	2
Williams	16	147	9.2	2
Fenner	14	92	6.6	0
Shedd	10	115	11.5	0
Truitt	7	91	13.0	1
Howard	4	30	7.5	0
Davison	2	34	17.0	0
Levitt	2	24	12.0	0
Hall	1	9	9.0	0
Raiders	294	3,944	13.4	29
Opponents	324	4,109	12.7	21

KICKOFF RETURNS
PLAYER	NO.	YDS.	AVG.	TD
Howard	61	1,318	21.6	0
Hall	9	182	20.2	0
Aska	2	46	23.0	0
Shedd	2	38	19.0	0
Truitt	2	51	25.5	0
Biekert	1	16	16.0	0
T. Brown	1	7	7.0	0
Holmberg	1	15	15.0	0
Levitt	1	12	12.0	0
Morton	1	14	14.0	0
Raiders	81	1,699	21.0	0
Opponents	48	1,124	23.4	0

PUNT RETURNS
PLAYER	NO.	YDS.	AVG.	TD
Howard	27	210	7.8	0
Raiders	27	210	7.8	0
Opponents	52	431	8.3	0

PUNTING
PLAYER	NO.	YDS.	AVG.
Araguz	93	4,189	45.0
Raiders	93	4,189	45.0
Opponents	77	3,035	39.4

PASSING
PLAYER	ATT.	COMP.	YDS.	PCT.	TD	INT.	RAT.
George	521	290	*3,917	55.7	29	9	91.2
Klingler	7	4	27	57.1	0	1	26.2
Kaufman	1	0	0	0.0	0	0	39.6
Raiders	529	294	3,944	55.6	29	10	89.9
Opponents	552	324	4,109	58.7	21	10	87.1

SACKS: Smith 6.5, Maryland 4.5, McGlockton 4.5, Raiders 31.0, Opponents 58.0

*League Leaders   (All individuals may not be represented.)

RECORD HOLDERS

INDIVIDUAL RECORDS—CAREER

CATEGORY	NAME	PERFORMANCE
Rushing (Yds.)	Marcus Allen, 1982-1992	8,545
Passing (Yds.)	Ken Stabler, 1970-79	19,078
Passing (TDs)	Ken Stabler, 1970-79	150
Receiving (No.)	Tim Brown, 1988-1997	599
Receiving (Yds.)	Fred Biletnikoff, 1965-1978	8,974
Interceptions	Willie Brown, 1967-1978	39
	Lester Hayes, 1977-1986	39
Punting (Avg.)	Leo Araguz, 1996-97	44.5
Punt Return (Avg.)	Claude Gibson, 1963-65	12.6
Kickoff Return (Avg.)	Jack Larscheid, 1960-61	28.4
Field Goals	Chris Bahr, 1980-88	162
Touchdowns (Tot.)	Marcus Allen, 1982-1992	98
Points	George Blanda, 1967-1975	863

INDIVIDUAL RECORDS—SINGLE SEASON

CATEGORY	NAME	PERFORMANCE
Rushing (Yds.)	Marcus Allen, 1985	1,759
Passing (Yds.)	Jeff George, 1997	3,917
Passing (TDs)	Daryle Lamonica, 1969	34
Receiving (No.)	Tim Brown, 1997	104
Receiving (Yds.)	Tim Brown, 1997	1,408
Interceptions	Lester Hayes, 1980	13
Punting (Avg.)	Ray Guy, 1973	45.3
Punt Return (Avg.)	Claude Gibson, 1964	14.4
Kickoff Return (Avg.)	Harold Hart, 1975	30.5
Field Goals	Jeff Jaeger, 1993	35
Touchdowns (Tot.)	Marcus Allen, 1984	18
Points	Jeff Jaeger, 1993	132

INDIVIDUAL RECORDS—SINGLE GAME

CATEGORY	NAME	PERFORMANCE
Rushing (Yds.)	Napoleon Kaufman, 10-19-97	227
Passing (Yds.)	Jeff Hostetler, 10-31-93	424
Passing (TDs)	Tom Flores, 12-22-63; Daryle Lamonica, 10-19-69	6
Receiving (No.)	Tim Brown, 12-21-97	14
Receiving (Yds.)	Art Powell, 12-22-63	247
Interceptions	Many times, last time by Terry McDaniel, 10-9-94	3
Field Goals	Jeff Jaeger, 12-11-94	5
Touchdowns (Tot.)	Art Powell, 12-22-63; Marcus Allen, 9-24-84	4
	Harvey Williams, 11-16-97	4
Points	Art Powell, 12-22-63; Marcus Allen, 9-24-84	24
	Harvey Williams, 11-16-97	24

PHILADELPHIA EAGLES

Veterans Stadium
3501 South Broad Street
Philadelphia, PA 19148
Telephone: (215) 463-2500
Website: nfl.com

Team Colors: Midnight Green, Silver, Black, and White
NFC East
1997 Record 6-9-1
Home: 6-2
Away: 0-7-1
Stadium: Veterans Stadium
Capacity: 65,352

1997 Regular-Season Attendance:
Home: 480,437 Away: 535,783
Playing Surface: AstroTurf-8
Training Camp:
Lehigh University
Bethlehem, PA 18015

1997 RESULTS

DATE	RESULT	OPPONENT	ATT.
8/31	L 17-31	at N.Y. Giants	70,296
9/7	W 10-9	GREEN BAY	66,803
9/15	L 20-21	at Dallas	63,942
9/28	L 19-28	at Minnesota	55,149
10/5	W 24-10	WASHINGTON	67,008
10/12	L 21-38	at Jacksonville	69,150
10/19	W 13-10*	ARIZONA	66,860
10/26	W 13-12	DALLAS	67,106
11/2	L 21-31	at Arizona	39,549
11/10	L 12-24	SAN FRANCISCO	67,133
11/16	T 10-10*	at Baltimore	63,546
11/23	W 23-20	PITTSBURGH	67,166
11/30	W 44-42	CINCINNATI	66,623
12/7	L 21-31	N.Y. GIANTS	67,084
12/14	L 17-20	at Atlanta	42,866
12/21	L 32-35	at Washington	75,939

*Overtime

1998 SCHEDULE

REGULAR SEASON

Sept. 6	SEATTLE	1:01
Sept. 13	at Atlanta	1:01
Sept. 20	**at Arizona**	**5:20**
Sept. 27	KANSAS CITY	1:01
Oct. 4	**at Denver**	**2:15**
Oct. 11	WASHINGTON	1:01
Oct. 18	at San Diego	1:15
Oct. 25	OPEN DATE	
Nov. 2	**DALLAS (Mon.)**	**8:20**
Nov. 8	DETROIT	1:01
Nov. 15	at Washington	1:01
Nov. 22	at New York Giants	1:01
Nov. 29	**at Green Bay**	**3:15**
Dec. 3	**ST. LOUIS (Thurs.)**	**8:20**
Dec. 13	ARIZONA	1:01
Dec. 20	**at Dallas**	**3:15**
Dec. 27	NEW YORK GIANTS	4:05

Nationally Televised Games in **Bold**/All times local

COACHING STAFF

Head Coach—Ray Rhodes; Assistant Coaches—Dana Bible, Jim Bollman, Gerald Carr, Juan Castillo, John Harbaugh, Chuck Knox, Jr., Sean Payton, Danny Smith, Emmitt Thomas, Mike Trgovac, Joe Vitt, Ted Williams, Mike Wolf, Ken Zampese.

1998 SCOUTING REPORT

In 1995 and 1996, the Eagles were considered overachievers for making the playoffs each year. In 1997, a supposedly more talented Philadelphia team underachieved to a 6-9-1 record.

Head coach Ray Rhodes knows players such as defensive end Mike Mamula (8 sacks in '96 and only 4 last year) and 1997 first-round draft choice Jon Harris (only 1 sack in limited duty) need to step up if the Eagles are going to return to the playoffs. Defensive end Hugh Douglas, who was the 1995 NFL defensive rookie of the year, comes over from the Jets to strengthen the pass rush.

There also are high expectations for third-year quarterback Bobby Hoying, who becomes the Eagles' starter after strong showings late last season.

1998 DRAFT CHOICES

RD. NAME	POS.	COLLEGE	RD. NAME	POS.	COLLEGE
1. Tra Thomas	T	Florida St.	4b. Clarence Love	CB	Toledo
3a. Jeremiah Trotter	LB	Stephen F. Austin	5. Ike Reese	LB	Michigan St.
3b. Allen Rossum	CB	Notre Dame	7a. Chris Akins	DT	Texas
4a. Brandon Whiting	DT	California	7b. Melvin Thomas	G	Colorado

Thomas is massive (6-8, 350) athlete who can dominate as both run and pass blocker... Trotter is hitter who gives 100 percent on every play. He was fastest inside linebacker at scouting combine (4.65 seconds in 40 yards)...Rossum has good cover skills and is dangerous return man...Love may not start as rookie, but could start by 1999.

KEY ACQUISITIONS

NAME	POS.	PREVIOUS NFL TEAM	NAME	POS.	PREVIOUS NFL TEAM
Mike Caldwell (FA)	LB	Cardinals	George Hegamin (FA)	T	Cowboys
Hugh Douglas (Trade)	DE	Jets	Bill Johnson (FA)	DT	Rams
Jeff Graham (Trade)	WR	Jets	Keith Sims (FA)	G	Redskins

KEY LOSSES

NAME	POS.	NEW NFL TEAM	NAME	POS.	NEW NFL TEAM
Ty Detmer (FA)	QB	49ers	Darrin Smith (FA)	LB	Seahawks
Jeff Herrod (FA)	LB	Colts	Ricky Watters (FA)	RB	Seahawks
Joe Panos (FA)	G	Bills			

(FA) = Free Agent

1997 STATISTICAL LEADERS

SCORING

PLAYER	TD	PAT	FG	PTS.
Boniol	0	33/33	22/31	99
Watters	7	0/0	0/0	42
Fryar	6	0/0	0/0	36
Lewis	4	0/0	0/0	24
Solomon	3	0/0	0/0	20
Garner	3	0/0	0/0	18
Turner	3	0/0	0/0	18
Dunn	2	0/0	0/0	12
Timpson	2	0/0	0/0	12
Clark	1	0/0	0/0	6
Dawkins	1	0/0	0/0	6
T. Detmer	1	0/0	0/0	6
Johnson	1	0/0	0/0	6
Seay	1	0/0	0/0	6
Eagles	36	33/33	22/31	317
Opponents	43	42/42	24/33	372

2-Point conversions: Eagles 1-3, Opponents 0-1

RUSHING

PLAYER	ATT.	YDS.	AVG.	TD
Watters	285	1,110	3.9	7
Garner	116	547	4.7	3
Turner	18	96	5.3	0
Hoying	16	78	4.9	0
T. Detmer	14	46	3.3	1
Peete	8	37	4.6	0
Staley	7	29	4.1	0
Eagles	465	1,943	4.2	11
Opponents	476	2,009	4.2	16

INTERCEPTIONS

PLAYER	NO.	YDS.	AVG.	TD
Dawkins	3	76	25.3	1
Vincent	3	14	4.7	0
Dimry	2	25	12.5	0
Eagles	14	186	13.3	1
Opponents	16	425	26.6	4

RECEIVING

PLAYER	ATT.	YDS.	AVG.	TD
Fryar	86	1,316	15.3	6
Turner	48	443	9.2	3
Watters	48	440	9.2	0
Timpson	42	484	11.5	2
Solomon	29	455	15.7	3
Garner	24	225	9.4	0
Johnson	14	177	12.6	1
Seay	13	187	14.4	1
Lewis	12	94	7.8	4
Dunn	7	93	13.3	2
C. Jones	5	73	14.6	0
Staley	2	22	11.0	0
Vincent	0	0	—	0
Eagles	330	4,009	12.1	22
Opponents	259	3,201	12.4	20

KICKOFF RETURNS

PLAYER	NO.	YDS.	AVG.	TD
Staley	47	1,139	24.2	0
Witherspoon	9	171	19.0	0
Johnson	3	22	7.3	0
Turner	3	48	16.0	0
Dunn	2	32	16.0	0
Wyatt	2	50	25.0	0
Gray	1	8	8.0	0
Eagles	69	1,520	22.0	1
Opponents	66	1,548	23.5	0

PUNT RETURNS

PLAYER	NO.	YDS.	AVG.	TD
Seay	16	172	10.8	0
Gray	2	17	8.5	0
Eagles	31	234	7.5	0
Opponents	48	515	10.7	1

PUNTING

PLAYER	NO.	YDS.	AVG.
Hutton	87	3,660	42.1
Eagles	88	3,660	41.6
Opponents	87	3,603	41.4

PASSING

PLAYER	ATT.	COMP.	YDS.	PCT.	TD	INT.	RAT.
T. Detmer	244	134	1,567	54.9	7	6	73.9
Hoying	225	128	1,573	56.9	11	6	83.8
Peete	118	68	869	57.6	4	4	78.0
Johnson	0	0	0	—	0	0	
Eagles	587	330	4,009	56.2	22	16	78.5
Opponents	490	259	3,201	52.9	20	14	75.1

SACKS: Hall 8.0, W. Thomas 5.0, Dent 4.5, Eagles 43.0, Opponents 64.0

(All individuals may not be represented.)

RECORD HOLDERS

INDIVIDUAL RECORDS—CAREER

CATEGORY	NAME	PERFORMANCE
Rushing (Yds.)	Wilbert Montgomery, 1977-1984	6,538
Passing (Yds.)	Ron Jaworski, 1977-1986	26,963
Passing (TDs)	Ron Jaworski, 1977-1986	175
Receiving (No.)	Harold Carmichael, 1971-1983	589
Receiving (Yds.)	Harold Carmichael, 1971-1983	8,978
Interceptions	Bill Bradley, 1969-1976	34
	Eric Allen, 1988-1994	34
Punting (Avg.)	Joe Muha, 1946-1950	42.9
Punt Return (Avg.)	Steve Van Buren, 1944-1951	13.9
Kickoff Return (Avg.)	Steve Van Buren, 1944-1951	26.7
Field Goals	Paul McFadden, 1984-87	91
Touchdowns (Tot.)	Harold Carmichael, 1971-1983	79
Points	Bobby Walston, 1951-1962	881

INDIVIDUAL RECORDS—SINGLE SEASON

CATEGORY	NAME	PERFORMANCE
Rushing (Yds.)	Wilbert Montgomery, 1979	1,512
Passing (Yds.)	Randall Cunningham, 1988	3,808
Passing (TDs)	Sonny Jurgensen, 1961	32
Receiving (No.)	Irving Fryar, 1996	88
Receiving (Yds.)	Mike Quick, 1983	1,409
Interceptions	Bill Bradley, 1971	11
Punting (Avg.)	Joe Muha, 1948	47.2
Punt Return (Avg.)	Steve Van Buren, 1944	15.3
Kickoff Return (Avg.)	Al Nelson, 1972	29.1
Field Goals	Paul McFadden, 1984	30
Touchdowns (Tot.)	Steve Van Buren, 1945	18
Points	Paul McFadden, 1984	116

INDIVIDUAL RECORDS—SINGLE GAME

CATEGORY	NAME	PERFORMANCE
Rushing (Yds.)	Steve Van Buren, 11-27-49	205
Passing (Yds.)	Randall Cunningham, 9-17-89	447
Passing (TDs)	Adrian Burk, 10-17-54	*7
Receiving (No.)	Don Looney, 12-1-40	14
Receiving (Yds.)	Tommy McDonald, 12-10-60	237
Interceptions	Russ Craft, 9-24-50	*4
Field Goals	Tom Dempsey, 11-12-72	6
Touchdowns (Tot.)	Many times.	4
	Last time by Irving Fryar, 10-20-96	
Points	Bobby Walston, 10-17-54	25

*NFL Record

PITTSBURGH STEELERS

1997 Regular-Season Attendance:
Home: 462,532 Away: 519,955
Playing Surface: AstroTurf
Training Camp:
St. Vincent College
Latrobe, Pennsylvania 15650

**Three Rivers Stadium
300 Stadium Circle
Pittsburgh, PA 15212
Telephone: (412) 323-0300
Website:** nfl.com

Team Colors: Black and Gold
**AFC Central
1997 Record 11-5
Home:** 7-1
Away: 4-4
Stadium: Three Rivers Stadium
Capacity: 59,600

1997 RESULTS

DATE	RESULT	OPPONENT	ATT.
8/31	L 7-37	DALLAS	60,396
9/7	W 14-13	WASHINGTON	58,059
9/22	L 21-30	at Jacksonville	73,016
9/28	W 37-24	TENNESSEE	57,507
10/5	W 42-34	at Baltimore	64,421
10/12	W 24-22	INDIANAPOLIS	57,925
10/19	W 26-10	at Cincinnati	60,020
10/26	W 23-17*	JACKSONVILLE	57,011
11/3	L 10-13	at Kansas City	78,301
11/9	W 37-0	BALTIMORE	56,669
11/16	W 20-3	CINCINNATI	55,226
11/23	L 20-23	at Phil.	67,166
11/30	W 26-20*	at Arizona	66,341
12/7	W 35-24	DENVER	59,739
12/13	W 24-21*	at N.E.	60,013
12/21	L 6-16	at Tennessee	50,677

POSTSEASON

1/3	W 7-6	NEW ENGLAND	61,228
1/11	L 21-24	DENVER	61,382

*Overtime

1998 SCHEDULE

REGULAR SEASON

Sept. 6	at Baltimore 1:01
Sept. 13	CHICAGO 1:01
Sept. 20	at Miami 1:01
Sept. 27	SEATTLE 4:05
Oct. 4	OPEN DATE
Oct. 11	at Cincinnati 1:01
Oct. 18	BALTIMORE 1:01
Oct. 26	**at Kansas City (Mon.) . 7:20**
Nov. 1	TENNESSEE 1:01
Nov. 9	**GREEN BAY (Mon.) . . . 8:20**
Nov. 15	at Tennessee 12:01
Nov. 22	JACKSONVILLE 12:01
Nov. 26	**at Detroit (Thurs.) . . 12:35**
Dec. 6	NEW ENGLAND 1:01
Dec. 13	at Tampa Bay 1:01
Dec. 20	CINCINNATI 1:01
Dec. 28	**at Jacksonville (Mon.) . 8:20**

Nationally Televised Games in **Bold**/All times local

COACHING STAFF

Head Coach—Bill Cowher; Assistant Coaches—Mike Archer, Dave Culley, Jim Haslett, Dick Hoak, Tim Lewis, Mike Mularkey, John Mitchell, Ray Sherman, Kent Stephenson, Ron Zook.

1998 SCOUTING REPORT

It doesn't seem to matter how many free agents the Steelers lose each year, they just continue to win. General manager Tom Donohoe's keen eye for talent in the draft and head coach Bill Cowher's indomitable spirit are two reasons why Cowher joined Paul Brown as the only coaches in NFL history to guide their teams to the playoffs in their first six seasons. In 1997, Pittsburgh advanced to the AFC title game for the third time in four years.

Kordell Stewart proved he was more than just a talented player as he demonstrated superb leadership and decision making in his first full season as the Steelers' starting quarterback. Pittsburgh used "The Bus" (Jerome Bettis) to lead the NFL in team rushing. Bettis finished second in the AFC in rushing yards. Stewart and Bettis will be expected to carry similar loads again.

The Steelers' defense, which ranked first in the NFL against the run in '97, could be even better this year.

1998 DRAFT CHOICES

RD. NAME	POS.	COLLEGE	RD. NAME	POS.	COLLEGE
1. Alan Faneca	G	Louisiana St.	4b. Carlos King	RB	N. Carolina St.
2. Jeremy Staat	DE	Arizona St.	5. Jason Simmons	CB	Arizona St.
3a. Chris Conrad	T	Fresno St.	6a. C. Fuamatu-Ma'afala	RB	Utah
3b. Hines Ward	WR	Georgia	6b. Ryan Olson	LB	Colorado
4a. Deshea Townsend	CB	Alabama	7. Angel Rubio	DE	S.W. Missouri

In Faneca and Conrad, Steelers drafted two premier blockers who could anchor their offensive line for many years…Staat is powerful lineman who loves to bull rush. He played defensive tackle in college…Ward has offensive skills similar to Kordell Stewart.

KEY ACQUISITIONS

NAME	POS.	PREVIOUS NFL TEAM	NAME	POS.	PREVIOUS NFL TEAM
ger Duffy (FA)	C	Jets	Dewayne Washington (FA)	CB	Vikings

KEY LOSSES

NAME	POS.	NEW NFL TEAM	NAME	POS.	NEW NFL TEAM
Randy Fuller (FA)	CB	Unsigned	Tom Myslinski (FA)	G	Colts
John Jackson (FA)	T	Chargers	Yancey Thigpen (FA)	WR	Oilers

(FA) = Free Agent

1997 STATISTICAL LEADERS

SCORING

PLAYER	TD	PAT	FG	PTS.
N. Johnson	0	40/40	22/25	106
Stewart	11	0/0	0/0	66
Bettis	9	0/0	0/0	54
Thigpen	7	0/0	0/0	44
Bruener	6	0/0	0/0	36
Hawkins	3	0/0	0/0	18
Blackwell	2	0/0	0/0	12
C. Johnson	2	0/0	0/0	12
G. Jones	2	0/0	0/0	12
Gildon	1	0/0	0/0	6
Lake	1	0/0	0/0	6
Steelers	44	40/40	22/25	372
Opponents	31	28/28	29/35	307

2-Point conversions: Steelers 1-2, Opponents 2-3

RUSHING

PLAYER	ATT.	YDS.	AVG.	TD
Bettis	*375	1,665	4.4	7
Stewart	88	476	5.4	11
G. Jones	72	235	3.3	1
McAfee	13	41	3.2	0
Hawkins	5	17	3.4	0
Blackwell	2	14	7.0	0
Tomczak	7	13	1.9	0
Witman	5	11	2.2	0
Lester	2	9	4.5	0
Thigpen	1	3	3.0	0
Marsh	1	2	2.0	0
Jo. Miller	1	-7	-7.0	0
Steelers	572	2,479	4.3	19
Opponents	403	1,318	3.3	5

INTERCEPTIONS

PLAYER	NO.	YDS.	AVG.	TD
Woolford	4	91	22.8	0
Perry	4	77	19.3	0
Lake	3	16	5.3	0
Steelers	20	253	12.7	0
Opponents	19	270	14.2	0

RECEIVING

PLAYER	ATT.	YDS.	AVG.	TD
Thigpen	79	1,398	17.7	7
C. Johnson	46	568	12.3	2
Hawkins	45	555	12.3	3
Bruener	18	117	6.5	6
G. Jones	16	96	6.0	1
Bettis	15	110	7.3	2
Blackwell	12	168	14.0	1
Lester	10	51	5.1	0
Lyons	4	29	7.3	0
McAfee	2	44	22.0	0
Marsh	2	14	7.0	0
Adams	1	39	39.0	0
Sadowski	1	12	12.0	0
Botkin	1	11	11.0	0
Witman	1	3	3.0	0
Steelers	253	3,215	12.7	22
Opponents	295	3,681	12.5	24

KICKOFF RETURNS

PLAYER	NO.	YDS.	AVG.	TD
Blackwell	32	791	24.7	1
Coleman	24	487	20.3	0
Adams	10	215	21.5	0
Vrabel	1	0	0.0	0
Steelers	67	1,493	22.3	1
Opponents	74	1,556	21.0	1

PUNT RETURNS

PLAYER	NO.	YDS.	AVG.	TD
Blackwell	23	149	6.5	0
Coleman	5	5	1.0	0
Hawkins	4	68	17.0	0
Steelers	32	222	6.9	0
Opponents	23	271	11.8	0

PUNTING

PLAYER	NO.	YDS.	AVG.
Jo. Miller	64	2,729	42.6
Steelers	64	2,729	42.6
Opponents	66	2,804	42.5

PASSING

PLAYER	ATT.	COMP.	YDS.	PCT.	TD	INT.	RAT.
Stewart	440	236	3,020	53.6	21	17	75.2
Tomczak	24	16	185	66.7	1	2	68.9
Quinn	2	1	10	50	0	0	64.6
Steelers	466	253	3,215	54.3	22	19	74.8
Opponents	554	295	3,681	53.2	24	20	73.5

SACKS: Lake 6.0, Gildon 5.0, Kirkland 5.0, Steelers 48.0, Opponents 20.0

*League Leader   (All individuals may not be represented.)

RECORD HOLDERS

INDIVIDUAL RECORDS—CAREER

CATEGORY	NAME	PERFORMANCE
Rushing (Yds.)	Franco Harris, 1972-1983	11,950
Passing (Yds.)	Terry Bradshaw, 1970-1983	27,989
Passing (TDs)	Terry Bradshaw, 1970-1983	212
Receiving (No.)	John Stallworth, 1974-1987	537
Receiving (Yds.)	John Stallworth, 1974-1987	8,723
Interceptions	Mel Blount, 1970-1983	57
Punting (Avg.)	Bobby Joe Green, 1960-61	45.7
Punt Return (Avg.)	Bobby Gage, 1949-1950	14.9
Kickoff Return (Avg.)	Lynn Chandnois, 1950-56	29.6
Field Goals	Gary Anderson, 1982-1994	309
Touchdowns (Tot.)	Franco Harris, 1972-1983	100
Points	Gary Anderson, 1982-1994	1,343

INDIVIDUAL RECORDS—SINGLE SEASON

CATEGORY	NAME	PERFORMANCE
Rushing (Yds.)	Barry Foster, 1992	1,690
Passing (Yds.)	Terry Bradshaw, 1979	3,724
Passing (TDs)	Terry Bradshaw, 1978	28
Receiving (No.)	Yancey Thigpen, 1995	85
Receiving (Yds.)	Yancey Thigpen, 1997	1,398
Interceptions	Mel Blount, 1975	11
Punting (Avg.)	Bobby Joe Green, 1961	47.0
Punt Return (Avg.)	Bobby Gage, 1949	16.0
Kickoff Return (Avg.)	Lynn Chandnois, 1952	35.2
Field Goals	Norm Johnson, 1995	34
Touchdowns (Tot.)	Louis Lipps, 1985	15
Points	Norm Johnson, 1995	141

INDIVIDUAL RECORDS—SINGLE GAME

CATEGORY	NAME	PERFORMANCE
Rushing (Yds.)	John Fuqua, 12-20-70	218
Passing (Yds.)	Bobby Layne, 12-3-58	409
Passing (TDs)	Terry Bradshaw, 11-15-81	5
	Mark Malone, 9-8-85	5
Receiving (No.)	J.R. Wilburn, 10-22-67	12
Receiving (Yds.)	Buddy Dial, 10-22-61	235
Interceptions	Jack Butler, 12-13-53	*4
Field Goals	Gary Anderson, 10-23-88	6
Touchdowns (Tot.)	Ray Mathews, 10-17-54	4
	Roy Jefferson, 11-3-68	4
Points	Ray Mathews, 10-17-54	24
	Roy Jefferson, 11-3-68	24

ST. LOUIS RAMS

One Rams Way
St. Louis County, MO 63045
Telephone: (314) 982-7267
Website: nfl.com

Team Colors: Royal Blue, Gold, and White

1997 Regular-Season Attendance:
Home: 518,468 Away: 465,021
Playing Surface: AstroTurf
Training Camp:
Western Illinois University
Macomb, Illinois 61455

NFC West
1997 Record 5-11
Home: 2-6 **Away:** 3-5
Stadium: Trans World Dome at America's Center
Capacity: 66,000

1997 RESULTS

DATE	RESULT	OPPONENT	ATT.
8/31	W 38-24	New Orleans	64,575
9/7	L 12-15	San Francisco	64,630
9/14	L 14-35	at Denver	74,338
9/21	W 13-3	N.Y. Giants	64,642
9/28	L 17-35	at Oakland	42,506
10/12	L 10-30	at S.F.	63,825
10/19	L 9-17	Seattle	64,819
10/26	L 20-28	Kansas City	64,864
11/2	L 31-34	at Atlanta	36,583
11/9	L 7-17	at Green Bay	60,093
11/16	L 21-27	Atlanta	64,299
11/23	L 10-16	Carolina	64,609
11/30	W 23-20	at Washington	74,772
12/7	W 34-27	at N.O.	54,803
12/14	L 10-13	Chicago	66,030
12/20	W 30-18	at Carolina	58,101

1998 SCHEDULE

REGULAR SEASON

Sept. 6	NEW ORLEANS	12:01
Sept. 13	MINNESOTA	12:01
Sept. 20	at Buffalo	1:01
Sept. 27	ARIZONA	12:01
Oct. 4	OPEN DATE	
Oct. 11	NEW YORK JETS	3:15
Oct. 18	at Miami	4:15
Oct. 25	SAN FRANCISCO	12:01
Nov. 1	at Atlanta	1:01
Nov. 8	at Chicago	12:01
Nov. 15	at New Orleans	12:01
Nov. 22	CAROLINA	3:05
Nov. 29	ATLANTA	12:01
Dec. 3	**at Phila. (Thurs.)**	**8:20**
Dec. 13	NEW ENGLAND	12:01
Dec. 20	at Carolina	1:01
Dec. 27	at San Francisco	1:05

Nationally Televised Games in **Bold**/All times local

COACHING STAFF
Head Coach—Dick Vermeil; Assistant Coaches—Steve Brown, John Bunting, Chris Clausen, Dick Coury, Frank Gansz, Peter Giunta, Kerry Goode, Carl Hairston, Jim Hanifan, Todd Howard, Wilbert Montgomery, John Ramsdell, Jerry Rhome, Lynn Stiles, Ed White, Mike White.

1998 SCOUTING REPORT

The Rams have one of the NFL's youngest teams and it showed last season as they stumbled to a 5-11 record. (St. Louis was 2-7 in games decided by eight points or fewer.) Dick Vermeil, who joined St. Louis in 1997 after a 14-year absence from the NFL coaching ranks, expects more from his players in '98.

Second-year quarterback Tony Banks typified the Rams' play last year. In his first seven games, he had a 59.7 passer rating. In his last nine games, his rating was 81.0. A full season from Pro Bowl wide receiver Isaac Bruce, who missed four games and was slowed at the beginning of last season because of a hamstring injury, will add to Banks's development. Wide receiver Eddie Kennison, who scored 11 touchdowns as a rookie in 1996, needs to regain his stride.

1998 DRAFT CHOICES

RD.	NAME	POS.	COLLEGE
1.	Grant Wistrom	DE	Nebraska
2.	Robert Holcombe	RB	Illinois
3.	Leonard Little	LB	Tennessee
4a.	Az-zahir Hakim	WR	San Diego St.
4b.	Roland Williams	TE	Syracuse
5.	Raymond Priester	RB	Clemson
6.	Glenn Rountree	G	Clemson
7.	Jason Chorak	LB	Washington

Wistrom is versatile enough to play as down lineman or stand-up defensive end/outside linebacker. Missouri native is relentless competitor who gives maximum effort on every play… Holcombe is determined runner who'll be main ball carrier in Rams' offense…Little has skills to play end, but his size makes him better suited for linebacker.

KEY ACQUISITIONS

NAME	POS.	PREVIOUS NFL TEAM
Ray Agnew (FA)	DT	Giants
Steve Bono (Trade)	QB	Packers
John Flannery (FA)	C	Cowboys
Eric Hill (FA)	LB	Cardinals
Ricky Proehl (FA)	WR	Bears

KEY LOSSES

NAME	POS.	NEW NFL TEAM
Keith Crawford (FA)	WR	Falcons
Bill Johnson (FA)	DT	Eagles
Leslie O'Neal (FA)	DE	Chiefs
Mark Rypien (FA)	QB	Falcons
Torrance Small (FA)	WR	Colts

(FA) = Free Agent

1997 STATISTICAL LEADERS

SCORING

PLAYER	TD	PAT	FG	PTS.
Wilkins	0	32/32	25/37	107
Phillips	8	0/0	0/0	48
Bruce	5	0/0	0/0	30
Conwell	4	0/0	0/0	24
Lee	3	0/0	0/0	18
J. Moore	3	0/0	0/0	18
Banks	1	0/0	0/0	6
Heyward	1	0/0	0/0	6
Laing	1	0/0	0/0	6
McNeil	1	0/0	0/0	6
R. Moore	1	0/0	0/0	6
O'Neal	1	0/0	0/0	6
Small	1	0/0	0/0	6
Thompson	1	0/0	0/0	6
Rams	32	32/32	25/37	299
Opponents	39	31/31	26/31	359

2-Point conversions: Rams 0-0, Opponents 7-8

RUSHING

PLAYER	ATT.	YDS.	AVG.	TD
Phillips	183	633	3.5	8
J. Moore	104	380	3.7	3
Banks	47	186	4.0	1
Lee	28	104	3.7	1
R. Moore	24	103	4.3	1
Heyward	34	84	2.5	1
Crawford	2	32	16.0	0
Thompson	16	30	1.9	1
Kennison	3	13	4.3	0
Rypien	1	1	1.0	0
Rams	443	1,563	3.5	15
Opponents	440	1,687	3.8	10

INTERCEPTIONS

PLAYER	NO.	YDS.	AVG.	TD
McNeil	*9	127	14.1	1
Lyle	8	102	12.8	0
Lyght	4	25	6.3	0
Rams	25	281	11.2	1
Opponents	15	85	5.7	0

RECEIVING

PLAYER	ATT.	YDS.	AVG.	TD
Lee	61	825	13.5	3
Bruce	56	815	14.6	5
Conwell	38	404	10.6	4
Small	32	488	15.3	1
Kennison	25	404	16.2	0
Crawford	11	232	21.1	0
Phillips	10	33	3.3	0
Heyward	8	77	9.6	0
J. Moore	8	69	8.6	0
Laing	5	31	6.2	1
Floyd	4	39	9.8	0
R. Moore	4	34	8.5	0
Ross	3	37	12.3	0
Thomas	2	25	12.5	0
Jacoby	2	10	5.0	0
Wiegert	1	1	1.0	0
Rams	271	3,524	13.0	14
Opponents	288	3,675	12.8	26

KICKOFF RETURNS

PLAYER	NO.	YDS.	AVG.	TD
Thompson	49	1,110	22.7	0
Ross	6	130	21.7	0
Thomas	5	97	19.4	0
Lee	4	71	17.8	0
Kennison	1	14	14.0	0
Rams	68	1,454	21.4	0
Opponents	54	1,262	23.4	1

PUNT RETURNS

PLAYER	NO.	YDS.	AVG.	TD
Kennison	34	247	7.3	0
Floyd	4	15	3.8	0
Rams	40	274	6.9	0
Opponents	60	618	10.3	1

PUNTING

PLAYER	NO.	YDS.	AVG.
Horan	53	2,272	42.9
Brice	41	1,713	41.8
Rams	95	3,985	41.9
Opponents	82	3,648	44.5

PASSING

PLAYER	ATT.	COMP.	YDS.	PCT.	TD	INT.	RAT.
Banks	487	252	3,254	51.7	14	13	71.5
Rypien	39	19	270	48.7	0	2	50.2
Rams	526	271	3,524	51.5	14	15	69.9
Opponents	543	288	3,675	53.0	26	25	71.3

SACKS: O'Neal 10.0, Carter 7.5, Bill Johnson 4.0, Rams 38.0, Opponents 44.0

*League Leader   (All individuals may not be represented.)

RECORD HOLDERS

INDIVIDUAL RECORDS—CAREER

CATEGORY	NAME	PERFORMANCE
Rushing (Yds.)	Eric Dickerson, 1983-87	7,245
Passing (Yds.)	Jim Everett, 1986-1993	23,758
Passing (TDs)	Roman Gabriel, 1962-1972	154
Receiving (No.)	Henry Ellard, 1983-1993	593
Receiving (Yds.)	Henry Ellard, 1983-1993	9,761
Interceptions	Ed Meador, 1959-1970	46
Punting (Avg.)	Danny Villanueva, 1960-64	44.2
Punt Return (Avg.)	Henry Ellard, 1983-1992	11.3
Kickoff Return (Avg.)	Tom Wilson, 1956-1961	27.1
Field Goals	Mike Lansford, 1982-1990	158
Touchdowns (Tot.)	Eric Dickerson, 1983-87	58
Points	Mike Lansford, 1982-1990	789

INDIVIDUAL RECORDS—SINGLE SEASON

CATEGORY	NAME	PERFORMANCE
Rushing (Yds.)	Eric Dickerson, 1984	*2,105
Passing (Yds.)	Jim Everett, 1989	4,310
Passing (TDs)	Jim Everett, 1988	31
Receiving (No.)	Isaac Bruce, 1995	119
Receiving (Yds.)	Isaac Bruce, 1995	1,781
Interceptions	Dick (Night Train) Lane, 1952	*14
Punting (Avg.)	Danny Villanueva, 1962	45.5
Punt Return (Avg.)	Woodley Lewis, 1952	18.5
Kickoff Return (Avg.)	Verda (Vitamin T) Smith, 1950	33.7
Field Goals	David Ray, 1973	30
Touchdowns (Tot.)	Eric Dickerson, 1983	20
Points	David Ray, 1973	130

INDIVIDUAL RECORDS—SINGLE GAME

CATEGORY	NAME	PERFORMANCE
Rushing (Yds.)	Eric Dickerson, 1-4-86	248
Passing (Yds.)	Norm Van Brocklin, 9-28-51	*554
Passing (TDs)	Many times, last time by Jim Everett, 9-25-88	5
Receiving (No.)	Tom Fears, 12-3-50	*18
Receiving (Yds.)	Willie Anderson, 11-26-89	*336
Interceptions	Many times, last time by Keith Lyle, 12-15-96	3
Field Goals	Bob Waterfield, 12-9-51	5
Touchdowns (Tot.)	Bob Shaw, 12-11-49; Elroy (Crazylegs) Hirsch, 9-28-51	4
	Harold Jackson, 10-14-73	4
Points	Bob Shaw, 12-11-49;	24
	Elroy (Crazylegs) Hirsch, 9-28-51	24
	Harold Jackson, 10-14-73	24

*NFL Record

SAN DIEGO CHARGERS

Qualcomm Stadium
P.O. Box 609609
San Diego, CA 92160-9609
Telephone: (619) 874-4500
Website: nfl.com

Team Colors: Navy Blue, White, and Gold

AFC West
1997 Record 4-12
Home: 2-6
Away: 2-6
Stadium: Qualcomm Stadium
Capacity: 71,000

1997 Regular-Season Attendance:
Home: 465,906 Away: 482,485
Playing Surface: Grass
Training Camp: University of California-San Diego
La Jolla, California 92037

1997 RESULTS

DATE	RESULT	OPPONENT	ATT.
8/31	L 7-41	at N.E.	60,190
9/7	W 20-6	at N.O.	65,760
9/14	L 7-26	CAROLINA	63,149
9/21	L 22-26	at Seattle	51,110
9/28	W 21-17	BALTIMORE	54,094
10/5	W 25-10	at Oakland	43,648
10/16	L 3-31	at Kansas City	77,196
10/26	W 35-19	INDIANAPOLIS	63,177
11/2	L 31-38	at Cincinnati	53,754
11/9	L 31-37	SEATTLE	64,616
11/16	L 13-38	OAKLAND	65,714
11/23	L 10-17	at S.F.	61,195
11/30	L 28-38	DENVER	54,245
12/7	L 3-14	ATLANTA	46,317
12/14	L 7-29	KANSAS CITY	54,594
12/21	L 3-38	at Denver	69,632

1998 SCHEDULE

REGULAR SEASON

Sept. 6	BUFFALO	1:15
Sept. 13	at Tennessee	12:01
Sept. 20	at Kansas City	12:01
Sept. 27	NEW YORK GIANTS	1:15
Oct. 4	at Indianapolis	12:01
Oct. 11	at Oakland	1:15
Oct. 18	PHILADELPHIA	1:15
Oct. 25	SEATTLE	1:15
Nov. 1	OPEN DATE	
Nov. 8	**at Denver**	**2:15**
Nov. 15	BALTIMORE	1:05
Nov. 22	KANSAS CITY	1:15
Nov. 29	**DENVER**	**5:20**
Dec. 6	at Washington	1:01
Dec. 13	at Seattle	1:05
Dec. 20	OAKLAND	1:05
Dec. 27	at Arizona	2:15

*Nationally Televised Games in **Bold**/All times local*

COACHING STAFF
Head Coach—Kevin Gilbride; Assistant Coaches—Joe Bugel, June Jones, Bill Macdermott, Nick Nicolau, Frank Novak, Wayne Nunnely, Joe Pascale, Rod Perry, Mike Sheppard, Jim Vechiarella, Ollie Wilson.

1998 SCOUTING REPORT

San Diego is turning over a new leaf in 1998. Starting quarterback Stan Humphries retired after the 1997 season, so the Chargers traded up one spot with Arizona in this year's NFL draft, then made Washington State quarterback Ryan Leaf the second overall choice. San Diego paid a high price for Leaf, who last year led the Cougars to the Rose Bowl for the first time since the 1930 season. The Chargers gave the Cardinals the third overall choice and a second-round selection in this year's draft, a 1999 first-round pick, and two players. Helping speed along Leaf's development will be June Jones, who was hired as offensive coordinator and quarterbacks coach.

Running back Natrone Means, who powered the Chargers to Super Bowl XXIX, returns to anchor the running game after two seasons in Jacksonville.

1998 DRAFT CHOICES

RD.	NAME	POS.	COLLEGE	RD.	NAME	POS.	COLLEGE
1.	Ryan Leaf	QB	Washington St.	6.	Clifford Ivory	CB	Troy State
2.	Mikhael Ricks	WR	Stephen F. Austin	7a.	Jon Haskins	LB	Stanford
5.	Cedric Harden	DE	Florida A&M	7b.	Kio Sanford	WR	Kentucky

Chargers traded third overall selection and second-round pick in 1998, first-round choice in 1999, wide receiver Eric Metcalf, and linebacker Patrick Sapp to Arizona for second overall selection in 1998 NFL draft, which they used to take Washington State quarterback Leaf. Leaf is big as tight end and tough as linebacker. He has strong arm and throws with velocity on deep balls...Ricks has size (6-5, 237) and speed to play both receiver and H-back.

KEY ACQUISITIONS

NAME	POS.	PREVIOUS NFL TEAM	NAME	POS.	PREVIOUS NFL TEAM
Gerald Dixon (FA)	LB	Bengals	Natrone Means (FA)	RB	Jaguars
Roman Fortin (FA)	C	Falcons	Aaron Taylor (FA)	G	Packers
John Jackson (FA)	T	Steelers			

KEY LOSSES

NAME	POS.	NEW NFL TEAM	NAME	POS.	NEW NFL TEAM
Aaron Craver (FA)	RB	Saints	Patrick Sapp (Trade)	LB	Cardinals
Eric Metcalf (Trade)	WR	Cardinals			

(FA) = Free Agent

1997 STATISTICAL LEADERS

SCORING

PLAYER	TD	PAT	FG	PTS.
G. Davis	0	21/22	19/24	78
Martin	6	0/0	0/0	36
Metcalf	5	0/0	0/0	30
Carney	0	5/5	7/7	26
Brown	4	0/0	0/0	24
Harrison	3	0/0	0/0	18
Bradford	2	0/0	0/0	12
Jackson	2	0/0	0/0	12
F. Jones	2	0/0	0/0	12
Hartley	1	0/0	0/0	6
C. Jones	1	0/0	0/0	6
Chargers	27	26/27	26/31	266
Opponents	50	46/46	25/26	425

2-Point conversions: Chargers: 0-0, Opponents 1-4

RUSHING

PLAYER	ATT.	YDS.	AVG.	TD
Brown	253	945	3.7	4
Fletcher	51	161	3.2	0
Bynum	30	97	3.2	0
Craver	20	71	3.6	0
C. Jones	4	42	10.5	0
Whelihan	13	29	2.2	0
Humphries	13	24	1.8	0
Pegram	9	23	2.6	1
Gardner	7	20	2.9	0
Everett	5	6	1.2	0
Philcox	1	3	3.0	0
Chargers	409	1,416	3.5	5
Opponents	453	1,698	3.7	12

INTERCEPTIONS

PLAYER	NO.	YDS.	AVG.	TD
Harrison	2	75	37.5	1
Bradford	2	56	28.0	1
Harper	2	43	21.5	0
Chargers	15	257	17.1	3
Opponents	21	387	18.4	3

RECEIVING

PLAYER	ATT.	YDS.	AVG.	TD
Martin	63	904	14.3	6
F. Jones	41	505	12.3	2
Metcalf	40	576	14.4	0
Fletcher	39	292	7.5	0
C. Jones	32	423	13.2	1
Still	24	324	13.5	0
Brown	21	137	6.5	0
Hartley	19	246	12.9	1
Craver	4	26	6.5	0
Gardner	2	10	5.0	0
Pegram	2	7	3.5	0
Bynum	2	4	2.0	0
Mitchell	1	14	14.0	0
Pupunu	1	7	7.0	0
Chargers	291	3,475	11.9	12
Opponents	297	3,632	12.2	31

KICKOFF RETURNS

PLAYER	NO.	YDS.	AVG.	TD
Bynum	38	814	21.4	0
Metcalf	16	355	22.2	0
Rachal	15	336	22.4	0
Craver	3	68	22.7	0
Bordelon	2	0	0.0	0
Harrison	1	40	40.0	1
Chargers	75	1,613	21.5	1
Opponents	63	1,517	24.1	1

PUNT RETURNS

PLAYER	NO.	YDS.	AVG.	TD
Metcalf	45	489	10.9	3
Harrison	1	0	0.0	0
Chargers	47	489	10.4	3
Opponents	39	416	10.7	0

PUNTING

PLAYER	NO.	YDS.	AVG.
Bennett	89	3,972	44.6
Chargers	90	3,972	44.1
Opponents	85	3,702	43.6

PASSING

PLAYER	ATT.	COMP.	YDS.	PCT.	TD	INT.	RAT.
Whelihan	237	118	1,357	49.8	6	10	58.3
Humphries	225	121	1,488	53.8	5	6	70.8
Everett	75	36	457	48	1	4	49.7
Philcox	28	16	195	57.1	0	1	60.6
Team	565	291	3,475	51.5	12	21	62.2
Opponents	568	297	3,632	52.3	31	15	79.5

SACKS: Seau 7.0, Harrison 4.0, Parrella 3.5, Chargers 27.0, Opponents 51.0

(All individuals may not be represented.)

RECORD HOLDERS

INDIVIDUAL RECORDS—CAREER

CATEGORY	NAME	PERFORMANCE
Rushing (Yds.)	Paul Lowe, 1960-67	4,965
Passing (Yds.)	Dan Fouts, 1973-1987	43,040
Passing (TDs)	Dan Fouts, 1973-1987	254
Receiving (No.)	Charlie Joiner, 1976-1986	586
Receiving (Yds.)	Lance Alworth, 1962-1970	9,585
Interceptions	Gill Byrd, 1983-1992	42
Punting (Avg.)	Darren Bennett, 1995-97	45.2
Punt Return (Avg.)	Darrien Gordon, 1993-96	13.6
Kickoff Return (Avg.)	Leslie (Speedy) Duncan, 1964-1970	25.3
Field Goals	John Carney, 1990-97	186
Touchdowns (Tot.)	Lance Alworth, 1962-1970	83
Points	John Carney, 1990-97	783

INDIVIDUAL RECORDS—SINGLE SEASON

CATEGORY	NAME	PERFORMANCE
Rushing (Yds.)	Natrone Means, 1994	1,350
Passing (Yds.)	Dan Fouts, 1981	4,802
Passing (TDs)	Dan Fouts, 1981	33
Receiving (No.)	Tony Martin, 1995	90
Receiving (Yds.)	Lance Alworth, 1965	1,602
Interceptions	Charlie McNeil, 1961	9
Punting (Avg.)	Darren Bennett, 1996	45.6
Punt Return (Avg.)	Leslie (Speedy) Duncan, 1965	15.5
Kickoff Return (Avg.)	Keith Lincoln, 1962	28.4
Field Goals	John Carney, 1994	34
Touchdowns (Tot.)	Chuck Muncie, 1981	19
Points	John Carney, 1994	135

INDIVIDUAL RECORDS—SINGLE GAME

CATEGORY	NAME	PERFORMANCE
Rushing (Yds.)	Gary Anderson, 12-18-88	217
Passing (Yds.)	Dan Fouts, 10-19-80, 12-11-82	444
Passing (TDs)	Dan Fouts, 11-22-81	6
Receiving (No.)	Kellen Winslow, 10-7-84	15
Receiving (Yds.)	Wes Chandler, 12-20-82	260
Interceptions	Many times.	3
	Last time by Dwayne Harper, 11-27-95	
Field Goals	John Carney, 9-5-93, 9-18-93	6
	Greg Davis, 10-5-97	6
Touchdowns (Tot.)	Kellen Winslow, 11-22-81	5
Points	Kellen Winslow, 11-22-81	30

SAN FRANCISCO 49ERS

4949 Centennial Boulevard
Santa Clara, California 95054
Telephone: (408) 562-4949
Website: nfl.com

Team Colors: Forty-Niners Gold and Cardinal

1997 Regular-Season Attendance:
Home: 501,641 Away: 522,898
Playing Surface: Grass
Training Camp:
University of Pacific
Stockton, California 95211

NFC West
1997 Record 13-3
Home: 8-0
Away: 5-3
Stadium: 3Com Park
Capacity: 70,140

1997 RESULTS

DATE	RESULT	OPPONENT	ATT.
08/31	L 6-13	at Tampa Bay	62,554
09/7	W 15-12	at St. Louis	64,630
09/14	W 33-7	NEW ORLEANS	61,838
09/21	W 34-7	ATLANTA	60,404
09/29	W 34-21	at Carolina	70,972
10/12	W 30-10	ST. LOUIS	63,825
10/19	W 35-28	at Atlanta	53,378
10/26	W 23-0	at N.O.	60,443
11/2	W 17-10	DALLAS	68,657
11/10	W 24-12	at Phil.	67,133
11/16	W 27-19	CAROLINA	61,500
11/23	W 17-10	SAN DIEGO	61,195
11/30	L 9-44	at Kansas City	77,535
12/7	W 28-17	MINNESOTA	55,761
12/15	W 34-17	DENVER	68,461
12/21	L 9-38	at Seattle	66,253

POSTSEASON

1/3	W 38-22	MINNESOTA	65,018
1/11	L 10-23	GREEN BAY	68,987

1998 SCHEDULE

REGULAR SEASON

Sept. 6	NEW YORK JETS	1:15
Sept. 14	at Washington (Mon.)	8:20
Sept. 20	OPEN DATE	
Sept. 27	ATLANTA	1:15
Oct. 4	at Buffalo	1:01
Oct. 11	at New Orleans	12:01
Oct. 18	INDIANAPOLIS	1:05
Oct. 25	at St. Louis	12:01
Nov. 1	**at Green Bay**	**3:15**
Nov. 8	CAROLINA	1:01
Nov. 15	at Atlanta	1:01
Nov. 22	**NEW ORLEANS**	**5:20**
Nov. 30	**N.Y. GIANTS (Mon.)**	**5:20**
Dec. 6	at Carolina	1:01
Dec. 14	**DETROIT (Mon.)**	**5:20**
Dec. 20	at New England	1:01
Dec. 27	ST. LOUIS	1:05

*Nationally Televised Games are in **Bold**/All times local*

COACHING STAFF

Head Coach—Steve Mariucci; Assistant Coaches—Jerry Attaway, Mike Barnes, Dwaine Board, Jaime Hill, Larry Kirksey, Greg Knapp, John Marshall, Bobb McKittrick, Bill McPherson, Jim Mora, Jr., Marty Mornhinweg, Pat Morris, Tom Rathman, Richard Smith, George Stewart, Andy Sugarman.

1998 SCOUTING REPORT

Steve Mariucci did well in his first season as San Francisco's head coach, guiding the 49ers to a 13-3 record and into the NFC Championship Game. If quarterback Steve Young and wide receiver Jerry Rice—two of the best players in NFL history—can stay healthy, San Francisco has a good shot at making Mariucci's second season a super one.

Rice is recovering from knee injuries that forced him to miss 14 games last year. Despite being bothered by a concussion early in the 1997 season, Young won his sixth NFL passing title.

1998 DRAFT CHOICES

RD. NAME	POS.	COLLEGE	RD. NAME	POS.	COLLEGE
1. R.W. McQuarters	CB	Oklahoma St.	5. Phil Ostrowski	G	Penn State
2. Jeremy Newberry	C	California	6. Fred Beasley	RB	Auburn
3. Chris Ruhman	T	Texas A&M	7. Ryan Thelwell	WR	Minnesota
4. Lance Shulters	S	Hofstra			

There are few things McQuarters doesn't do well. He excels in man-for-man coverage as defender, and is dangerous receiver and kick returner…Newberry also can play guard…Ruhman has size (6-5, 313) and quickness to help improve depth at tackle…Shulters loves to hit and will make presence felt as rookie…Beasley will run over defenders.

KEY ACQUISITIONS

NAME	POS.	PREVIOUS NFL TEAM	NAME	POS.	PREVIOUS NFL TEAM
Jamie Brown (Trade)	T	Broncos	Irv Smith (FA)	TE	Saints
Ty Detmer (FA)	QB	Eagles	Winfred Tubbs (FA)	LB	Saints
Antonio Langham (FA)	CB	Ravens	Gabe Wilkins (FA)	DE	Packers
Anthony Peterson (Trade)	LB	Bears			

KEY LOSSES

NAME	POS.	NEW NFL TEAM	NAME	POS.	NEW NFL TEAM
Gary Anderson (FA)	K	Vikings	Rod Milstead (FA)	G	Redskins
Justin Armour (FA)	WR	Broncos	Kevin Mitchell (FA)	LB	Saints
Tyronne Drakeford (FA)	CB	Saints	Kirk Scrafford (Retired)	T	None
William Floyd (FA)	RB	Panthers	Dana Stubblefield (FA)	DT	Redskins
Kevin Greene (FA)	LB	Panthers	Marvin Washington (FA)	DT	Broncos
Brent Jones (Retired)	TE	None	Rod Woodson (FA)	CB	Ravens
Terry Kirby (FA)	RB	Unsigned			

(FA) = Free Agent

1997 STATISTICAL LEADERS

SCORING

PLAYER	TD	PAT	FG	PTS.
Anderson	0	38/38	29/36	125
Kirby	8	0/0	0/0	52
Owens	8	0/0	0/0	48
Hearst	6	0/0	0/0	36
Floyd	4	0/0	0/0	24
Stokes	4	0/0	0/0	24
S. Young	3	0/0	0/0	18
Hanks	2	0/0	0/0	12
Jones	2	0/0	0/0	12
Clark	1	0/0	0/0	6
Greene	1	0/0	0/0	6
Levy	1	0/0	0/0	6
Rice	1	0/0	0/0	6
49ers	41	38/38	29/36	375
Opponents	31	29/29	16/20	265

2-Point conversions: 49ers 2-3, Opponents 0-2

RUSHING

PLAYER	ATT.	YDS.	AVG.	TD
Hearst	234	1,019	4.4	4
Kirby	125	418	3.3	6
Floyd	78	231	3.0	3
S. Young	50	199	4.0	3
Levy	16	90	5.6	0
Edwards	5	17	3.4	0
Brohm	4	11	2.8	0
Druckenmiller	10	-6	-.6	0
Rice	1	-10	-10.0	0
49ers	523	1,969	3.8	16
Opponents	386	1,366	3.5	5

INTERCEPTIONS

PLAYER	NO.	YDS.	AVG.	TD
Hanks	6	103	17.2	1
Drakeford	5	15	3.0	0
Woodson	3	81	27.0	0
Walker	3	49	16.3	0
49ers	25	366	14.6	1
Opponents	11	169	15.4	2

RECEIVING

PLAYER	ATT.	YDS.	AVG.	TD
Owens	60	936	15.6	8
Stokes	58	733	12.6	4
Floyd	37	321	8.7	1
Jones	29	383	13.2	2
Kirby	23	279	12.1	1
Hearst	21	194	9.2	2
Uwaezuoke	14	165	11.8	0
Clark	8	96	12.0	1
Rice	7	78	11.1	1
Edwards	6	48	8.0	0
Fann	5	78	15.6	0
Levy	5	68	13.6	0
Harris	5	53	10.6	0
49ers	278	3,432	12.3	20
Opponents	258	3,011	11.7	23

KICKOFF RETURNS

PLAYER	NO.	YDS.	AVG.	TD
Levy	36	793	22.0	0
Uwaezuoke	6	131	21.8	0
Kirby	3	124	41.3	1
Owens	2	31	15.5	0
Drakeford	1	24	24.0	0
Edwards	1	30	30.0	0
49ers	50	1,133	22.7	1
Opponents	82	1,746	21.3	0

PUNT RETURNS

PLAYER	NO.	YDS.	AVG.	TD
Uwaezuoke	34	373	11.0	0
Levy	6	109	18.2	1
Woodson	1	0	0.0	0
49ers	41	482	11.8	1
Opponents	41	307	7.5	0

PUNTING

PLAYER	NO.	YDS.	AVG.
Thompson	78	3,182	40.8
49ers	79	3,182	40.3
Opponents	83	3,473	41.8

PASSING

PLAYER	ATT.	COMP.	YDS.	PCT.	TD	INT.	RAT.
S. Young	356	241	3,029	*67.7	19	6	*104.7
Druckenmiller	52	21	239	40.4	1	4	29.2
Brohm	24	16	164	66.7	0	1	68.8
49ers	432	278	3,432	64.4	20	11	93.6
Opponents	509	258	3,011	50.7	23	25	63.6

SACKS: Stubblefield 15.0, Doleman 12.0, Greene 10.5, 49ers 54.0, Opponents 44.0

*League Leader   (All individuals may not be represented.)

RECORD HOLDERS

INDIVIDUAL RECORDS—CAREER

CATEGORY	NAME	PERFORMANCE
Rushing (Yds.)	Joe Perry, 1950-1960, 1963	7,344
Passing (Yds.)	Joe Montana, 1979-1992	35,124
Passing (TDs)	Joe Montana, 1979-1992	244
Receiving (No.)	Jerry Rice, 1985-1997	*1,057
Receiving (Yds.)	Jerry Rice, 1985-1997	*16,455
Interceptions	Ronnie Lott, 1981-1990	51
Punting (Avg.)	Tommy Davis, 1959-1969	44.7
Punt Return (Avg.)	Dana McLemore, 1982-87	10.8
Kickoff Return (Avg.)	Abe Woodson, 1958-1964	29.4
Field Goals	Ray Wersching, 1977-1987	190
Touchdowns (Tot.)	Jerry Rice, 1985-1997	*166
Points	Jerry Rice, 1985-1997	1,000

INDIVIDUAL RECORDS—SINGLE SEASON

CATEGORY	NAME	PERFORMANCE
Rushing (Yds.)	Roger Craig, 1988	1,502
Passing (Yds.)	Steve Young, 1993	4,023
Passing (TDs)	Steve Young, 1994	35
Receiving (No.)	Jerry Rice, 1995	122
Receiving (Yds.)	Jerry Rice, 1995	*1,848
Interceptions	Dave Baker, 1960	10
	Ronnie Lott, 1986	10
Punting (Avg.)	Tommy Davis, 1965	45.8
Punt Return (Avg.)	Dana McLemore, 1982	22.3
Kickoff Return (Avg.)	Joe Arenas, 1953	34.4
Field Goals	Jeff Wilkins, 1996	30
Touchdowns (Tot.)	Jerry Rice, 1987	23
Points	Jerry Rice, 1987	138

INDIVIDUAL RECORDS—SINGLE GAME

CATEGORY	NAME	PERFORMANCE
Rushing (Yds.)	Delvin Williams, 10-31-76	194
Passing (Yds.)	Joe Montana, 10-14-90	476
Passing (TDs)	Joe Montana, 10-14-90	6
Receiving (No.)	Jerry Rice, 11-20-94	16
Receiving (Yds.)	Jerry Rice, 12-18-95	289
Interceptions	Dave Baker, 12-4-60	*4
Field Goals	Ray Wersching, 10-16-83	6
	Jeff Wilkins, 9-29-96	6
Touchdowns (Tot.)	Jerry Rice, 10-14-90	5
Points	Jerry Rice, 10-14-90	30

*NFL Record

SEATTLE SEAHAWKS

11220 N.E. 53rd Street
Kirkland, Washington 98033
Telephone: (425) 827-9777
Websites: nfl.com and
www.footballnw.com

Team Colors: Blue, Green, and Silver
AFC West
1997 Record 8-8
Home: 4-4
Away: 4-4
Stadium: Kingdome
Capacity: 66,400

1997 Regular-Season Attendance:
Home: 462,124 Away: 475,730
Playing Surface: AstroTurf
Training Camp: Eastern Washington University Cheney, Washington 99004

1997 RESULTS

DATE	RESULT	OPPONENT	ATT.
8/31	L 3-41	N.Y. JETS	53,893
9/7	L 14-35	DENVER	55,859
9/14	W 31-3	at Ind.	49,194
9/21	W 26-22	SAN DIEGO	51,110
9/28	L 17-20*	at Kansas City	77,877
10/5	W 16-13	TENNESSEE	49,897
10/19	W 17-9	at St. Louis	64,819
10/26	W 45-34	OAKLAND	66,264
11/2	L 27-30	at Denver	74,212
11/9	W 37-31	at San Diego	64,616
11/16	L 17-20*	at N.O.	50,493
11/23	L 14-19	KANSAS CITY	66,264
11/30	L 17-24	ATLANTA	52,584
12/7	L 24-31	at Baltimore	54,395
12/14	W 22-21	at Oakland	40,124
12/21	W 38-9	SAN FRANCISCO	66,253

*Overtime

1998 SCHEDULE

REGULAR SEASON

Sept. 6	at Philadelphia	1:01
Sept. 13	ARIZONA	1:15
Sept. 20	WASHINGTON	1:05
Sept. 27	at Pittsburgh	4:05
Oct. 4	**at Kansas City**	**7:20**
Oct. 11	**DENVER**	**1:15**
Oct. 18	OPEN DATE	
Oct. 25	at San Diego	1:15
Nov. 1	**OAKLAND**	**5:20**
Nov. 8	KANSAS CITY	1:15
Nov. 15	at Oakland	1:05
Nov. 22	at Dallas	12:01
Nov. 29	TENNESSEE	1:05
Dec. 6	at New York Jets	1:01
Dec. 13	SAN DIEGO	1:05
Dec. 20	INDIANAPOLIS	1:05
Dec. 27	**at Denver**	**2:15**

Nationally Televised Games in **Bold**/All times local

COACHING STAFF

Head Coach—Dennis Erickson; Assistant Coaches—Tommy Brasher, Bob Bratkowski, Dave Brown, Keith Gilbertson, Milt Jackson, Jim Johnson, Darren Krein, Tim Lappano, Dana LeDuc, Greg McMakin, Bill Meyers, Rich Olson, Willy Robinson, Pete Rodriguez, Gregg Smith, Eric Yarber.

1998 SCOUTING REPORT

The Seahawks' fortunes in 1998 will ride on the arm of veteran quarterback Warren Moon. But this isn't your average 41-year-old arm. Last year Moon signed as a free agent with Seattle, supposedly to give the team an experienced backup. But the 14-year veteran, who is one of only four players to pass for more than 45,000 yards in NFL history, became the Seahawks' starter after John Friesz was injured in the first game. Moon set club records with 313 completions and 3,678 passing yards in Seattle's 8-8 season.

The Seahawks had the league's best passing offense and were third in total offense in 1997. Moon's favorite target, wide receiver Joey Galloway, has superstar potential. Running back Ricky Watters, who has rushed for 3,794 yards over the last three seasons, was signed to take some of the pressure off Moon.

1998 DRAFT CHOICES

RD. NAME	POS.	COLLEGE	RD. NAME	POS.	COLLEGE
1. Anthony Simmons	LB	Clemson	6a. Carl Hansen	DE	Stanford
2. Todd Weiner	T	Kansas St.	6b. Bobby Shaw	WR	California
3. Ahman Green	RB	Nebraska	7. Jason McEndoo	C	Washington St.
4. De Shone Myles	LB	Nevada-Reno			

Simmons is instinctive and aggressive playmaker who is effective on blitzes...Weiner is small tackle with enough speed to play guard...Green has good vision and excellent speed (4.4 seconds in 40 yards). He can go distance once he breaks through line of scrimmage...Myles plays better against run than pass...Shaw has soft hands and runs good routes.

KEY ACQUISITIONS

NAME	POS.	PREVIOUS NFL TEAM	NAME	POS.	PREVIOUS NFL TEAM
Kevin Glover (FA)	C	Lions	Darrin Smith (FA)	LB	Eagles
Chris Gray (FA)	G	Bears	Ricky Watters (FA)	RB	Eagles
Brian Habib (FA)	G	Broncos			

KEY LOSSES

NAME	POS.	NEW NFL TEAM	NAME	POS.	NEW NFL TEAM
Kevin Mawae (FA)	C	Jets	Rick Tuten (FA)	P	Rams
Lamar Smith (FA)	RB	Saints	Chris Warren (FA)	RB	Cowboys

(FA) = Free Agent

1997 STATISTICAL LEADERS

SCORING

PLAYER	TD	PAT	FG	PTS.
Peterson	0	37/37	22/28	103
Galloway	12	0/0	0/0	72
Broussard	6	0/0	0/0	36
McKnight	6	0/0	0/0	36
Warren	4	0/0	0/0	24
Smith	2	0/0	0/0	14
Br. Blades	2	0/0	0/0	12
C. Brown	2	0/0	0/0	12
Pritchard	2	0/0	0/0	12
Strong	2	0/0	0/0	12
Crumpler	1	0/0	0/0	6
Kitna	1	0/0	0/0	6
Moon	1	0/0	0/0	6
Sinclair	1	0/0	0/0	6
D. Williams	1	0/0	0/0	6
Seahawks	43	37/37	22/28	365
Opponents	38	35/35	31/34	362

2-Pt. Conversions: Seahawks 1-6, Opponents 2-3.

RUSHING

PLAYER	ATT.	YDS.	AVG.	TD
Warren	200	847	4.2	4
Broussard	70	418	6.0	5
Smith	91	392	4.3	2
Galloway	9	72	8.0	0
Moon	17	40	2.4	1
Pritchard	1	14	14.0	0
Kitna	10	9	0.9	1
Strong	4	8	2.0	0
Seahawks	404	1,800	4.5	13
Opponents	455	1,731	3.8	10

INTERCEPTIONS

PLAYER	NO.	YDS.	AVG.	TD
D. Williams	8	172	21.5	1
Be. Blades	2	11	5.5	0
Seahawks	13	196	15.1	1
Opponents	21	372	17.7	4

RECEIVING

PLAYER	ATT.	YDS.	AVG.	TD
Galloway	72	1,049	14.6	12
Pritchard	64	843	13.2	2
Warren	45	257	5.7	0
McKnight	34	637	*18.7	6
Crumpler	31	361	11.6	1
Br. Blades	30	319	10.6	2
Broussard	24	143	6.0	1
Smith	23	183	8.0	0
Strong	13	91	7.0	2
Fauria	10	110	11.0	0
Hobbs	5	44	8.8	0
Harris	4	81	20.3	0
Davis	2	48	24.0	0
May	2	21	10.5	0
Seahawks	359	4,187	11.7	26
Opponents	276	3,356	12.2	19

KICKOFF RETURNS

PLAYER	NO.	YDS.	AVG.	TD
Broussard	50	1,076	21.5	0
Harris	14	318	22.7	0
Coleman	3	65	21.7	0
Davis	2	25	12.5	0
R. Brown	1	16	16.0	0
Seahawks	76	1,550	20.4	0
Opponents	77	1,779	23.1	1

PUNT RETURNS

PLAYER	NO.	YDS.	AVG.	TD
Harris	21	144	6.9	0
Davis	16	104	6.5	0
Seahawks	37	248	6.7	0
Opponents	38	463	12.2	2

PUNTING

PLAYER	NO.	YDS.	AVG.
Tuten	48	2,007	41.8
Stark	20	813	40.7
Seahawks	78	3,144	40.3
Opponents	74	3,111	42.0

PASSING

PLAYER	ATT.	COMP.	YDS.	PCT.	TD	INT.	RAT.
Moon	528	313	3,678	59.3	25	16	83.7
Kitna	45	31	371	68.9	1	2	82.7
Friesz	36	15	138	41.7	0	3	18.1
Galloway	0	0	0	—	0	0	—
Seahawks	609	359	4,187	58.9	26	21	79.7
Opponents	462	276	3,356	59.7	19	13	84.1

SACKS: Sinclair 12.0, Adams 7.0, C. Brown 6.5, Seahawks 42.0, Opponents 36.0

*League Leader   (All individuals may not be represented.)

RECORD HOLDERS

INDIVIDUAL RECORDS—CAREER

CATEGORY	NAME	PERFORMANCE
Rushing (Yds.)	Chris Warren, 1990-97	6,706
Passing (Yds.)	Dave Krieg, 1980-1991	26,132
Passing (TDs)	Dave Krieg, 1980-1991	195
Receiving (No.)	Steve Largent, 1976-1989	819
Receiving (Yds.)	Steve Largent, 1976-1989	13,089
Interceptions	Dave Brown, 1976-1986	50
Punting (Avg.)	Rick Tuten, 1991-97	43.8
Punt Return (Avg.)	Paul Johns, 1981-84	11.4
Kickoff Return (Avg.)	Steve Broussard, 1995-97	22.9
Field Goals	Norm Johnson, 1982-1990	159
Touchdowns (Tot.)	Steve Largent, 1976-1989	101
Points	Norm Johnson, 1982-1990	810

INDIVIDUAL RECORDS—SINGLE SEASON

CATEGORY	NAME	PERFORMANCE
Rushing (Yds.)	Chris Warren, 1994	1,545
Passing (Yds.)	Warren Moon, 1997	3,678
Passing (TDs)	Dave Krieg, 1984	32
Receiving (No.)	Brian Blades, 1994	81
Receiving (Yds.)	Steve Largent, 1985	1,287
Interceptions	John Harris, 1981; Kenny Easley, 1984	10
Punting (Avg.)	Rick Tuten, 1995	45.0
Punt Return (Avg.)	Bobby Joe Edmonds, 1987	12.6
Kickoff Return (Avg.)	Steve Broussard, 1995	24.7
Field Goals	Todd Peterson, 1996	28
Touchdowns (Tot.)	Chris Warren, 1995	16
Points	Todd Peterson, 1996	111

INDIVIDUAL RECORDS—SINGLE GAME

CATEGORY	NAME	PERFORMANCE
Rushing (Yds.)	Curt Warner, 11-27-83	207
Passing (Yds.)	Dave Krieg, 11-20-83	418
Passing (TDs)	Dave Krieg, 12-2-84, 9-15-85, 11-28-88	5
	Warren Moon, 10-26-97	5
Receiving (No.)	Steve Largent, 10-18-87	15
Receiving (Yds.)	Steve Largent, 10-18-87	261
Interceptions	Kenny Easley, 9-3-84; Eugene Robinson, 12-6-92	3
	Darryl Williams, 9-21-97	3
Field Goals	Norm Johnson, 9-20-87, 12-18-88	5
Touchdowns (Tot.)	Daryl Turner, 9-15-85	4
	Curt Warner, 12-11-88	4
Points	Daryl Turner, 9-15-85	24
	Curt Warner, 12-11-88	24

TAMPA BAY BUCCANEERS

One Buccaneer Place
Tampa, Florida 33607
Telephone: (813) 870-2700
Website: nfl.com

Team Colors: Buccaneer Red, Pewter, Black, and Orange

1997 Regular-Season Attendance:
Home: 543,514 Away: 459,316
Playing Surface: Grass
Training Camp:
University of Tampa
Tampa, Florida 33606

NFC Central
1997 Record 10-6
Home: 5-3
Away: 5-3
Stadium: Name TBA
Capacity: 65,394

1997 RESULTS

DATE	RESULT	OPPONENT	ATT.
08/31	W 13-6	SAN FRANCISCO	62,554
09/7	W 24-17	at Detroit	58,234
09/14	W 28-14	at Minnesota	63,697
09/21	W 31-21	MIAMI	73,314
09/28	W 19-18	ARIZONA	53,804
10/5	L 16-21	at Green Bay	60,100
10/12	L 9-27	DETROIT	72,095
10/26	L 6-10	MINNESOTA	66,815
11/2	W 31-28	at Ind.	58,512
11/9	W 31-10	at Atlanta	46,018
11/16	W 27-7	NEW ENGLAND	70,479
11/23	L 7-13	at Chicago	43,955
11/30	W 20-8	at N.Y. Giants	68,678
12/7	L 6-17	GREEN BAY	73,523
12/14	L 0-31	at N.Y. Jets	60,122
12/21	W 31-15	CHICAGO	70,930

POSTSEASON

12/28	W 20-10	DETROIT	73,361
1/4	L 7-21	at Green Bay	60,327

1998 SCHEDULE

REGULAR SEASON

Sept. 6	at Minnesota	12:01
Sept. 13	at Green Bay	12:01
Sept. 20	CHICAGO	4:05
Sept. 28	**at Detroit (Mon.)**	**8:20**
Oct. 4	NEW YORK GIANTS	4:15
Oct. 11	OPEN DATE	
Oct. 18	CAROLINA	1:01
Oct. 25	at New Orleans	12:01
Nov. 1	MINNESOTA	1:01
Nov. 8	**TENNESSEE**	**8:20**
Nov. 15	at Jacksonville	4:15
Nov. 22	DETROIT	1:01
Nov. 29	at Chicago	12:01
Dec. 7	**GREEN BAY (Mon.)**	**8:20**
Dec. 13	PITTSBURGH	1:01
Dec. 19	**at Washington (Sat.)**	**4:05**
Dec. 27	at Cincinnati	1:01

*Nationally Televised Games in **Bold**/All times local*

COACHING STAFF

Head Coach—Tony Dungy; Assistant Coaches—Mark Asanovich, Clyde Christensen, Herman Edwards, Chris Foerster, Monte Kiffin, Joe Marciano, Rod Marinelli, Tony Nathan, Kevin O'Dea, Mike Shula, Lovie Smith, Ricky Thomas.

1998 SCOUTING REPORT

After 14 seasons without a winning record or an appearance in the NFL postseason, Tampa Bay finally broke through in 1997. Under second-year head coach Tony Dungy, the Buccaneers finished second in their division with a 10-6 record. They defeated Detroit in an NFC Wild Card Playoff Game before losing to Green Bay in a divisional playoff.

Eight Buccaneers, the most from any NFL team, were selected to the Pro Bowl—quarterback Trent Dilfer, fullback Mike Alstott, running back Warrick Dunn, linebackers Derrick Brooks and Hardy Nickerson, center Tony Mayberry, defensive tackle Warren Sapp, and safety John Lynch.

Tampa Bay's defense finished third in the NFL last year, but its offense, which ranked twenty-ninth, must improve if the Buccaneers want to go to the Super Bowl.

1998 DRAFT CHOICES

RD. NAME	POS.	COLLEGE	RD. NAME	POS.	COLLEGE
2a. Jacquez Green	WR	Florida	6a. James Cannida	DT	Nevada-Reno
2b. Brian Kelly	CB	USC	6b. Shevin Smith	S	Florida St.
3. Jamie Duncan	LB	Vanderbilt	7. Chance McCarty	DE	Texas Christian
4. Todd Washington	C	Virginia Tech			

Green has excellent quickness and instincts. At full speed, he is difficult to catch…Kelly is very aggressive and may be better suited to play safety…Duncan always seems to be around ball…Washington also can play guard…Cannida is fierce competitor…Smith is former walk-on at Florida State whose hustle and intensity should earn him spot on roster.

KEY ACQUISITIONS

NAME	POS.	PREVIOUS NFL TEAM	NAME	POS.	PREVIOUS NFL TEAM
Bert Emanuel (FA)	WR	Falcons	Lorenzo Neal (Trade)	RB	Jets

KEY LOSSES

NAME	POS.	NEW NFL TEAM	NAME	POS.	NEW NFL TEAM
Eric Curry (FA)	DE	Packers	Sean Landeta (FA)	P	Packers
Jackie Harris (FA)	TE	Oilers	Jim Pyne (FA)	C	Lions
Melvin Johnson (Trade)	S	Chiefs	Errict Rhett (Trade)	RB	Ravens

(FA) = Free Agent

1997 STATISTICAL LEADERS

SCORING

PLAYER	TD	PAT	FG	PTS.
Husted	0	32/35	13/17	71
Alstott	10	0/0	0/0	60
Dunn	7	0/0	0/0	42
Williams	5	0/0	0/0	30
Anthony	4	0/0	0/0	24
Moore	4	0/0	0/0	24
Rhett	3	0/0	0/0	18
Copeland	1	0/0	0/0	6
Dilfer	1	0/0	0/0	6
Hape	1	0/0	0/0	6
Harris	1	0/0	0/0	6
Singleton	1	0/0	0/0	6
Buccaneers	38	32/35	13/17	299
Opponents	29	25/25	18/29	263

2-Point conversions: Buccaneers 0-3, Opponents 4-4

RUSHING

PLAYER	ATT.	YDS.	AVG.	TD
Dunn	224	978	4.4	4
Alstott	176	665	3.8	7
Dilfer	33	99	3.0	1
Rhett	31	96	3.1	3
Anthony	5	84	16.8	0
Ellison	2	10	5.0	0
Williams	1	5	5.0	0
Hape	1	1	1.0	0
Walsh	6	-4	-.7	0
Buccaneers	479	1,934	4.0	15
Opponents	420	1,617	3.9	14

INTERCEPTIONS

PLAYER	NO.	YDS.	AVG.	TD
Abraham	5	16	3.2	0
Lynch	2	28	14.0	0
Brooks	2	13	6.5	0
Johnson	1	19	19.0	0
Mincy	1	14	14.0	0
Buccaneers	13	95	7.3	0
Opponents	12	370	30.8	4

RECEIVING

PLAYER	ATT.	YDS.	AVG.	TD
Dunn	39	462	11.8	3
Anthony	35	448	12.8	4
Williams	33	486	14.7	4
Copeland	33	431	13.1	1
Alstott	23	178	7.7	3
Moore	19	217	11.4	4
Harris	19	197	10.4	1
Thomas	13	129	9.9	0
Hape	4	22	5.5	1
Davis	3	35	11.7	0
Bouie	1	25	25.0	0
Ellison	1	8	8.0	0
Jordan	1	0	0.0	0
Buccaneers	224	2,638	11.8	21
Opponents	325	3,342	10.3	13

KICKOFF RETURNS

PLAYER	NO.	YDS.	AVG.	TD
Anthony	25	592	23.7	0
Williams	15	277	18.5	0
Dunn	6	129	21.5	0
Ellison	2	61	30.5	0
Alstott	1	0	0.0	0
Rhett	1	16	16.0	0
White	1	0	0.0	0
Buccaneers	51	1,075	21.1	0
Opponents	44	957	21.8	1

PUNT RETURNS

PLAYER	NO.	YDS.	AVG.	TD
Williams	46	597	13.0	1
Dunn	5	48	9.6	0
Buccaneers	51	645	12.6	1
Opponents	42	388	9.2	0

PUNTING

PLAYER	NO.	YDS.	AVG.
Landeta	54	2,274	42.1
Barnhardt	29	1,304	45.0
Buccaneers	84	3,578	42.6
Opponents	88	3,661	41.6

PASSING

PLAYER	ATT.	COMP.	YDS.	PCT.	TD	INT.	RAT.
Dilfer	386	217	2,555	56.2	21	11	82.8
Walsh	17	6	58	35.3	0	1	21.2
Barnhardt	1	1	25	100.0	0	0	118.8
Buccaneers	404	224	2,638	55.4	21	12	80.4
Opponents	518	325	3,342	62.7	13	13	79.2

SACKS: Sapp 10.5, Ahanotu 10.0, Culpepper 8.5, Buccaneers 44.0, Opponents 32.0

(All individuals may not be represented.)

RECORD HOLDERS

INDIVIDUAL RECORDS—CAREER

CATEGORY	NAME	PERFORMANCE
Rushing (Yds.)	James Wilder, 1981-89	5,957
Passing (Yds.)	Vinny Testaverde, 1987-1992	14,820
Passing (TDs)	Vinny Testaverde, 1987-1992	77
Receiving (No.)	James Wilder, 1981-89	430
Receiving (Yds.)	Mark Carrier, 1987-1992	5,018
Interceptions	Cedric Brown, 1977-1984	29
Punting (Avg.)	Frank Garcia, 1983-87	41.1
Punt Return (Avg.)	Karl Williams, 1996-97	14.8
Kickoff Return (Avg.)	Isaac Hagins, 1976-1980	21.9
Field Goals	Michael Husted, 1993-97	96
Touchdowns (Tot.)	James Wilder, 1981-89	46
Points	Donald Igwebuike, 1985-89	416

INDIVIDUAL RECORDS—SINGLE SEASON

CATEGORY	NAME	PERFORMANCE
Rushing (Yds.)	James Wilder, 1984	1,544
Passing (Yds.)	Doug Williams, 1981	3,563
Passing (TDs)	Trent Dilfer, 1997	21
Receiving (No.)	Mark Carrier, 1989	86
Receiving (Yds.)	Mark Carrier, 1989	1,422
Interceptions	Cedric Brown, 1981	9
Punting (Avg.)	Tommy Barnhardt, 1996	43.1
Punt Return (Avg.)	Karl Williams, 1996	21.1
Kickoff Return (Avg.)	Karl Williams, 1996	27.4
Field Goals	Michael Husted, 1994, 1996	25
Touchdowns (Tot.)	James Wilder, 1984	13
Points	Donald Igwebuike, 1989	99

INDIVIDUAL RECORDS—SINGLE GAME

CATEGORY	NAME	PERFORMANCE
Rushing (Yds.)	James Wilder, 11-6-83	219
Passing (Yds.)	Doug Williams, 11-16-80	486
Passing (TDs)	Steve DeBerg, 9-13-87	5
Receiving (No.)	James Wilder, 9-15-85	13
Receiving (Yds.)	Mark Carrier, 12-6-87	212
Interceptions	Many times.	2
	Last time by Martin Mayhew, 12-3-95	
Field Goals	Many times.	4
	Last time by Michael Husted, 11-17-96	
Touchdowns (Tot.)	Jimmie Giles, 10-20-85	4
Points	Jimmie Giles, 10-20-85	24

TENNESSEE OILERS

1997 Regular-Season Attendance:
Home: 224,221 Away: 459,008
Playing Surface: Turf
Training Camp: Hale Hall
Tennessee State University
Nashville, Tennessee 37209

Baptist Sports Park
7640 Highway 70 South
Nashville, Tennessee 37221
Telephone: (615) 673-1500
Website: nfl.com

Team Colors: Columbia Blue, Scarlet, and White
AFC West
1997 Record 8-8
Home: 6-2
Away: 2-6
Stadium: Vanderbilt Stadium
Capacity: 42,000

1997 RESULTS

DATE	RESULT	OPPONENT	ATT.
8/31	W 24-21*	OAKLAND	30,171
9/7	L 13-16*	at Miami	64,439
9/21	L 10-36	BALTIMORE	17,737
9/28	L 24-37	at Pittsburgh	57,507
10/5	L 13-16	at Seattle	49,897
10/12	W 30-7	CINCINNATI	17,071
10/19	W 28-14	WASHINGTON	31,042
10/26	W 41-14	at Arizona	44,030
11/2	L 24-30	JACKSONVILLE	27,208
11/9	W 10-6	N.Y. GIANTS	26,744
11/16	L 9-17	at Jacksonville	70,070
11/23	W 31-14	BUFFALO	23,571
11/27	W 27-14	at Dallas	63,421
12/4	L 14-41	at Cincinnati	49,086
12/14	L 19-21	at Baltimore	60,558
12/21	W 16-6	PITTSBURGH	50,677

*Overtime

1998 SCHEDULE

REGULAR SEASON

Sept. 6	at Cincinnati	1:01
Sept. 13	SAN DIEGO	12:01
Sept. 20	at New England	1:01
Sept. 27	JACKSONVILLE	12:01
Oct. 4	OPEN DATE	
Oct. 11	at Baltimore	1:01
Oct. 18	CINCINNATI	12:01
Oct. 25	CHICAGO	3:05
Nov. 1	at Pittsburgh	1:01
Nov. 8	**at Tampa Bay**	**8:20**
Nov. 15	PITTSBURGH	12:01
Nov. 22	NEW YORK JETS	3:15
Nov. 29	at Seattle	1:05
Dec. 6	BALTIMORE	3:15
Dec. 13	at Jacksonville	1:01
Dec. 20	at Green Bay	12:01
Dec. 26	**MINN. (Sat.)**	**11:35 A.M.**

*Nationally Televised Games in **Bold**/All times local*

COACHING STAFF
Head Coach—Jeff Fisher; Assistant Coaches—Bart Andrus, Greg Brown, O'Neill Gilbert, Jerry Gray, George Henshaw, Alan Lowry, Mike Munchak, Rex Norris, Russ Purnell, Sherman Smith, Les Steckel, Steve Watterson, Gregg Williams.

1998 SCOUTING REPORT

How far the Oilers go in 1998 will depend on how much quarterback Steve McNair progresses. Houston's first-round draft choice in 1996, McNair has put up a solid 76.3 career passer rating in three seasons, but the Oilers finished twenty-ninth in the NFL in passing offense last year. McNair's numbers should receive a big boost with the addition of Pro Bowl wide receiver Yancey Thigpen, who finished third in the NFL with a career-high 1,398 receiving yards for the Steelers in 1997.

The strength of the Oilers still remains the ground game, led by Pro Bowl running back Eddie George. In two NFL seasons, the former Heisman Trophy winner has gained 2,767 yards. McNair led all NFL quarterbacks with 674 rushing yards in 1997.

Houston head coach Jeff Fisher, a former defensive coordinator, has to upgrade the Oilers' defense, which ranked twenty-second in the NFL last year.

1998 DRAFT CHOICES

RD. NAME	POS.	COLLEGE	RD. NAME	POS.	COLLEGE
1. Kevin Dyson	WR	Utah	5. Benji Olson	G	Washington
2. Samari Rolle	CB	Florida St.	6. Lee Wiggins	DB	South Carolina
3. Dainon Sidney	CB	Ala.-Birmingham	7a. Jimmy Sprotte	LB	Arizona
4. Joe Salave'a	DT	Arizona	7b. Kevin Long	C	Florida St.

Oilers' "Air McNair" offense gets big-play weapon in Dyson. He has speed to stretch opposing defenses and will make acrobatic catches…Rolle will either intercept or knock down most balls thrown his way…Sidney is former college track star who's still learning how to be polished defensive back…Few athletes play with more heart than hard-working Salave'a.

KEY ACQUISITIONS

NAME	POS.	PREVIOUS NFL TEAM	NAME	POS.	PREVIOUS NFL TEAM
Jackie Harris (FA)	TE	Buccaneers	Yancey Thigpen (FA)	WR	Steelers
Craig Hentrich (FA)	P	Packers	Ricky Whittle (FA)	RB	Saints

KEY LOSSES

NAME	POS.	NEW NFL TEAM	NAME	POS.	NEW NFL TEAM
Kevin Donnalley (FA)	G	Dolphins			

(FA) = Free Agent

1997 STATISTICAL LEADERS

SCORING

PLAYER	TD	PAT	FG	PTS.
Del Greco	0	32/32	27/35	113
McNair	8	0/0	0/0	48
E. George	7	0/0	0/0	44
Wycheck	4	0/0	0/0	26
Davis	4	0/0	0/0	24
Sanders	3	0/0	0/0	18
Thomas	3	0/0	0/0	18
Robertson	2	0/0	0/0	12
Kent	1	0/0	0/0	6
D. Lewis	1	0/0	0/0	6
Norgard	1	0/0	0/0	6
Russell	1	0/0	0/0	6
D. Walker	1	0/0	0/0	6
Oilers	36	32/32	27/35	333
Opponents	35	34/34	22/30	310

2-Pt. Conversions: Oilers 2-4, Opponents 0-1

RUSHING

PLAYER	ATT.	YDS.	AVG.	TD
E. George	357	1,399	3.9	6
McNair	101	674	6.7	8
Thomas	67	310	4.6	3
Harmon	8	30	3.8	0
Roby	1	12	12.0	0
Ritchey	1	6	6.0	0
Krieg	4	-2	-.5	0
Mason	1	-7	-7.0	0
Sanders	1	-8	-8.0	0
Oilers	541	2,414	4.5	17
Opponents	414	1,573	3.8	12

INTERCEPTIONS

PLAYER	NO.	YDS.	AVG.	TD
Robertson	5	127	25.4	0
D. Lewis	5	115	23.0	1
D. Walker	2	53	26.5	1
Oilers	14	328	23.4	2
Opponents	13	48	3.7	0

RECEIVING

PLAYER	ATT.	YDS.	AVG.	TD
Wycheck	63	748	11.9	4
Davis	43	564	13.1	4
Sanders	31	498	16.1	3
Harmon	16	186	11.6	0
Mason	14	186	13.3	0
Thomas	14	111	7.9	0
Roan	12	159	13.3	0
Russell	12	141	11.8	1
E. George	7	44	6.3	1
Kent	6	55	9.2	1
R. Lewis	1	7	7.0	0
Norgard	1	2	2.0	1
Oilers	220	2,704	12.3	15
Opponents	321	3,898	12.1	21

KICKOFF RETURNS

PLAYER	NO.	YDS.	AVG.	TD
Mason	26	551	21.2	0
Thomas	17	346	20.4	0
Gray	8	185	23.1	0
Archie	2	24	12.0	0
Roan	2	20	10.0	0
Harmon	1	16	16.0	0
Layman	1	5	5.0	0
Oilers	58	1,150	19.8	0
Opponents	71	1,528	21.5	0

PUNT RETURNS

PLAYER	NO.	YDS.	AVG.	TD
Gray	17	144	8.5	0
Mason	13	95	7.3	0
Oilers	32	244	7.6	0
Opponents	36	430	11.9	0

PUNTING

PLAYER	NO.	YDS.	AVG.
Roby	73	3,049	41.8
Del Greco	1	32	32.0
Oilers	74	3,081	41.6
Opponents	69	3,007	43.6

PASSING

PLAYER	ATT.	COMP.	YDS.	PCT.	TD	INT.	RAT.
McNair	415	216	2,665	52.0	14	13	70.4
Krieg	2	1	2	50.0	0	0	56.3
Ritchey	2	2	15	100.0	0	0	97.9
Davis	1	1	22	100.0	1	0	158.3
Oilers	420	220	2,704	52.4	15	13	71.6
Opponents	543	321	3,898	59.1	21	14	83.4

SACKS: Holmes 7.0, G. Walker 7.0, Ford 5.0, Oilers 35.0, Opponents 32.0

(All individuals may not be represented.)

RECORD HOLDERS

INDIVIDUAL RECORDS—CAREER

CATEGORY	NAME	PERFORMANCE
Rushing (Yds.)	Earl Campbell, 1978-1984	8,574
Passing (Yds.)	Warren Moon, 1984-1993	33,685
Passing (TDs)	Warren Moon, 1984-1993	196
Receiving (No.)	Ernest Givins, 1986-1994	542
Receiving (Yds.)	Ernest Givins, 1986-1994	7,935
Interceptions	Jim Norton, 1960-68	45
Punting (Avg.)	Greg Montgomery, 1988-1993	43.6
Punt Return (Avg.)	Billy Johnson, 1974-1980	13.2
Kickoff Return (Avg.)	Bobby Jancik, 1962-67	26.5
Field Goals	Al Del Greco, 1991-97	162
Touchdowns (Tot.)	Earl Campbell, 1978-1984	73
Points	George Blanda, 1960-66	596

INDIVIDUAL RECORDS—SINGLE SEASON

CATEGORY	NAME	PERFORMANCE
Rushing (Yds.)	Earl Campbell, 1980	1,934
Passing (Yds.)	Warren Moon, 1991	4,690
Passing (TDs)	George Blanda, 1961	36
Receiving (No.)	Charlie Hennigan, 1964	101
Receiving (Yds.)	Charlie Hennigan, 1961	1,746
Interceptions	Fred Glick, 1963	12
	Mike Reinfeldt, 1979	12
Punting (Avg.)	Greg Montgomery, 1992	46.9
Punt Return (Avg.)	Billy Johnson, 1977	15.4
Kickoff Return (Avg.)	Ken Hall, 1960	31.3
Field Goals	Al Del Greco, 1996	32
Touchdowns (Tot.)	Earl Campbell, 1979	19
Points	Al Del Greco, 1996	131

INDIVIDUAL RECORDS—SINGLE GAME

CATEGORY	NAME	PERFORMANCE
Rushing (Yds.)	Billy Cannon, 12-10-61; Eddie George, 8-31-97	216
Passing (Yds.)	Warren Moon, 12-16-90	527
Passing (TDs)	George Blanda, 11-19-61	*7
Receiving (No.)	Charlie Hennigan, 10-13-61	13
	Haywood Jeffires, 10-13-91	13
Receiving (Yds.)	Charlie Hennigan, 10-13-61	272
Interceptions	Many times	3
	Last time by Marcus Robertson, 11-21-93	
Field Goals	Roy Gerela, 9-28-69	5
Touchdowns (Tot.)	Billy Cannon, 12-10-61	5
Points	Billy Cannon, 12-10-61	30

*NFL Record

WASHINGTON REDSKINS

Redskin Park
P.O. Box 17247
Washington, D.C. 20041
Telephone: (703) 478-8900
Websites: nfl.com and
www.redskins.com

1997 Regular-Season Attendance:
Home: 605,592 Away: 465,441
Playing Surface: Grass
Training Camp:
Frostburg State University
Frostburg, Maryland 21532

Team Colors: Burgundy, Gold
NFC East
1997 Record 8-7-1
Home: 5-2-1 **Away:** 3-5
Stadium: Jack Kent Cooke Stadium
Capacity: 80,116

1997 RESULTS

DATE	RESULT	OPPONENT	ATT.
8/31	W 24-10	at Carolina	72,633
9/7	L 13-14	at Pittsburgh	58,059
9/14	W 19-13*	ARIZONA	78,270
9/28	W 24-12	JACKSONVILLE	74,421
10/5	L 10-24	at Phil.	67,008
10/13	W 21-16	DALLAS	76,159
10/19	L 14-28	at Tennessee	31,042
10/26	L 17-20	BALTIMORE	75,067
11/2	W 31-8	at Chicago	53,032
11/9	W 30-7	DETROIT	75,261
11/16	L 14-17	at Dallas	64,559
11/23	T 7-7*	N.Y. GIANTS	75,703
11/30	L 20-23	ST. LOUIS	74,772
12/7	W 38-28	at Arizona	41,537
12/13	L 10-30	at N.Y. Giants	77,571
12/21	W 35-32	PHILADELPHIA	75,939

*Overtime

1998 SCHEDULE

REGULAR SEASON

Sept. 6	at New York Giants......1:01
Sept. 14	**S.F. (Mon.)..........8:20**
Sept. 20	at Seattle............1:05
Sept. 27	DENVER 1:01
Oct. 4	DALLAS..............1:01
Oct. 11	at Philadelphia 1:01
Oct. 18	at Minnesota 12:01
Oct. 25	OPEN DATE
Nov. 1	NEW YORK GIANTS 1:01
Nov. 8	at Arizona 2:05
Nov. 15	PHILADELPHIA.........1:01
Nov. 22	ARIZONA..............1:01
Nov. 29	at Oakland 1:15
Dec. 6	SAN DIEGO 1:01
Dec. 13	at Carolina 1:01
Dec. 19	**TAMPA BAY (Sat.) 4:05**
Dec. 27	**at Dallas............7:20**

Nationally Televised Games in **Bold**/All times local

COACHING STAFF

Head Coach—Norv Turner; Assistant Coaches—Jason Arapoff, Jeff Fitzgerald, Russ Grimm, Tom Hayes, Bobby Jackson, Earl Leggett, Dale Lindsey, Mike Martz, LeCharls McDaniel, Michael Nolan, Michael Pope, Dan Riley, Terry Robiskie, Ed Sidwell.

1998 SCOUTING REPORT

In the past two years Washington just missed making the playoffs, finishing 9-7 in 1996 and 8-7-1 in 1997. The Redskins' Achilles heel was a run defense that ranked last in the NFL in '96 and twenty-eighth in '97. To remedy that shortcoming, Washington signed free-agent 49ers defensive tackle Dana Stubblefield, a strong run defender who also had 15 sacks and was named the league's defensive player of the year last season. The Redskins also traded for Bengals defensive tackle Dan (Big Daddy) Wilkinson, the first overall selection in the 1994 NFL draft.

The burden of taking Washington to the playoffs now falls on quarterback Gus Frerotte, who played in the Pro Bowl after the 1996 season but struggled last year, and oft-injured running back Terry Allen, who also played in the Pro Bowl two seasons ago.

1998 DRAFT CHOICES

RD. NAME	POS.	COLLEGE	RD. NAME	POS.	COLLEGE
2. Stephen Alexander	TE	Oklahoma	6. Patrick Palmer	WR	NW Louisiana
3. Skip Hicks	RB	UCLA	7a. David Terrell	CB	Texas-El Paso
4. Shawn Barber	LB	Richmond	7b. Antwaune Ponds	LB	Syracuse
5. Mark Fischer	C	Purdue			

Redskins selected excellent pass-catching tight end in draft in Alexander…If he can stay healthy, Hicks could be one of steals of draft. He can break tackles and has deceptive speed. Hicks could see a lot of action as Redskins try to give Terry Allen more rest…Barber will be weakside or Nickel linebacker…Fischer played guard, tackle, and center in college.

KEY ACQUISITIONS

NAME	POS.	PREVIOUS NFL TEAM	NAME	POS.	PREVIOUS NFL TEAM
Rod Milstead (FA)	G	49ers	Dan Wilkinson (Trade)	DT	Bengals
Dana Stubblefield (FA)	DT	49ers			

KEY LOSSES

NAME	POS.	NEW NFL TEAM	NAME	POS.	NEW NFL TEAM
Jamie Martin (FA)	QB	Jaguars	Keith Sims (FA)	G	Eagles
Ed Simmons (FA)	T	Unsigned			

(FA) = Free Agent

1997 STATISTICAL LEADERS

SCORING

PLAYER	TD	PAT	FG	PTS.
Blanton	0	34/34	16/24	82
Allen	5	0/0	0/0	30
Shepherd	5	0/0	0/0	30
Bowie	4	0/0	0/0	24
Ellard	4	0/0	0/0	24
Mitchell	4	0/0	0/0	24
Davis	3	0/0	0/0	18
Jenkins	3	0/0	0/0	18
Westbrook	3	0/0	0/0	18
Connell	2	0/0	0/0	12
Frerotte	2	0/0	0/0	12
Pounds	2	0/0	0/0	12
Asher	1	0/0	0/0	6
Dishman	1	0/0	0/0	6
D. Green	1	0/0	0/0	6
Redskins	40	39/39	16/24	327
Opponents	32	28/28	21/25	289

2-Point conversions: Redskins: 0-0, Opponents: 3-4

RUSHING

PLAYER	ATT.	YDS.	AVG.	TD
Allen	210	724	3.4	4
Davis	141	567	4.0	3
Mitchell	23	107	4.7	1
Bowie	28	100	3.6	2
Frerotte	24	65	2.7	2
Hostetler	14	28	2.0	0
Shepherd	4	27	6.8	0
Logan	4	5	1.3	0
Connell	1	3	3.0	0
Redskins	453	1,615	3.6	12
Opponents	508	2,212	4.4	15

INTERCEPTIONS

PLAYER	NO.	YDS.	AVG.	TD
Dishman	4	47	11.8	1
Richard	4	28	7.0	0
Redskins	16	222	13.9	3
Opponents	22	262	11.9	1

RECEIVING

PLAYER	ATT.	YDS.	AVG.	TD
Asher	49	474	9.7	1
Mitchell	36	438	12.2	1
Westbrook	34	559	16.4	3
Bowie	34	388	11.4	2
Ellard	32	485	15.2	4
Shepherd	29	562	19.4	5
Allen	20	172	8.6	1
Davis	18	134	7.4	0
Thomas	11	93	8.5	0
Connell	9	138	15.3	2
Jenkins	4	43	10.8	3
Logan	3	6	2.0	0
Harper	2	65	32.5	0
Thrash	2	24	12.0	0
Raymer	0	0	—	0
Redskins	283	3,581	12.7	22
Opponents	267	3,098	11.6	14

KICKOFF RETURNS

PLAYER	NO.	YDS.	AVG.	TD
Mitchell	47	1,094	23.3	1
Logan	4	70	17.5	0
Davis	3	62	20.7	0
Asher	1	17	17.0	0
Bowie	1	15	15.0	0
D. Green	1	9	9.0	0
Jones	1	6	6.0	0
Redskins	59	1,283	21.7	1
Opponents	67	1,515	22.6	0

PUNT RETURNS

PLAYER	NO.	YDS.	AVG.	TD
Mitchell	38	442	11.6	1
Redskins	38	442	11.6	1
Opponents	33	237	7.2	0

PUNTING

PLAYER	NO.	YDS.	AVG.
M. Turk	84	3,788	45.1
Redskins	85	3,788	44.6
Opponents	95	4,038	42.5

PASSING

PLAYER	ATT.	COMP.	YDS.	PCT.	TD	INT.	RAT.
Frerotte	402	204	2,682	50.7	17	12	73.8
Hostetler	144	79	899	54.9	5	10	56.5
T. Green	1	0	0	0.0	0	0	39.6
Redskins	547	283	3,581	51.7	22	22	69.1
Opponents	513	267	3,098	52.0	14	16	66.7

SACKS: Harvey 9.5, M. Patton 4.5, Mims 4.0, Redskins 37.0, Opponents 33.0

(All individuals may not be represented.)

RECORD HOLDERS

INDIVIDUAL RECORDS—CAREER

CATEGORY	NAME	PERFORMANCE
Rushing (Yds.)	John Riggins, 1976-79, 1981-85	7,472
Passing (Yds.)	Joe Theismann, 1974-1985	25,206
Passing (TDs)	Sammy Baugh, 1937-1952	187
Receiving (No.)	Art Monk, 1980-1993	888
Receiving (Yds.)	Art Monk, 1980-1993	12,028
Interceptions	Darrell Green, 1983-1997	44
Punting (Avg.)	Sammy Baugh, 1937-1952	*45.1
Punt Return (Avg.)	Johnny Williams, 1952-53	12.8
Kickoff Return (Avg.)	Bobby Mitchell, 1962-68	28.5
Field Goals	Mark Moseley, 1974-1986	263
Touchdowns (Tot.)	Charley Taylor, 1964-1977	90
Points	Mark Moseley, 1974-1986	1,206

INDIVIDUAL RECORDS—SINGLE SEASON

CATEGORY	NAME	PERFORMANCE
Rushing (Yds.)	Terry Allen, 1996	1,353
Passing (Yds.)	Jay Schroeder, 1986	4,109
Passing (TDs)	Sonny Jurgensen, 1967	31
Receiving (No.)	Art Monk, 1984	106
Receiving (Yds.)	Bobby Mitchell, 1963	1,436
Interceptions	Dan Sandifer, 1948	13
Punting (Avg.)	Sammy Baugh, 1940	*51.4
Punt Return (Avg.)	Johnny Williams, 1952	15.3
Kickoff Return (Avg.)	Mike Nelms, 1981	29.7
Field Goals	Mark Moseley, 1983	33
Touchdowns (Tot.)	John Riggins, 1983	24
Points	Mark Moseley, 1983	161

INDIVIDUAL RECORDS—SINGLE GAME

CATEGORY	NAME	PERFORMANCE
Rushing (Yds.)	Gerald Riggs, 9-17-89	221
Passing (Yds.)	Sammy Baugh, 10-31-43	446
Passing (TDs)	Sammy Baugh, 10-31-43, 11-23-47	6
	Mark Rypien, 11-10-91	6
Receiving (No.)	Art Monk, 12-15-85	13
	Kelvin Bryant, 12-7-86	13
	Art Monk, 11-4-90	13
Receiving (Yds.)	Anthony Allen, 10-4-87	255
Interceptions	Sammy Baugh, 11-14-43; Dan Sandifer, 10-31-48	*4
Field Goals	Many times, last time by Chip Lohmiller, 10-25-92	5
Touchdowns (Tot.)	Dick James, 12-17-61, Larry Brown, 12-16-73	4
Points	Dick James, 12-17-61, Larry Brown, 12-16-73	24

*NFL Record

1998 NFL SCHEDULE

First Week
SUNDAY, SEPTEMBER 6
CBS-TV National Weekend
1. Arizona at Dallas 3:05
2. Atlanta at Carolina 1:01
3. Buffalo at San Diego 1:15
4. Detroit at Green Bay 12:01
5. Jacksonville at Chicago 12:01
6. Miami at Indianapolis 3:15
7. New Orleans at St. Louis 12:01
8. New York Jets at San Francisco 1:15
9. Pittsburgh at Baltimore 1:01
10. Seattle at Philadelphia 1:01
11. Tampa Bay at Minnesota 12:01
12. Tennessee at Cincinnati 1:01
13. Washington at New York Giants 1:01
14. Oakland at Kansas City .... (ESPN) 7:20

MONDAY, SEPTEMBER 7
15. New England at Denver .... (ABC) 6:20

Second Week
SUNDAY, SEPTEMBER 13
FOX-TV National Weekend
16. Arizona at Seattle 1:15
17. Baltimore at New York Jets 1:01
18. Buffalo at Miami 1:01
19. Carolina at New Orleans 12:01
20. Chicago at Pittsburgh 1:01
21. Cincinnati at Detroit 1:01
22. Dallas at Denver 2:15
23. Kansas City at Jacksonville 1:01
24. Minnesota at St. Louis 12:01
25. New York Giants at Oakland 1:15
26. Philadelphia at Atlanta 1:01
27. San Diego at Tennessee 12:01
28. Tampa Bay at Green Bay 12:01
29. Indianapolis at New England .... (ESPN) 8:20

MONDAY, SEPTEMBER 14
30. San Francisco at Washington .... (ABC) 8:20

Third Week
SUNDAY, SEPTEMBER 20
(Open Dates: Atlanta, Carolina, New Orleans, San Francisco)
CBS-TV National Weekend
31. Baltimore at Jacksonville 4:15
32. Chicago at Tampa Bay 4:05
33. Denver at Oakland 1:15
34. Detroit at Minnesota 12:01
35. Green Bay at Cincinnati 1:01
36. Indianapolis at New York Jets 1:01
37. Pittsburgh at Miami 1:01
38. St. Louis at Buffalo 1:01
39. San Diego at Kansas City 12:01
40. Tennessee at New England 1:01
41. Washington at Seattle 1:05
42. Philadelphia at Arizona .... (ESPN) 5:20

MONDAY, SEPTEMBER 21
43. Dallas at New York Giants .... (ABC) 8:20

Fourth Week
SUNDAY, SEPTEMBER 27
(Open Dates: Buffalo, Miami, New England, New York Jets)
FOX-TV National Weekend
44. Arizona at St. Louis 12:01
45. Atlanta at San Francisco 1:15
46. Denver at Washington 1:01
47. Green Bay at Carolina 1:01

*All times local

1998 NFL SCHEDULE

48. Jacksonville at Tennessee...12:01
49. Kansas City at Philadelphia...1:01
50. Minnesota at Chicago..3:15
51. New Orleans at Indianapolis..12:01
52. New York Giants at San Diego...1:15
53. Oakland at Dallas...12:01
54. Seattle at Pittsburgh..4:05
55. Cincinnati at Baltimore..(ESPN) 8:20

MONDAY, SEPTEMBER 28
56. Tampa Bay at Detroit..(ABC) 8:20

Fifth Week
SUNDAY, OCTOBER 4
(Open Dates: Baltimore, Cincinnati, Jacksonville, Pittsburgh, St. Louis, Tennessee)
FOX-TV National Weekend
57. Carolina at Atlanta..1:01
58. Dallas at Washington..1:01
59. Detroit at Chicago...12:01
60. Miami at New York Jets..1:01
61. New England at New Orleans...12:01
62. New York Giants at Tampa Bay..4:15
63. Oakland at Arizona..1:05
64. Philadelphia at Denver..2:15
65. San Diego at Indianapolis..12:01
66. San Francisco at Buffalo..1:01
67. Seattle at Kansas City...(ESPN) 7:20

MONDAY, OCTOBER 5
68. Minnesota at Green Bay..(ABC) 7:20

Sixth Week
SUNDAY, OCTOBER 11
(Open Dates: Detroit, Green Bay, Minnesota, Tampa Bay)
CBS-TV National Weekend
69. Buffalo at Indianapolis..12:01
70. Carolina at Dallas...12:01
71. Chicago at Arizona..1:05
72. Denver at Seattle...1:15
73. Kansas City at New England..1:01
74. New York Jets at St. Louis..3:15
75. Pittsburgh at Cincinnati..1:01
76. San Diego at Oakland..1:15
77. San Francisco at New Orleans...12:01
78. Tennessee at Baltimore..1:01
79. Washington at Philadelphia..1:01
80. Atlanta at New York Giants...(ESPN) 8:20

MONDAY, OCTOBER 12
81. Miami at Jacksonville...(ABC) 8:20

Seventh Week
THURSDAY, OCTOBER 15
(Open Dates: Denver, Kansas City, Oakland, Seattle)
FOX-TV National Weekend
82. Green Bay at Detroit...(ESPN) 8:20

SUNDAY, OCTOBER 18
83. Arizona at New York Giants..1:01
84. Baltimore at Pittsburgh...1:01
85. Carolina at Tampa Bay...1:01
86. Cincinnati at Tennessee..12:01
87. Dallas at Chicago...3:15
88. Indianapolis at San Francisco...1:05
89. Jacksonville at Buffalo...1:01
90. New Orleans at Atlanta..1:01
91. Philadelphia at San Diego...1:15
92. St. Louis at Miami..4:15
93. Washington at Minnesota..12:01

MONDAY, OCTOBER 19
94. New York Jets at New England..(ABC) 8:20

*All times local

1998 NFL SCHEDULE

Eighth Week
SUNDAY, OCTOBER 25
(Open Dates: Arizona, Dallas, Indianapolis, New York Giants, Philadelphia, Washington)
CBS-TV National Weekend
- 95. Atlanta at New York Jets 1:01
- 96. Baltimore at Green Bay 12:01
- 97. Chicago at Tennessee 3:05
- 98. Cincinnati at Oakland 1:15
- 99. Jacksonville at Denver 2:15
- 100. Minnesota at Detroit 1:01
- 101. New England at Miami 1:01
- 102. San Francisco at St. Louis 12:01
- 103. Seattle at San Diego 1:15
- 104. Tampa Bay at New Orleans 12:01
- 105. Buffalo at Carolina .... (ESPN) 8:20

MONDAY, OCTOBER 26
- 106. Pittsburgh at Kansas City .... (ABC) 7:20

Ninth Week
SUNDAY, NOVEMBER 1
(Open Dates: Chicago, San Diego)
FOX-TV National Weekend
- 107. Arizona at Detroit 1:01
- 108. Denver at Cincinnati 1:01
- 109. Jacksonville at Baltimore 1:01
- 110. Miami at Buffalo 1:01
- 111. Minnesota at Tampa Bay 1:01
- 112. New England at Indianapolis 1:01
- 113. New Orleans at Carolina 1:01
- 114. New York Giants at Washington 1:01
- 115. New York Jets at Kansas City 3:05
- 116. St. Louis at Atlanta 1:01
- 117. San Francisco at Green Bay 3:15
- 118. Tennessee at Pittsburgh 1:01
- 119. Oakland at Seattle .... (ESPN) 5:20

MONDAY, NOVEMBER 2
- 120. Dallas at Philadelphia .... (ABC) 8:20

Tenth Week
SUNDAY, NOVEMBER 8
CBS-TV National Weekend
- 121. Atlanta at New England 1:01
- 122. Buffalo at New York Jets 4:15
- 123. Carolina at San Francisco 1:01
- 124. Cincinnati at Jacksonville 1:01
- 125. Detroit at Philadelphia 1:01
- 126. Indianapolis at Miami 1:01
- 127. Kansas City at Seattle 1:15
- 128. New Orleans at Minnesota 12:01
- 129. New York Giants at Dallas 12:01
- 130. Oakland at Baltimore 1:01
- 131. St. Louis at Chicago 12:01
- 132. San Diego at Denver 2:15
- 133. Washington at Arizona 2:05
- 134. Tennessee at Tampa Bay .... (ESPN) 8:20

MONDAY, NOVEMBER 9
- 135. Green Bay at Pittsburgh .... (ABC) 8:20

Eleventh Week
SUNDAY, NOVEMBER 15
FOX-TV National Weekend
- 136. Baltimore at San Diego 1:05
- 137. Cincinnati at Minnesota 12:01
- 138. Dallas at Arizona 2:15
- 139. Green Bay at New York Giants 4:15
- 140. Miami at Carolina 1:01
- 141. New England at Buffalo 1:01

All times local

142. New York Jets at Indianapolis	1:01
143. Philadelphia at Washington	1:01
144. Pittsburgh at Tennessee	12:01
145. St. Louis at New Orleans	12:01
146. San Francisco at Atlanta	1:01
147. Seattle at Oakland	1:05
148. Tampa Bay at Jacksonville	4:15
149. Chicago at Detroit	(ESPN) 8:20

MONDAY, NOVEMBER 16

150. Denver at Kansas City	(ABC) 7:20

Twelfth Week
SUNDAY, NOVEMBER 22
CBS-TV National Weekend

151. Arizona at Washington	1:01
152. Baltimore at Cincinnati	4:15
153. Carolina at St. Louis	3:05
154. Chicago at Atlanta	1:01
155. Detroit at Tampa Bay	1:01
156. Green Bay at Minnesota	12:01
157. Indianapolis at Buffalo	1:01
158. Jacksonville at Pittsburgh	1:01
159. Kansas City at San Diego	1:15
160. New York Jets at Tennessee	3:15
161. Oakland at Denver	2:15
162. Philadelphia at New York Giants	1:01
163. Seattle at Dallas	12:01
164. New Orleans at San Francisco	(ESPN) 5:20

MONDAY, NOVEMBER 23

165. Miami at New England	(ABC) 8:20

Thirteenth Week
THURSDAY, NOVEMBER 26
FOX-TV National Weekend

166. Minnesota at Dallas	(FOX) 3:05
167. Pittsburgh at Detroit	(CBS) 12:35

SUNDAY, NOVEMBER 29

168. Arizona at Kansas City	12:01
169. Atlanta at St. Louis	12:01
170. Buffalo at New England	4:05
171. Carolina at New York Jets	1:01
172. Indianapolis at Baltimore	1:01
173. Jacksonville at Cincinnati	1:01
174. New Orleans at Miami	1:01
175. Philadelphia at Green Bay	3:15
176. Tampa Bay at Chicago	12:01
177. Tennessee at Seattle	1:05
178. Washington at Oakland	1:15
179. Denver at San Diego	(ESPN) 5:20

MONDAY, NOVEMBER 30

180. New York Giants at San Francisco	(ABC) 5:20

Fourteenth Week
THURSDAY, DECEMBER 3
CBS-TV National Weekend

181. St. Louis at Philadelphia	(ESPN) 8:20

SUNDAY, DECEMBER 6

182. Baltimore at Tennessee	3:15
183. Buffalo at Cincinnati	1:01
184. Dallas at New Orleans	12:01
185. Detroit at Jacksonville	1:01
186. Indianapolis at Atlanta	1:01
187. Kansas City at Denver	2:15
188. Miami at Oakland	1:15
189. New England at Pittsburgh	1:01
190. New York Giants at Arizona	2:05
191. San Diego at Washington	1:01

All times local

1998 NFL SCHEDULE

    192. San Francisco at Carolina...1:01
    193. Seattle at New York Jets..1:01
    194. Chicago at Minnesota...(ESPN) 7:20
MONDAY, DECEMBER 7
    195. Green Bay at Tampa Bay.....................................(ABC) 8:20

Fifteenth Week
SUNDAY, DECEMBER 13
FOX-TV National Weekend
    196. Arizona at Philadelphia...1:01
    197. Atlanta at New Orleans..12:01
    198. Chicago at Green Bay..12:01
    199. Cincinnati at Indianapolis..1:01
    200. Dallas at Kansas City..3:15
    201. Denver at New York Giants...1:01
    202. Minnesota at Baltimore..4:15
    203. New England at St. Louis..12:01
    204. Oakland at Buffalo..1:01
    205. Pittsburgh at Tampa Bay...1:01
    206. San Diego at Seattle..1:05
    207. Tennessee at Jacksonville..1:01
    208. Washington at Carolina..1:01
    209. New York Jets at Miami.......................................(ESPN) 8:20
MONDAY, DECEMBER 14
    210. Detroit at San Francisco.......................................(ABC) 5:20

Sixteenth Week
SATURDAY, DECEMBER 19
FOX-TV National Weekend
    211. New York Jets at Buffalo.....................................(CBS) 12:35
    212. Tampa Bay at Washington...................................(FOX) 4:05
SUNDAY, DECEMBER 20
    213. Atlanta at Detroit..1:01
    214. Baltimore at Chicago..12:01
    215. Cincinnati at Pittsburgh..1:01
    216. Indianapolis at Seattle..1:05
    217. Kansas City at New York Giants.......................................1:01
    218. New Orleans at Arizona...2:15
    219. Oakland at San Diego...1:05
    220. Philadelphia at Dallas..3:15
    221. St. Louis at Carolina..1:01
    222. San Francisco at New England..1:01
    223. Tennessee at Green Bay..12:01
    224. Jacksonville at Minnesota....................................(ESPN) 7:20
MONDAY, DECEMBER 21
    225. Denver at Miami...(ABC) 8:20

Seventeenth Week
SATURDAY, DECEMBER 26
CBS-TV National Weekend
    226. Kansas City at Oakland.......................................(CBS) 1:05
    227. Minnesota at Tennessee...............................(FOX) 11:35 A.M.
SUNDAY, DECEMBER 27
    228. Buffalo at New Orleans...12:01
    229. Carolina at Indianapolis..1:01
    230. Detroit at Baltimore..1:01
    231. Green Bay at Chicago..12:01
    232. Miami at Atlanta...1:01
    233. New England at New York Jets.......................................1:01
    234. New York Giants at Philadelphia......................................4:05
    235. St. Louis at San Francisco...1:05
    236. San Diego at Arizona...2:15
    237. Seattle at Denver..2:15
    238. Tampa Bay at Cincinnati..1:01
    239. Washington at Dallas..(ESPN) 7:20
MONDAY, DECEMBER 28
    240. Pittsburgh at Jacksonville.....................................(ABC) 8:20

All times local